Deep Trance Identification

Unconscious Modeling and Mastery for Hypnosis Practitioners, Coaches, and Everyday People

By

Shawn Carson
Jess Marion
With
John Overdurf

Changing Mind Publishing
New York, New York

Deep Trance Identification: Unconscious modeling and Mastery for Hypnosis Practitioners, Coaches, and Everyday People

Table of Contents

Cautions and Disclaimer

This book describes techniques using Deep Trance Identification. By its very definition this involves trance and hypnosis. Therefore common sense rules should be followed when engaging in any of the techniques described, whether as the hypnotist or the client.

Many issues that could arise during a DTI can be easily avoided by following the protocols laid out in this book. In particular, always contextualize any change to a specific context, always carry out full ecology checks before commencing a DTI, and always reintegrate the client or modeler back into his or her own self, fully and completely (including integrating any clashes in values and so on), before concluding the DTI work. We will be discussing each of these safeguards in more detail later in the book.

In addition, follow the cautions below:

Firstly: Although this book does not include formal trance inductions, it does contain hypnotic language. Do not listen to any audio version of this book while driving a car or other motor vehicle, operating machinery, or indeed doing anything else that requires your full external attention.

Secondly: This book contains techniques that can be used to deal with personal problems of various kinds, such as lack of confidence, fears, and other every day issues. However, it is not intended to deal with any medical or psychological issues, and if you believe you have any such issue you should consult a medical professional. This goes for hypnotists as well. If you are not medically qualified, do not try to deal with a medically diagnosed issue (or one you believe should be diagnosed) without a medical referral, and/or whatever else is required in your legal jurisdiction.

Thirdly: Everyone has their own experience of trance in general, and DTI in particular. We have had completely positive experiences in our own DTI journeys, and positive experiences with regard to the DTI's we have lead clients through. However, it is possible that you or clients may have less positive experiences, including potential 'abreactions'. Therefore only engage in DTI if you/your hypnotist are properly qualified through an appropriate hypnosis organization, and have received appropriate training, including how to handle abreactions.

Fourthly: Hypnosis is not appropriate for everyone. Some people should not be put into hypnosis or trance at all (including and especially DTI), for example if they have fragile or borderline personalities. If you are in any doubt about your own, or a client's, suitability for DTI then get an expert medical opinion before proceeding.

In conclusion, only engage in hypnosis and DTI if you are totally confident of your ability to handle anything that comes up for yourself and your client. We cannot and do not take any responsibility for your work as a hypnotist, or your experience as the client of another hypnotist.

"This book by Carson, Marion, and Overdurf is an excellent exploration of the extraordinary trance process of deep trance identification. It is thorough, practical, and clear, thereby providing an excellent guide for those seeking far-reaching transformational changes. I highly recommend it!"

Stephen Gilligan, Ph.D.
Author, Generative Trance

FOREWARNED

By Michael Watson

I was honored when I was asked to write an introduction to this book. But then I got a look at it, and as I hungrily went through it I realized that it should come with a warning.

I don't know how you've found your way here, or what you're hoping to discover in these pages, but I'm pretty certain that your life is about to change.

When I was too young to know better (before I had learned my way out of the idea), I could be a cowboy, an astronaut, Robin Hood, and Elliot Ness on a moment's notice ... all before my mother called me in for lunch. I hadn't realized how much learning was taking place as I entered whole-heartedly into those experiences, yet through it all I was discovering and developing aspects of myself that would remain with me in life. I was learning about roles and relationships, nurturing interests and abilities, acquiring perspectives and shaping my character. Then came the dark ages of my adolescence and I put aside my childish ways in favor of a more "realistic, serious, and grown-up" way of being.

Perhaps you can relate. Maybe you've had similar adventures that can inform you as you make your way into this remarkable book.
Because this is the kind of thing that stays with you. As a serious young adult with spiritual aspirations, I'd meditated with the aim of integrating peace, love, devotion and other qualities into my life ... and one day I found myself going a step farther and asking my students, "What would Jesus do?", or "Gandhi?" or "John Lennon?"

10

or "your mother?" ... and I was back to my old tricks. Only now I had the skills of a disciplined meditator, so I didn't need to run around the room like my childhood self. I could do it while sitting in a chair! I had rediscovered this intrinsic ability. And it had some real-world, practical applications!

There were few people talking about Deep Trance Identification in those days. And there was very little published material about it. I read what I could find, studied with whoever I could learn more from. And consulted with my inner child and other experts ... and mostly I practiced, finding my best teachers through the experience itself.
This book satisfies a deep need for useful material on the subject so that you can start exploring right away. The methods presented here are straightforward and easy to master ... and best of all, they are creative and delightful.

DTI can help you acquire skills and abilities, it can help you solve problems and respond better to challenges, it can help you achieve a richer understanding of yourself and others - it is a vehicle for personal evolution.

This book is about waking up a natural talent, loosening self-limiting identities, and opening up to new perspectives and endless possibilities
It is a portal. You've been warned.

Opening Thoughts

Welcome to the first step on your journey of discovering just how easily you can learn and grow. Reading this book will lay a foundation of skills, beliefs, and values that will transform your life. And what those skills, beliefs, and values are, you get to choose!

This book is intended for both your conscious mind and your *unconscious* mind. Your conscious mind can enjoy diving deeply into the theories and techniques of *deep trance identification*. While *your unconscious* mind does something else, something amazing that can tranceform your life. And we will leave it to your unconscious mind to choose the best way to *do that now*.

As you go through this book you may notice consciously some very interesting things about the text itself. For example there may be some sentences that consciously appear to not make sense, this is particularly true as you read through the demos of the techniques. You can *rest assured* knowing that the sentences are meant for your unconscious mind. You may also notice that some words are italicized. You could consciously note them as *unconscious tranceformation* takes place, or you can simply trust your unconscious mind to understand the positive suggestions being made. Your unconscious mind may also come across other positive suggestions not marked out and that part of you can revel in knowing that those suggestions are just for the unconscious.

As you move *deeper* into the book if your conscious mind should forget to remember to track all of those italicizations you can know that you are in just the right place to *relax into new learning*. And if you should find yourself comfortably in trance as you continue on, really learning something of great importance about who you are on a deep level, then of course we cannot stop you.

For example, you could *imagine* standing in the space in front of you is the future you. This is the you who has learned how to effortlessly DTI. This is a version of you who has practiced DTIing with countless models. This is the you who has *profoundly changed* in amazing, fun, and unexpected ways. This future *you have accomplished all of your reasons for learning how to DTI*. We are curious, what does this version of you look like? What is the expression on your face? How are you being in the world that is different from how you've been right now?

Because you could, as a consciousness, drift outside of you so you can see you and you could see the future you, facing each other. Wouldn't it be amazing if you were to *step into* the future you and really feel it from the inside out. What thoughts will you be having and what feelings are you experiencing as a result? What are you believing about yourself and the world around you. What's most important to you about that? As you look back at the you who is reading this book, you can see they are already *beginning to change*. How could that you over there stay the same? You are here having this experience of being masterful at deep trance identification, and that you there is just beginning to learn on a deep level. That you there is changing into the version of you that knows that your *potential is infinite*, that you can pretend anything and master it, and you are ready for all of the wonderful changes about to take place.

Stepping outside of that future you can understand that this is a journey well worth experiencing from the inside out. As you drift back into the present moment, the you who is changing you may find the sense of delight in the fact that you are embarking on the journey where the destination is even more splendid than what you think now. And going forward all of your deep trance identification experiences can build a well-traveled path so that each and every time you DTI it becomes easier and easier. And the future you who has already changed can simply wait for you to arrive.

It is time to begin your journey. As you go on to the first chapter your conscious mind can explore the history, neuroscience, and structure of deep trance identification while your unconscious mind continues to implement positive lasting changes in you.

Chapter 1: Introducing DTI

There is a wise Chinese proverb that says, 'A journey of a thousand miles begins with a single step'. As you begin this journey into Deep Trance Identification (DTI) by taking this first step, I wonder what it would be like if you could walk this journey in someone else's shoes, or a thousand people's shoes, or even fly through part of it as Superman or Superwoman? What amazing things would you discover in fantastic new ways, and how would you trance-form as a person?

These questions can only be answered through experience and it is this experience that is at the heart of DTI.

For the first six or seven years of your life you were *living* DTI in the most basic and organic way, pretty much 24/7. DTI is the fundamental way we learn—in other words we imitate. No formal trance is required to experience DTI; everything we *are* is the result of accelerated learning through DTI. Neuroscientists estimate you learn more information in the first eighteen months of your life, than you will for the remainder of your time here on the planet, no matter how long you live.

So what's the difference between who you were then, as a young baby, and who you are now? One difference is in that early developmental period when, you were largely living in theta brain wave patterns, associated with creativity, dreaming, and dream-like states. You had not yet formed the reality boundaries/distinctions that establish themselves as your brain develops physically. You had not developed the capacity to generate alpha or beta waves, correlated with consciousness, and reflexive awareness; what hypnotists call the conscious mind.

The net effect of these early-year differences is that you did not have the filters that develop only in adulthood, filters that can get in the way of a having direct experience of something and someone. What this means is that as a child you could easily identify with another's experience. Of course, the downside to the lack of filters at that early developmental period is that a child can take on a lot of nasty stuff too! However, for the rest of this book we will be using our filters to select positive experiences to model, before we drop those filters to take those experiences on.

The reason we need 'deep-trance' as part of DTI (at least as an adult) is that by building our filters, we have necessarily forgotten how to suspend judgment in the way we did easily and naturally as small children. Our adult filters are largely associated with the dominant hemisphere, generally our left-brain or 'conscious mind', and prevent us from fully identifying with any model. Said another way, DTI is our best attempt as an adult to 'open our filters', and step back into the experience of a child. But there is an important difference, which is this, when experiencing DTI we are going to do so for a specific reason, to apply specific skills in a specific context, and to integrate these with our own experiences and lives.

So what exactly is Deep Trance Identification? DTI is a process through which you have the opportunity to 'be' someone else for a while, to learn what they have learned, and to grow by absorbing their skills. DTI is a phenomenon that fascinates many hypnotists and laypeople alike, and yet there is very little written on it. In fact the bulk of the written information available is written in Russian—, Russia being the birthplace of DTI as we understand it today. This book is our attempt to bridge the gap and bring to the western hypnosis and coaching world both a clear understanding of what DTI is, how to do it effectively both for short and long term modeling projects, and finally to provide you with a number of different techniques you

can integrate into your hypnosis or coaching practice.

Why DTI?

When I (Jess) was first learning hypnosis I came across a saying attributed to Milton Erickson. Out of all of the amazing works I had read detailing his linguistic magic, this one small phrase is the one that has stayed with me all of these years. He said, *"Pretend anything and master it."* This one line impacted me on such a deep level that to this day I call it to mind when I want to learn something new.

I held this view so strongly that I used it as a springboard to propel me forward in the learning process. In fact I can remember the first time I hypnotized someone, or more accurately didn't hypnotize someone. I was at a large training and had never done hypnosis consciously up to that point. I can remember I felt so intimidated by my practice partner, who I saw as being way more skilled than me, that I could barely utter a word. I sat there nearly silent for the entire exercise, my thoughts running wild and my state anywhere other than where it should have been. By the end of the exercise I wanted to run back to the comfort of my seat, conveniently located behind a very tall gentleman, where I could hide my 'failure' from the rest of the room. To top it off my client asked me, "Did you forget to hypnotize me?" I felt utterly defeated, and it was only the first morning of class! Realizing this wasn't the most resourceful frame of mind, I remembered that quote from Erickson and like a flash it occurred to me: if I couldn't hypnotize someone as myself, what if I hypnotized them by being someone else?

I made the decision to step into Erickson's shoes; he could definitely hypnotize people, even if I believed I couldn't. When I did this, something amazing happened: it was as if everything I had been studying just poured out. 'Being Erickson' meant that I could be playful and curious about my 'clients' and most importantly, anything that happened could and would be hypnotic.

17

Of course, if I was Erickson that also meant I couldn't have those old limiting beliefs. It was as if the experience in the previous exercise never happened and I could enjoy a new emotional and hypnotic flexibility. For me this was a naturally occurring DTI, and a powerful one at that. It had completely changed my thoughts, state, behaviors and beliefs and made me feel infinitely more resourceful.

Since that day, I have used DTI whenever I want to learn something new. Deep Trance Identification is an amazing way to bring out your natural resourcefulness. DTI frees you, and can free your client, from limiting beliefs and thoughts, and install new beliefs and behaviors that can trance-form your life.

The ability to fully associate into another person can have a tremendously generative effect; think of children pretending to be superheroes, doctors, or princesses. These are much more than just games. Children use naturally occurring DTI's to learn important values and life lessons, to try-on different social roles, and practice problem solving. The natural flexibility in identity that children have makes it easy for them to try on being others, and learning new ideas, states, and behaviors. This is a flexibility we need to rediscover if we are to successfully DTI as adults.

The good news is that Deep Trance Identification uses your brain's natural learning strategies to inductively become more resourceful. One of the beliefs Neuro Linguistic Programming (NLP) holds is that anything anyone can do, you can also learn to do. DTI gives you a means of supercharging that learning process.

Traditionally, DTI has been a means of skills acquisition and enhancement. However, this isn't its only use because the DTI experience has huge implications for the therapeutic world as well. Consider, if your client could step into their idol's shoes, what would happen to the problem they had brought to you? Or how powerful would it be for your client to be able to step fully and completely into the shoes of her future-self, who has already solved that problem; who has already changed? In this book we will be exploring both the generative and therapeutic uses of Deep Trance Identification as a means of personal transformation.

Inside This Book

This work is designed to give you a treasure trove of skills that you can use in your own modeling projects, as well as with your clients. The book is comprised of three sections: in the first we will introduce you to the amazing world of DTI. We will explore its history, the neuroscience behind DTI, and the framework of DTI. This will place DTI within the scope of human experience, as well as giving you a solid footing to proceed further into this amazing world of experience.

In the second section we will present our basic strategy for doing a complete DTI. The process we present is designed to help you fully associate into your chosen model. When you use this process in its entirety, DTI becomes easy and utterly transformative. It also ensures that the DTI is ecological and that your unconscious mind is fully onboard with the DTI experience.

Finally, the third section is comprised of techniques and patterns you can use both as a means of DTIing and also as a way of using DTI to create change and help clients and yourself build powerful new skill sets. In this section we will explore esoteric topics such as DTI as a resiliency strategy, the double Reverse-DTI, and how to use archetypes to create lasting change.

How To Use This Book

You may notice as you read on that we often switch between referring to you as the one experiencing the DTI, and you acting as coach leading your client through the DTI experience. If you find yourself wondering in any section if we are referring to you, or your client, you will be right in realizing that we are.

With this in mind, if you should find yourself going into trance as you read and trying on the experiences we describe, you are once again correct in understanding that the easiest way to learn anything is to experience it within your own physiology. You can enjoy allowing your unconscious mind to play with the ideas in any way that helps you learn.

As mentioned above, this book is designed to firmly root you in the field as a DTI facilitator. We recommend reading the entire book first, not skipping chapters. Afterward feel free to return to any chapter you want to reread, or simply for reference.

Many students find it useful to put ideas into action through practice. It may be of value to you to find a partner with whom you can practice, after all, as with anything, practice is key. And if you should find that your skills grow exponentially by deep trance identifying with a master hypnotist, or perhaps DTI-ing with your future-self who is gifted both as a facilitator as well as someone who can experience DTI with ease, then of course we can't stop you.

When you are ready to take the next step on your journey to mastering DTI as a hypnotist and as someone who is already a skilled learner, then step into the next chapter. Just know that going forward you are stepping into a new world, one where anything is possible and you can learn from anyone. This is a world that very few people have consciously traversed, and yet you will find it comfortably familiar.

Chapter 2: The History of DTI

In this chapter we will focus on the history and development of Deep Trance Identification as a learning strategy, as well as a cultural phenomenon.

DTI, in some form or another, has been around as long as recorded human experience. We have a natural tendency to empathize with others, to wonder what it would be like to be them, and to model ourselves after them.

We have all had the experience as children watching a movie, or TV show, and imagining ourselves as the hero. Growing up one of my (Shawn) favorite shows was the old Batman and Robin TV show, with Adam West as Batman and Burt Ward as Robin. I remember one Christmas my older brother Simon and I received Batman and Robin outfits, of course he was Batman being the older brother and I was Robin, and we spent many a happy hour battling the Joker, the Penguin, and Catwoman. As children these experiences were completely real to us, my brother Simon 'became' Batman and I 'became' Robin. We saw the super villains who were fighting in life-size three-dimensional Technicolor with wraparound sound. Imagine you are somebody you are not, and seeing things that aren't actually there, this is called 'positive hallucinations' in hypnosis, and is proof of trance, as far as a hypnotist is concerned! No doubt even our caveman ancestors, when they were children, looked up to the great hunters in the tribe and imagined being them, pulling a pointed stick from a tree to represent a spear so they could play 'hunt the mammoth'!

DTI in an Anthropological Context

We will be coming back to superheroes as role models for DTI in a later chapter. For now we just want you to understand that deep trance identification is an entirely natural process we all used when we were children, we just forgot our natural ability as we aged. One purpose of this book is to help you remember what you knew as a child. In hypnosis, reverting to childhood is called a 'regression', and can be an incredibly valuable hypnotic experience. Regression to childhood is a theme we will come back to repeatedly in this book.

During my (Jess) time as an anthropologist, one of the things that drew my interest was the pan-cultural phenomenon of Deep Trance Identification. Of course, as anthropologists, we didn't call it that; we typically used terms like 'spirit possession'. The idea of becoming someone else through ritual has been a part of most, if not all, cultures since ancient times. We only have to look at spiritual traditions from around the world, from the jungles of Indonesia to the plains of Africa, to the mega churches of the American Midwest, to find examples. DTI unites each of these diverse cultural expressions.

Balinese Dancers meet Milton Erickson

One of the legendary examples of trance in general, and DTI specifically, comes from the work of renowned anthropologists Margaret Mead and Gregory Bateson. In the 1930s Mead journeyed to remote villages in Bali where she filmed a sacred drama in which the actors believed they became the witches and gods spoken of in the story. This ritual drama was done as a means of healing the community [Jess Marion will be releasing a book on the anthropology of trance early in 2015]. Mead and Bateson observed the proceedings but were left with more questions than answers, because as the play progressed, the actors, one by one, began to act in unscripted ways. The refined choreography of Balinese dance gave way to a chaotic explosion of movement. The dance culminated in many of the participants' breaking ceremonial daggers on their bodies without being harmed. By reenacting this sacred drama and becoming gods and witches, the Balinese were able to heal sickness and avert calamities that threatened the village.

Upon their return to the US, Bateson enlisted Milton Erickson's help in understanding the trance phenomena in Mead's films. Erickson was able to discern the mechanisms of trance involved in the dance, as well as the process through which the Balinese 'became' their gods.

This is just one example of how DTI has been used over the centuries for therapeutic reasons. If we were to look across the span of history, most of these DTIs are actually what we will refer to as 'Reverse-DTI', meaning that rather than 'becoming' somebody else, somebody else actually 'becomes' you. We will discuss these types of Reverse-DTI techniques in detail in chapter 23; how to use them and when. These early instances of DTI occurred when somebody became possessed by a god or a spirit. Rather than 'becoming' the God, that God 'became' them, hence the term 'Reverse-DTI'.

The Greeks and their Daemons

While the Bali case was an instance of therapeutic 'Reverse-DTI' we can look to the ancient Greeks for the generative approach to Reverse-DTI. In this tradition the Reverse-DTI happens by the power of a Daemon. A Daemon is a spirit, or being that typically inhabited the walls of a house, and was capable of temporarily taking over the person who lived in the house. This idea sounds very strange, even scary, to our modern ears because the idea of a Daemon 'possession' was reinterpreted negatively by the early Christian church. But in

23

fact, to the Greeks, a Daemon was entirely benevolent. The Daemon was a creative spirit that lived in the walls of a house owned by a poet, musician, painter, writer, scientist or other creative person. It possessed that person to inspire them to write poetry, music, paint, or whatever the particular muse provided. That person's creativity was caused by them being taken over by the Daemon—it was a kind of emissary between gods and men, in this case literally providing 'divine inspiration'.

The Dionysian Mysteries

The Greeks were also happy to experience Reverse-DTI with the gods themselves. A great example is the festival of Dionysus, the god of the grape harvest. Followers of Dionysius would engage in the festival called the Dionysian Mysteries, during which the God would come upon them, and the spirit of the God would enter into them. The result of this process was a state known as 'enthous', literally to be possessed by 'theos', possessed by God. This gives us the modern word 'enthusiasm'! The Dionysian Mysteries were continued by the Romans under the auspices of their own wine god, Bacchus. Bacchus was the Roman version of Dionysus and followers of Bacchus would engage in what was known as the Bacchanalia, where they too would be possessed by the God. Interestingly we can see a remnant of the festival of Dionysus in the Holy Sacrament of the Eucharist. There are many other examples from antiquity of cultures and events where it's perfectly acceptable, even normal, to experience a Reverse-DTI and to be possessed by a God or Spirit.

The Ignatian Exercises

DTI was also a feature of Christianity through the work of Ignatius of Loyola. Ignatius was a Spanish knight who became a priest and went on to found the Jesuit order in 1540. One of his principal contributions to Christian spirituality was the development of a series of meditative exercises designed to promote a proper understanding of Christian teaching. In these exercises the meditator would imagine scenes from the New Testament from various perspectives, for example from the perspective of an apostle listening to Jesus teach, or even from the perspective of Jesus himself.

These exercises were to be performed over a period of four weeks in conjunction with prayer, contemplation and spiritual meditation as segues, creating 'altered states' of heightened spirituality. In conjunction with the perceptual position shifts, these produced temporary dissolution of boundaries between the meditator and the object of meditation. The exercises were intended to elicit strong emotional responses in the meditator, as they imagined being in the biblical scene, fully associating into their role and making the scene their own.

Although 500 years old, the Spiritual Exercises of Ignatius are still one of the best ways to develop your ability to DTI. Of course you can replace the New Testament scenes with others more appropriate to your own needs. We will not be laying out the Spiritual Exercises in this book; however there are several excellent free online resources that can lead you through the Spiritual Exercises in detail (simply search for the Spiritual Exercises of Ignatius of Loyola) for those interested in learning more.

In modern times, DTI was built into many different approaches to spirituality. On the behavioral and emotional level, sayings like "be more Christ (or Buddha)-like" come to mind. In the late 1990s, "What Would Jesus Do" bracelets were very popular in the U.S. The "WWJD" phenomenon invited Christians to shift perceptual positions and step into the shoes of Jesus before making a decision, speaking or acting.

In Tantric Buddhism, meditators focus on a personal deity, to whom they perform rituals and develop a deep devotion. The meditation experience culminates in merging with that deity. The recognition that the human mind is

25

in fact the Buddha mind, leads to spiritual liberation within that tradition.

If we look across the world's great religious traditions we come across countless stories of gods DTI-ing with humans, and humans 'becoming' gods; DTI, as a modality for personal trance-formation, is as relevant to us today as it was to our most ancient of human ancestors.

DTI in the Theater

The theater has been around for thousands of years, and probably much longer. In fact, theater almost certainly predates written language, and served the purpose of teaching shared tribal beliefs, values, and theology, as well as day-to-day skills and roles to members of the tribe. As anyone who has experience in theater will know, the real skill in acting is to separate the personality of the actor from the personality of the character being played.

When the actor actually becomes the character, often called method acting, the outcome is a form of DTI. In method acting, the actor adopts the beliefs, values, thoughts, feelings and behaviors of the character. Method acting is so called because it was originally based upon the 'Method' created by the great Russian actor Konstantin Stanislavski. Stanislavski began to develop his ideas in the 1880s, and immortalized these in his classic book published in the 1920s, *An Actors Work.*

In *An Actor's Work*, Stanislavski discusses this very issue, namely how an actor puts aside his own personality and takes on that of the character he is playing. Stanislavski recognizes that 'personality' must include the thoughts, emotions, physiology, focus, and actions of the character for a coherent whole. If any of these elements belong solely to the actor, rather than the character, then the reality of the role is lost. Of course the actor does bring portions of himself and his own experience into the role as we will discuss in Chapter 19. Stanislavski stated that 'these elements [of personality] must be indivisible at the creative moment, when you are in the proper inner state, and that state is almost indistinguishable from life'. Stanislavsky taught a particular technique, which he called his 'psychotechnique', for creating and maintaining this creative indivisibility of the character's personality.

We will discuss Stanislavski's work in detail in Chapter 19.

Raikov and the Russian Revolution in DTI

Our next thread in exploring the tapestry of DTI takes us all the way to Russia a country separated from Western Europe by alphabet and language, as well as by the animosity of imperial powers.

Russia has always had a fascination with hypnosis, going back at least as far as the infamous Rasputin, the mystical advisor to the family of the Russian Czar Nicholas. Rasputin held a special fascination for the Czarina, Alexandra Feodorovna, and while Rasputin was not a hypnotist in the strict sense of the word, he seemed to have exerted a hypnotic influence over the Romanovs. The story of Rasputin ended badly for all concerned, but shows the fascination of the Russian mind with the unconscious.

Psychiatrists and psychologists in Russia began to develop their own theories of hypnosis more or less independently of the West, although following similar lines—for example the theory of animal magnetism (Mesmerism).

As theories of hypnosis developed in Russia, areas of mind control using psychology, hypnosis, and telepathy developed as areas of fascination for the Russian military. This fascination resulted in the Russian military engaging in extensive research, going back at least to the 1930s. When the Iron Curtain descended on Eastern Europe following World War II, and Russia and America began to jockey for global leadership through the Korean and Vietnam Wars, it is not surprising that Russia's mind control programs became a matter of concern for the US military. This resulted in the US military creating its own programs, about which books have been written and movies made, such as the George Clooney 2009 movie, '*The Men Whose Stare at Goats*'.

While neither side seemed to make much progress on the telepathic front, Russia's research in this area was a matter of intense fascination, at least through the 1970s. I (Shawn) recall as a small boy playing competitive chess and avidly following the exploits of one of my early heroes, Bobby Fischer, when he defeated the reigning world chess champion, the Russian player Boris Spassky in Reykjavík, Iceland. I clearly remember the story circulating at the time that the Russians had brought along a 'parapsychologist' whose role was to sit in the front row of the audience and beam negative telepathic waves in Fischer's direction! Whatever the truth of this story, it does demonstrate the aura of mystery that surrounded Russian parapsychology.

At the same time the unnamed Russian parapsychologist was beaming his mind rays at Bobby Fischer, another Russian was experimenting with an entirely different, and much more positive, type of mind control. Alexander Raikov was a Russian hypnotist who was fascinated with the unconscious mind's creative acts through music, art, and language—and yes, chess.

Raikov's most famous research involved students at the Moscow Conservatory of Music in the 1960's. Raikov used hypnosis to improve the technical music skills of the students, as well as their interpretative abilities.

Raikov studied the effects of hypnosis and DTI on several thousand people. Not only was Raikov able to improve the skills of the students with hypnosis, but he also carried out double-blind studies to support his theories. For example, at the Moscow Conservatory of Music he would induce a deep trance in highly hypnotizable subjects, and over the course of one to three sessions would get them to identify with ('be in the skin of', as Raikov describes it) a musician who was a master of the instrument the student was studying. So for example, students of the piano would DTI with Rachmaninov students of the violin would DTI with Kreisler, and students of the cello would DTI with Casals.

There are several extremely interesting aspects to Raikov's technique. For one thing, he would regress the students back to childhood as part of his protocol. He would also get the students to engage in a physical activity, either playing the instrument, or playing an imaginary instrument while in trance. He referred to these deep trances where the subject would undertake a physical activity as 'active hypnotic somnambulism'. Raikov strongly held to the opinion that deep-trance was required to experience a true DTI.

Before and after the sessions, the students would play a piece of music for expert examiners who would rank their performance. Some of the students had completed the protocol, whilst others went through a control experience that was similar, but did not involve trance and DTI. Raikov was therefore able to determine exactly the effect of the DTI on the musical skills of the students.

Raikov published a number of papers on his research at the Moscow Conservatory, as well as similar research carried out at language schools and arts schools. Unfortunately these papers were available only in Russian so there is very little information available in the West detailing his work. Nevertheless, Raikov's work became widely discussed by those developing the new field called NLP, in particular Richard Bandler, John Grinder, and one of their students, Stephen Gilligan.

Gilligan Models Milton Erickson

As a result of Raikov's work and the stories circulating in the NLP community in California in the early 1970s, Stephen Gilligan decided to DTI with Milton Erickson, with whom he was studying hypnosis. Gilligan describes the process in an interview he gave with Chris and Jules Collingwood, during which he revealed several fascinating insights into the outcome of his DTI, and the difference between DTI and conscious modeling as used in NLP.

Gilligan says DTI is a process wherein the modeler develops a deep trance, goes to a safe place, sets aside his or her regular personality, and assumes another personality for 30 minutes or so. Gilligan describes how, within DTI, you let go of your normal identity, the way you think, the way you hold your body, the way you talk, the way you react. Your whole sense of self drops to a much *deeper level*, so that everything else *becomes malleable*.

Gilligan recalled Gregory Bateson, who was good friends with Milton Erickson, walking in the first time Gilligan was doing his DTI, 'being Erickson'. Gilligan, 'being Erickson', said something to Bateson, which scared the living daylights out of Bateson, because it was something that only Erickson and Bateson knew. Gilligan was channeling Erickson in a way that defies rational explanation.

The thing about Gilligan's experience that is most notable is that it was nothing like he consciously expected it would be. He had expected on a conscious level that Milton Erickson's mind would be racing at full speed as he considered all the ways he could take a person into a trance. Instead, what Gilligan actually experienced during the DTI was a state of extreme *calm*, the opposite of what he had been expecting.

Another fascinating insight from Gilligan's experience was that it changed how he actually perceived the world around him. After his DTI he literally saw everyone as already being in trance. Please note that this was way more than an intellectual insight into Milton Erickson's world, it was a literal change in Gilligan's visual perception.

Dilts, NLP and Modeling

Following Gilligan's experiences DTIing with Milton Erickson, it may be fair to say that the mainstream NLP community moved away from DTI as a main instrument of modeling, and moved to a more analytical approach.

This shift was exemplified by Robert Dilts who developed a more left brain approach to modeling. Dilts used this new left brain strategy to model several figures from history, including Walt Disney (Dilts' famous "Disney Strategy'), and also Aristotle and Mozart, as well as fictional characters such as Sherlock Holmes.

Dilts' protocol for modeling included something that he called Unconscious Uptake, which involved stepping into the person to be modeled and experiencing his world from the inside. However, the use of explicit deep trance to achieve this Unconscious Uptake was not stressed. Rather, under Dilts' protocol, the modeler adopts the physiology, especially the micro-physiology, of the model. While it can certainly be argued that mirroring the micro-physiology is a trance experience, at the same time it is not necessarily 'deep-trance' in the way that Raikov suggested was necessary for DTI, or in the way that Gilligan experienced DTI with Erickson.

John Overdurf Brings It Back Home

I (John) first started teaching DTI as a part of the workshop called Hypnosis II, which became known as the book, Training Trances. Later on Julie (Silverthorn) and I started teaching 'PhotoReading and More'. Julie was a Photoreading instructor and I did the 'More' which added the idea of unconscious activation of what was read using perceptual positions, particularly DTI with the author of the book that was being photo read.

PhotoReading was primarily one way to 'upload' large amounts of information through reading, much of which was absorbed unconsciously, then activated using specific activation techniques. So the real challenge was developing ways to bring what was 'uploaded' into conscious awareness, and in the area of skills into practical application. That lead to hypnotic modeling, which was a protocol based around DTI. Hypnotic modeling could be done with or without PhotoReading of course.

When we decided to do Hypnosis III, the next level of our hypnosis training, I decided to add a significant amount of time for each participant to DTI with Milton Erickson. As I was laying out the exercises for the course, I started thinking, "*This is going to be so cool*" and realized I was becoming very envious about what the students were going to experience at the training. I wanted to *have a similar experience* but still have it be integrated into my role as the teacher. "No big deal, *you can do that*," I thought to myself. So I decided I'd set up a request to my unconscious mind to create a *DTI experience at some point during this training* using ideomotor signals to verify my unconscious mind's full participation. You can find out exactly what happened when I did it in the later chapter on ecology!

A week later the training happened. It was several days into the training and we'd provided the participants some articles detailing Erickson's life as well as listening to some audios and watching the "Monde" video in evening sessions. We'd also set-up dream incubation (more about that later on). We were now at the point to do the ecology protocol (which I modeled after my own experience), and then do the DTI.

I asked if someone would be willing to volunteer for a demonstration of DTI with Erickson. A psychologist raised her hand and indicated she had a chronic physical condition that was not improving. She wanted to DTI with Erickson's "healing abilities and attitude toward life." If you are wondering how effective the demo was, she experienced considerable relief and her healing accelerated, although she later did some more work to reinforce it. I went on to use DTI as an effective way to initiate and *accelerate healing* with a good number of clients with serious physical issues. In any case, this is where the big surprise came, and the story becomes about the power and "genius" of our unconscious minds. I started the demo with her and kind of felt 'trancey'. The next thing I knew I was doing some sort of post hypnotic suggestion to future pace the results to the contexts she wanted. I felt a little disoriented.

She returned to her seat and I began the typical Q&A about the demo with the class. As questions were asked, I could not remember much of anything about the demo, except a few bits in the beginning and the post hypnotic suggestion at the end. Oops! This is unusual for me; usually my recall is pretty clear about what transpired in demos. Every time I tried to answer a detailed question, I'd space-out, have a fleeting glimpse of something, then just say, "I'm not sure," or when I could say something, it was as if it wasn't me saying it. After a few exchanges like this, I realized, "Oh my God, that's when I did the DTI!" In my unconscious mind I thought the best time for me having a DTI experience of Erickson was when I was demo-ing 'DTI-with-Erickson' with someone else! As Erickson himself used to say, "Your unconscious mind is a lot smarter than you." In this case I had to humbly agree.

That demo was recorded and I remember the struggle I had trying to listen to it months later, to figure out what I did with her. It took quite a few listening sessions to stay conscious enough to know what happened—a very compelling convincer and something I hope you will experience in your own way through the help of this book. There is so substitute for the conviction you develop when you *have the experience* you want others to have, first with yourself.

How This Book Fits In

I (Jess) can remember clearly sitting in a class with John in 2012. During this course John mentioned DTI in passing and I was instantly drawn to the concept. I texted Shawn immediately, saying we should teach a course on

33

DTI. That led to a year of intense exploration of DTI experiences and techniques to create a DTI protocol Shawn and I felt was good enough to share with others. We carried out a series of experiments using different trance-protocols, both with each other and our clients. As part of this process, we began experimenting seriously with DTI in the context of Superheroes, a subject close to both our hearts (much more on that later!).

Shawn and I taught our first DTI course in the fall of 2013. We were in the middle of teaching the course when John Overdurf visited New York to teach his own hypnosis workshop (not on DTI). We were fortunate enough to have dinner with John at Uncle Nick's Greek Restaurant on 8th Avenue. During dinner Shawn and I described our DTI workshop to John. As we talked, John began to light up and described his own DTI protocol. We spent most of the meal comparing and contrasting our approaches. By combining and taking the best of both approaches, we were fortunate enough to have convinced John to co-author this book: which brings us back to the present and the neuroscience of DTI, which we will discuss in the next chapter.

Chapter 3: The Neuroscience of Deep Trance Identification

We are lucky to be writing this book about DTI in 2014 because the vital, expanding field of neuroscience is literally exploding with ground-breaking research that helps us understand how our brains really work.

In this chapter we will be touching of some of the relevant research which provides a deeper understanding of DTI and related processes.
At the foundation of the neuroscientific research we will cover the phenomena called neuroplasticity. Neuroplasticity is the brain's ability to be flexible and to rewire in response to experience. Neuroplasticity starts before we are born, in utero. It never sleeps. It never stops for one moment of your life. In fact, your brain is re-wiring itself as you read this text.

As a field, it is the study of how life experience and/or self-directed attention, like hypnosis, can create physical, structural changes in our brains. The brain is constantly changing not only in function but in physical structure!

Think of it this way: your mind, attention, is different from your brain, the physical organ. The physical organ called the brain can also be changed through something, which is not physical at all: *our attention.* Your mind is using your brain to change itself.

Your brain has functions like other organs in your body. The two primary functions of the organ, called your brain, are to:

1. Learn something as quickly as possible through sufficient repetition and/or intensity of experience.

2. Consolidate those learnings so they become automatic programs.

Just like training an athlete for a specific sport, the coach takes the athlete through specific drills to develop optimal reactions or maneuvers. Through repetition "muscle memory" gets developed and now the athlete can respond automatically at the right time.

The fact of the matter is your brain's neurons are more like muscles in body, than we ever thought. Through proper training, your neurons will get more "muscular and coordinated." They'll grow bigger, stronger, fire more efficiently and be more sensitive to being triggered at the right time.

So as you learn the protocols and maneuvers in this book, you will be physically sculpting, training and conditioning the DTI neural networks in your brain. As time goes on your brain's DTI "muscles" will become bigger, stronger, more efficient and easily triggered at the right time. Your life will change in amazing ways as a result. How cool is that? So, now, let's take a closer look at some research findings that will provide you with valuable background and "pointers" to make your work more effective.

Mirror Neurons

In the early 1990's, researchers at the University of Palma in Italy used brain scanning technology to study the behavior of monkeys in the laboratory. They would scan the brains of the monkeys while training them to perform certain tasks, and of course would reward them with fruit and other treats when they performed the task correctly. The researchers therefore had brain scans of the monkeys not only performing those tasks, but also picking up and eating the fruit. One day, one of the researchers happened to pick up and eat a fruit treat in front of one of the monkeys. The researchers were amazed to see that the readout of the monkey's brain scan while watching the researcher was similar to the readout of the monkey's brain scan when it picked up and ate a piece of fruit itself.

At first, the researchers could not understand how the monkey's brain could be doing exactly the same thing while watching an action, as it did when performing the same action. Happily, they did not simply put this down to a fluke, or a badly calibrated machine, but instead pursued this line of inquiry. They indeed found that the monkeys' brains responded to watching an action being done by another monkey or a human in much the same way as if monkey itself were doing it. The Palma researchers had discovered Mirror Neurons.

Today we are fortunate in that much research has been done on Mirror Neurons so that we have a good understanding of how they work, and what they do. Now, those readers who are students of the game will know that there is also a good deal of debate about Mirror Neurons. For example, it is scientifically uncertain as to whether Mirror Neurons exist in human beings. The reason for this uncertainty is in fact because Mirror Neurons fire essentially as individual neurons so are not as easily seen by brain scans that scan large brain regions. So while it is easy to measure Mirror Neuron activity in monkeys, by placing a probe inside the monkey's brain, such research is considered unethical if performed on a healthy human being. (We could of course argue as to whether, and to what extent, it is ethical to do the same thing to our monkey cousins). In any case, the real source of the scientific disputes regarding Mirror Neurons arises as a result of over-reach by certain neuroscientists regarding the state of research in the area. For example, one well-known neuroscientist has argued that the Mirror Neuron is responsible for human civilization!

As hypnotists, we have always thought that the discovery of Mirror Neurons should not have been such a surprise to the researchers at the University of Palma. After all, as long ago as the nineteenth century the famous psychologist William James suggested that the best way to discover what another person is feeling is to take on their physiology or facial expression. In fact James proposed that emotions were actually caused by changes in physiology or facial expression, a theory known as the James-Lange theory of emotion after its two developers. This theory is no longer thought to be completely accurate. Nevertheless, we all have personal experiences of our own Mirror Neurons. For example, if you see another person trip, or hit his thumb with a hammer, you may have a visceral reaction as if it were you who had fallen, or are hurt.

Mirror Neurons appear to be designed to allow us understand other people, both on a behavioral and an emotional level. When we see another person engaged in some behavior, specific Mirror Neurons inside our own brains begin to fire off, as if we were doing the behavior ourselves. Similarly, if we see somebody experiencing an emotion, for example smiling or laughing, then we begin to feel that emotion ourselves.

Mirror Neurons have several other interesting properties from the perspective of DTI. For example, one set of Mirror Neurons are designed to react to sound. If you were to imagine the sound of somebody drinking, a part of your brain would begin to provide you an experience as if you too were drinking. Perhaps this explains why good Hollywood Foley artists, those magicians tasked with adding realistic sound effects to movies, are so sought after!

Another interesting aspect of Mirror Neurons is that they react in a way that is context specific. Imagine seeing a person across the room with a coffee-cup in front of them, they pick up the cup... What is it that you experience? It turns out that the answer depends upon the context of what you actually saw in your imagination. For example, if you saw a coffee cup full of hot coffee, then your Mirror Neurons would likely have provided you with an experience of sipping from the cup. On the other hand if you had imagined an empty coffee cup was being picked up, then it is more likely that your Mirror Neurons would have provided you with an experience of putting the cup in the sink or the dishwasher!

This will be an important principle when we begin to experience Deep Trance Identification within a context from our own life, as the following quick examples may demonstrate:

Imagine seeing the Incredible Hulk in front of you, big green and immensely strong. Imagine floating out of yourself and into the Incredible Hulk, becoming the Incredible Hulk. As the Incredible Hulk you find yourself surrounded by evil bad guys and villains... What is your experience?

Now float back into yourself. Once more, imagine seeing the Incredible Hulk in front of you. Float out of yourself and into the Incredible Hulk, becoming the Incredible Hulk. This time imagine you are sitting at a table with three elderly ladies' you are all drinking tea and playing bridge. You are holding a card in one hand, and a fine china teacup in the other, as you listen to your partner bid... What is your experience this time?

For many, the experience of becoming the Incredible Hulk within the context of the old ladies' bridge party can be a very jarring experience because there is a mismatch between the expected behavior of the Incredible Hulk, and the expected behavior in the context. This has important implications for the DTI process, which we will get to later.

The Holistic Brain

It is said that we only use 5% of our brain. This is actually not true, our whole brain is active all the time, with neurons firing and seeking to become part of a wider firing of neural networks that we call a thought. The more neurons and neural networks that can be recruited into any one thought, the more likely it is the thought will have the energy to come to our awareness, and therefore be acted upon.

What does this have to do with DTI? It's simple, by experiencing a DTI with somebody we know well, or someone we have studied extensively (as we will suggest you do with anyone you choose to model using DTI), you recruit all the neural networks associated with that model. If the model is confident, your neural network associated with confidence will be recruited to fire as part of the DTI process. If the model is intensely focused on his goal, then the part of your brain responsible for focusing on goals will be recruited, and so on.

Therefore the DTI process, whereby the subject puts her whole, undivided attention on a particular model, not just consciously but also unconsciously, provides a mechanism allowing the brain's natural 'thought process' to be used to make profound changes in feelings, behaviors and abilities.

Working Memory

Your brain has a wonderful mechanism comprised of several 'moving parts', which acts as a sort of control panel for everything that you do, and everything that you feel. This control panel is referred to as your 'working memory'.

Your working memory is constantly active, reviewing the past for meaning, planning the future, and reviewing actions you are about to take. Working memory is comprised of three parts: firstly there is a sort of movie screen, called a 'visiospatial sketchpad', on which a short movie plays. This may be a memory of the past, some action you are just about to take, your plan for the future, your fears of the future, or simply a daydream. The second part of

40

working memory is a sound loop that goes along with the movie. For example, if you were to imagine a movie of a car door slamming, chances are your brain will automatically provide an appropriate soundtrack! Did you notice that? SLAM!

The final part of working memory is in many ways the most important. This is the meaning associated with the movie, you can think of it as being the 'movie title'. Let's consider an example: if you make wonderful pictures in your mind of your bright future, it does not mean it will come true, or even that it is more likely to come true. In fact, there is research that shows exactly the opposite in many cases, picturing what you want to happen has the reverse effect, making it less likely you will achieve your goal. Why is this? Because the movie you play in your mind has an inappropriate title! For example, researchers at the University of California asked students to imagine getting a high grade on an upcoming exam. Rather than helping them to get good grades, the visualization actually was counterproductive and the students' grades went down because they spent less time studying. The problem with the visualization was that the title the researchers had suggested was something along the lines of, "I will get a high grade in the upcoming exam." With this in mind the students had less motivation to study than if they had not visualized at all. In contrast, a second group of students was asked to visualize studying prior to the exam, and their results improved, a visualization which communicated the title 'studying = success'.

At its heart, DTI is a visualization that relies on working memory to generate reference experiences from the life of the model. This allows the subject to step into these reference experiences. Therefore, when building these experiences it is important not only that the subject visualize the scene clearly, but to also have a soundtrack. It is also vital that the 'title' of the DTI is clear, in this case what the subject expects to get out of the DTI process. We will be talking about this more in a later chapter.

Dopamine

Dopamine is a neuro-transmitter that has several important functions in the brain. One of these functions—the one we will be concerned about in context of DTI, is to assist in learning.

Dopamine has two important purposes in the context of learning. The first is that dopamine stabilizes working memory; it keeps the appropriate movie playing on the movie screen, with the appropriate soundtrack and the appropriate title. This allows the subject to more fully and completely *experience the DTI.* The second important function of dopamine is that it tells the hippocampus, the part of the brain where long-term memories begin to be laid down, that what the brain is experiencing right now is important and should be remembered. This signal starts the process of long-term memory formation.

Given these two vital roles of dopamine, wouldn't it be wonderful to be able to supply as much dopamine as the brain needs whenever we want to learn something important?

How can you train your dopamine neurons to become more muscular, so that you will feel more excitement in life more often, and have better memory function? The answer: sort for what is new and different in your environment. The research indicates that novelty is the breakfast of champions for dopamine neurons.

There's another way, too. Have FUN. That's right, when you have fun you are automatically generating dopamine inside your brain, locking the attention of your working memory on whatever it is that you're doing, and kick-starting the process of forming a long-term memory about it.

Fortunately DTI by its nature is a lot of fun! This is especially true when we DTI with a colorful character such as Superman, Steve Jobs, Michael Jordan, or whoever you personally find fascinating. So remember, when you are in a

DTI, or leading another person through a DTI as hypnotist, make it as much fun as possible!!!

Hebb's Law: Neurons That Fire Together Wire Together

If you're familiar with only one rule of neuroscience it may well be Hebb's Law. In general, neuroscientists disagree about almost everything to do with the brain, with the exception of this one rule, which they agree on enough to call it a law! When two neurons, or two neural networks, fire off at the same time they become more sensitive to each other, a process known as long-term potentiation or LTP. Over time, and we can be talking a relatively short amount of time, these neurons or neural networks become permanently wired together, part of the same circuit.

When you study a model as part of the DTI process, the various aspects of that model's being, their physical movements and gestures, their emotions, their beliefs, their values, and their very identity, are represented on a neural level by neural networks within your brain. You literally build a model of the model within your brain, using neurons that represent various aspects of the model. These diverse neural networks become wired together by virtue of firing together, as you study the model as a single individual. Once you have had the DTI experience, this neural-model is activated on a deep unconscious level. However, this is not the end of the wiring that takes place under Hebb's Law. You see, you then take the DTI experience and bring those skills, and experience them within the context in which you want the abilities of the model. This context is also represented by a network within your brain, and this context becomes linked to the DTI model.

What this means is that the capabilities of the model are available to you whenever you are in that context, a very desirable state of affairs!

Ideomotor Responses

Let's take a moment to talk about ideomotor responses as we specifically use them to check the ecology of the DTI.

Physical actions are under unconscious control. You may think that you consciously pick up a coffee cup, or consciously walk across the room, but actually the programs for physical actions and motions are controlled by the unconscious mind (see for example Benjamin Libet's widely discussed work on this topic).

We discussed above how all parts of the brain are constantly firing off, seeking to become part of a recognized thought. This is as true of neurons and circuits within the motor cortex, as anywhere else. As a result we are constantly making movements, large and small, from gestures that we make when we speak, to micro-expressions that reveal our innermost emotions, to imperceptible micro-movements of our body, arms, legs, hands and fingers.

These unconscious movements can be used to reveal unconscious responses in a process called ideomotor signals. Ideomotor signals are simply small movements such as finger twitches for example. We can link these movements with wider brain states, such as a state of agreement or disagreement. Sometimes the ideomotor responses are already associated with these states, for example, a micro-head nod is often associated with agreement in the Western world because we nod our head while agreeing! But ideomotor Responses can also be linked with wider brain states using long-term potentiation, which is discussed in the section on Hebb's Law above.

Simply asking the unconscious mind to show a 'yes' signal, while for example holding the pendulum, will lead to the pendulum swinging in one direction. That is enough to link that direction of swing with the brain state 'yes' agreement, at least for the duration of discovering whether the subject's unconscious mind is committed to the DTI process. We discuss how to use this process in Chapter 8.

Chapter 4: Overview of the DTI Protocol

In this chapter we go over the complete protocol so that you have an understanding of how the pieces fit together, before we get into details of each piece.

A DTI is an awesome opportunity to *absorb a complete skill set* from someone who is a master in the field that you want to master. In preparing for, experiencing, integrating, applying, testing and refining your DTI, you will absorb a vast skill-set in a way that is natural and allows those skills to be incorporated in the very fabric of your being on the deepest unconscious level. When I (Shawn) am doing a DTI, I love spending the time needed to really get under the skin and inside the mind of the model.

The DTI process is a form of Hero's Journey. First you feel the call to adventure, either because you face a problem in your own life or because you simply see the possibility for more. So pack your bags and prepare for your journey, then step out into new exciting experiences. At some point, you change and become a new person having absorbed those experiences on a deep level. Ultimately you return to the real world, bringing these new skills with you.

Obviously, not everyone wants to immerse themselves in the DTI process for the amount of time that it takes to 'become' the master you are emulating on such a deep level. Some people prefer to dive into a quick DTI, for rapid access to the master's skills. This is perfectly understandable. We call this approach 'Instant DTI' which we will present in the next chapter.

But for the remainder of this chapter we will talk about how to do a complete, in-depth, amazingly profound, and utterly life transforming DTI, skipping no steps and leaving out no details. For these purposes, we will be structuring the DTI into four phases:

Phase 1: Preparing for the DTI

There is no point in getting on the train unless your bags are packed. You are going to want to take everything you will need on your journey. You'll want to decide on your destination, make sure you really want to go there, take stock of your inventory, carefully choose your traveling companions, and plan the itinerary, before you leave.

Phase 2: The DTI Experience

Having carefully prepared, you can fully immerse yourself in the journey, meet the locals, and ask lots of questions about their experiences. Enjoy each and every stop along the way. Remember to take lots of photographs and video to remind you of the journey.

Phase 3: Integration

Now that the trip is completed, you'll want to begin to take what you've learned and integrate it with your own personality. After all, the journey you have just taken is now a part of your own experiences, your own memories, a part of yourself.

Phase 4: Application, Testing, and Refinement

Now it's back to the real world. You will want to apply those skills you just learned to real life. You will want to apply them to the actual situations you face on a day-to-day basis. You will want to see how well they work, to test them out, and to the extent they don't work as well as you would wish to refine them to make them better, and to improve them by cutting out any unnecessary steps.

Within each of these phases there will be several steps as follows:

Phase 1: Preparing for the DTI

A list of questions to ask yourself, or your client, that will assist you in preparing for the DTI is included as Appendix 1. These questions cover the following areas:

Step 1: Defining the Context For The DTI

During this step you will decide why you want to do the DTI, and in what area of your life you wish to have the master's skills available. You will also take stock of your own resources, emotions, beliefs and values that may support, or undermine your journey.

Step 2: Therapeutic versus Generative DTI

We think of DTI's as falling into two broad categories, generative and therapeutic. In a therapeutic DTI you are bringing certain unwanted baggage; there is some feeling, belief, or value that is making you less than who you want to be, something you wish to be transformed as a result of the DTI.

A generative DTI on the other hand, carries no such unwanted baggage. You step out locked and loaded, seeking only to step to the next level of your evolution and personal development.

Of course, no DTI is purely therapeutic; every DTI offers the opportunity for amazing personal evolution. After all, you never know how far a change may go! Equally no DTI is entirely generative. If you are seeking personal evolution there is always the question of what is stopping you from being that already?

Step 3: Choosing the model

Who do you wish to model? Who is the master of the skill you want to attain? We are fortunate to be part of a species that includes giants; intellectual giants, creative giants, business giants, artistic giants, scientific giants, giants who have mastered the use of their bodies, minds, emotions, and spirit. Many of these giants themselves stand on the shoulders of earlier giants, and this has allowed mankind to create incredible works of art, paintings, books, music, and architecture; to travel at unprecedented speeds over land, water, and through the air; to walk on the moon and the ocean floor, to peer into the depths of space, and into the heart of atoms. Choose wisely!

As if the giants of history were not enough for you to choose from, other creative minds have provided even more choice. Idealized human beings exist in literature and religious texts; perhaps you will choose the observational skills of Sherlock Holmes, or maybe Tony Stark's engineering and business brilliance that allowed him to become Iron Man, or even Jesus Christ's ability to love his fellow man. You can even, if you wish, DTI with the very gods.

Nor are you limited to human beings, or even beings imagined by human beings. You can DTI with the animal kingdom; how would it feel to become a jaguar? Or perhaps you would like to experience something more elemental, such as the life of a giant Sequoia tree? Will you DTI with a tornado and feel the raw energy of nature? The possibilities are only limited by your imagination.

We will be talking about how to choose a DTI model in Chapter 9.

Step 4: Choosing a counter model

The idea of a DTI with a counter model is something that, we believe, makes our protocol absolutely unique. There are many reasons to use a counter model within your DTI process, so many reasons in fact that we can't even begin to discuss them here, so you'll have to wait for Chapter 10.

Step 5: Are You Unconsciously Aligned With the DTI Process?

DTI is a process that requires, indeed relies on, the active involvement of the unconscious mind. If your unconscious mind is not on board with the entire process, the DTI is at best going to be less effective than it could be, at worst ineffective, and possibly even worse than worst, counterproductive. So we better make absolutely sure that the unconscious mind gets on board the train at the same time we do!

Phase 2: The DTI Experience

Step 1: Building Rapport with the model

To maximize the benefits of the effect of the DTI there needs to be a high level of rapport between you and the model. This may sound odd given that you may have never met the model, but it is important to realize that this rapport exists within you, meaning it is rapport between your representation of yourself, and your representation of the model.

The research on Mirror Neurons shows a DTI is less effective when there is no rapport between you and the model. In short, if you don't like the model, your conscious mind is very unlikely to take on the attributes of the model. Hopefully, this particular point will be dealt with when you check the unconscious alignment and ecology, because your unconscious will likely refuse to DTI with someone you don't like or respect!

The research also shows that the DTI is most effective when you have deep rapport with the model. And the deeper you can make that rapport, the more effective and more profound the DTI becomes. Therefore, we will be discussing methods to deepen rapport with the model before you begin your DTI in Chapter 11.

Step 2: Dream Incubation

One of the most effective ways of experiencing the DTI is actually within your dreams. All three of the authors actively use dream incubation, lucid dreaming or shared dreaming to install generative experiences on an unconscious level. And this includes DTI within dreams.

I (John) modeled Milton Erickson both consciously and unconsciously over a number of years. Part of this modeling involved a series of dreams during which Erickson supervised my training as a psychologist working within a prison. Having Milton Erickson actually teach you in this way, even in dreams, is truly a life-changing experience.

We will discuss Dream Incubation for DTI in Chapter 12.

Step 3: Selecting the DTI Technique

The second part of this book will be spent discussing various DTI techniques, from Alexander Raikov's original protocol, through John's Quantum Perceptual Positions DTI, through the various protocols developed by Shawn and Jess, including BEAT DTI, Reverse-DTI, Future Self DTI, Symbolic DTI and several more.

When originally discussing this book the three authors debated at length the issue of simplicity versus variety, "How many DTI techniques should we include? Should we only include one and the book should be about how to apply this most effectively? Or should we include several?" In the end (and not necessarily with unanimous agreement!), we decided to include a number of DTI techniques for you to play with.

No doubt you will like some more than others. Perhaps you will be lucky and find one to immediately fall in love with, and use exclusively. Perhaps you'll be even luckier and get to play with several of them, or even all of them. You may find that one technique is ideal for you and when working with clients a different approach yields better results.

Whatever your preference, there are enough techniques included in the book to satisfy all tastes, including the taste for infinite variety! However, all the DTI techniques described are ultimately based on John's Quantum Perceptual Positions DTI, discussed in Chapter 13.

Step 3: Building and Absorbing the Model

Another one of the aspects of our DTI protocol, which makes it different to most or all other discussions of DTI, is our firm belief that in order to understand a person on a deep enough level to truly model them, you need to understand their personal history, and the life events that have made them the master they are. This idea was brought out by our love of biography. When we read a biography we don't simply want to read about how that person behaved at the peak of their power. We also want to understand where they came from, their childhood, their early lives and the mistakes and lessons that made them the person they are at the peak of that power.

As we build our model, we are going to do so not just by considering how the master did what he did so masterfully, we are also going to consider how he gained that mastery. This gives our own unconscious the opportunity not to simply learn from them, but to learn in the way that they learned. We will be using an approach we call the Event Matrix to build our model. The Event Matrix is discussed in Chapters 14 and 15.

Step 4: Unconscious Activation of the model

Finally we have the portion of the DTI process that you would normally think of as DTI: trance, visualizations (positive hallucinations), inner dialoguing, perceptual position shifts, and so on.

Step 5: Conscious Activation of the model

Now comes a very important and frequently neglected part of the DTI process. There is a point in time where the subject has absorbed the mastery of the model on a deep unconscious level. The skills of the model are available to them, but on a latent basis; almost like a gene that has not yet chosen to express itself. This DTI 'gene' now needs to be 'switched on' in order to express itself on an emotional and behavioral level.

The method of switching on the DTI can be simple, a mere expression of an emotion or action that arises from the model, from the master, and not from the subject's normal repertoire of emotional or behavioral responses. One way of doing this is by using the BEAT pattern described in Chapter 20.

Phase 3: Integration

Step 1: Integrating the model

You have already tested for the ecology of the DTI by making sure that you were consciously aligned with the process. You have had the DTI experience; the skills and other qualities of the master have been experienced and installed on a deep unconscious level. You have carefully selected on a conscious and unconscious level exactly those skills and abilities, beliefs and values, and other qualities you wish to take back with you.

But it is still possible that there may be some clashes between your beliefs, your values, and your identity, and those that you have absorbed through the DTI process, within a real-world context you may face.

You may actually have chosen to DTI with this model precisely because they had beliefs, values, meta-programs and other qualities that you do not, but that you wish to absorb. Sometimes the DTI process by itself can be sufficient to install these new beliefs and values, or meta-programs within the specific context where you want the change to take place. After all, to install a new belief, value, or meta program you need the conscious and unconscious intention to do so, a reference experience of the new belief, value, or meta program in practice, and a self-experience either in reality—or as an imagined 'future place' using the new belief, value or mentor program.

In any case, you will wish to fully and completely integrate the model into your own neurology, physiology, behaviors and identity. At the same time you will want to reconcile and resolve any clashes between your beliefs, values and Meta programs and those of the model. We will be using a technique called the Mind Meld to resolve any such clashes that may arise (named after the famous Vulcan Mind Meld of Star Trek!). We will devote an entire chapter to this technique, Chapter 21. Of course, if the DTI works well and does not cause any inner conflicts, the Mind Meld will be unnecessary.

Step 2: Connecting the model with the Real-World Context

In this step we are going to 'attach' the activated DTI gene onto the context where the skills and behaviors are desired. We will do this using some well-known NLP techniques, including a variation of the Swish pattern. See Chapter 21 for details.

Phase 4: Application, Testing, and Refinement

Step 1: Application and testing

Of course, a DTI is of no use whatsoever unless it provides skills and abilities that can actually be used in the real world. The subject has to step into the real world context and find out what happens.

If all goes to plan, the skills and capabilities of the model will arise and operate exactly as hoped.

Step 2: Refinement

As with most things, in practice some aspect of the experience may be less than perfect, and some issue arises that could be improved upon. This is to be expected and offers an opportunity to revisit the DTI, to see how the model will deal with that issue!

Chapter 5: Instant DTI – Shawn Meets Superman

In this chapter we are going to jump right in and give you a quick and easy way to *experience DTI*. We are going to set it up first by talking about Superman, although if you are terribly anxious to get on with the process you can fly ahead a few pages (a little Superman humor there!).

I (Shawn) have always had a fascination with comic books. Even as a child, reading the Beano and Dandy in England, I loved the 'pictures that tell a story'. I always imagined being the characters as they lived through their adventures. I remember reading about Desperate Dan, a larger-than-life cowboy, when I was five or six years old, and feeling my first razor burn as I watched him shave with a blowtorch!

Many people believe that my favorite comic book character is Superman, probably because most days you'll find me wearing a Superman T-shirt. Even when I'm wearing a shirt and tie on top, I'm likely wearing a Superman T-shirt underneath (I like to be prepared!). There are other comic book characters I love reading about as well, but it is certainly true that Superman captures my imagination in respect to his character, his beliefs, and his values. On a deep unconscious level I certainly identify with Superman!

The Purpose of the Superman DTI

People often ask me about my affiliation with Superman, particularly when I am attending hypnosis conferences, and they see me wearing a seemingly endless series of Superman T-shirts from my extensive collection! "How many Superman T-shirts do you own?" I am frequently asked, a question to which there is no good answer because it depends on whether my birthday is approaching or has just passed, and how many of my T-shirts have worn out over the prior year. This is usually followed by the question, "Why Superman?"

Why Superman indeed? I have several answers depending upon my mood and who is asking me. I may say, "Superman cares, he believes he can save the world," or perhaps, "The Buddhists believe that to do good you have to have the courage of the superhero, but the heart of a child." Or I might talk about the creator of Superman, Jerry Siegel, whose father died whilst his store was being robbed, when Siegel was a child attending school; how things might've been different if young Jerry had been able to use super-hearing to hear the robbery in process, super-speed to get there in time, and super-strength to overpower the robbers. Talk about finding resources to deal with a past event!

Whatever the truth about Superman and me, my unconscious mind certainly has reasons of its own to identify with Superman. And yet, if I am to do a contextual DTI with Superman, I need to pull those reasons somewhat into conscious awareness as well. Once my conscious mind is aware of the reasons, I will be able to place the super-resources in the context, or contexts, in which they will serve me best.

The Context for the Change

So really, why Superman? As an Englishman in New York, I know what it's like to be a stranger in a strange land. And with my unusual mix of corporate consulting and hypnosis, I feel the dichotomy that comes with wearing a Superman T-shirt underneath that shirt and tie!

There are moments in my day when I am in the midst of an ordinary conversation when suddenly I find myself entering my coaching state, and seeing the people around me in a different way, x-ray vision if you will, and listening in a different way, a type of x-ray hearing. These are times when I catch a glimpse, not a full understanding perhaps, but at least a glimpse of what it must be like to be Clark Kent at the moment that Clark Kent becomes Superman. You probably have the same experience at some points in your day, a moment of transition where you move from the mundane to the sublime, a time when you enter your flow state, your skill, your expertise. What is that like for you?

Superman's Behaviors and Capabilities

So I ask myself, "If you were Superman, what would you be doing differently to what you do now? How would you be feeling that's different to how you feel now? If you know that you can leap tall buildings in the single bound, that you have super strength, that you can fly, how would your life be different? How much confidence can you feel, knowing that now?"

I ponder the question, "If I knew I couldn't fail, if I was certain that I would succeed what would I attempt? In fact, is there anything I would not attempt???"

My Values and Beliefs

What do I believe when I am wearing that Superman T-shirt? What's important about wearing that? Is it helping others? Is it protecting the weak? Or is it about being powerful, knowing I personally am safe as the Man of

Steel to take risks?

Again, the questions make me think deeply about my beliefs, and what is really important to me?

Commitment to the Change and Unconscious Alignment

And with all of that I ask myself, "Are you ready to gain a deeper understanding of how it feels to be Superman? Are you committed to following this path to see where it leads? Because if you're not, don't bother starting!" You may be starting to realize that this is anything but a casual exploration; anything but a casual relationship with Superman. You may be starting to realize that this could change who you are.

So I want to be sure, I want to be certain, not just intellectually but on a deeper level, that this is what I want. I go inside and I listen, I listen to my inner voice, my inner wisdom. I listen to my heart and I listen to my gut. And only when I'm sure do I take the next step.

DTI and Identity

You see, if you're going to do a DTI, you can't help but change who you are; your identity. Because after all a DTI is a deep trance IDENTIFICATION. When you identify with another person on a deep unconscious level, you take on a piece of who they are, and that changes you. So you should DTI with another person only when you are sure that you are fully aligned with this, not only consciously, but also unconsciously.

The other side of this coin is that your unconscious mind can protect you. Your unconscious mind is designed to filter out and reject information that is not aligned with who you are. So, if your unconscious mind is not on board with the DTI, then it may well reject what you were consciously hoping to gain from the DTI.

Why Superman?

Let's return to the question of why Superman? I have an affinity with him to be sure, based on my love of comic books and my feeling of being a stranger transplanted into an alien environment. But will being Superman help me to better manage those transitions in time, when I have to center myself in my coaching state to help another person? Are those points in time when Clark Kent becomes Superman such a transition? Or are the differences so great that no such parallel can be drawn?

Very often when somebody looks for a model to learn from, somebody to 'become', to improve a skill, they look for somebody who is good at that skill. If they want to sell more real estate they look for somebody who's good at selling real estate. If they want to be a great hypnotist they look for somebody who's a great hypnotist. If they want to be a great baseball pitcher they look for someone who is a great baseball pitcher, and so on.

On one level this makes sense. However, there is another point of view, because very often the people who make the biggest impact in a field actually come from outside the field. Such outsiders bring in skills that are outside the norm for that field, just as Superman brings a skill set which is unique to the planet Earth and yet can help to solve the problems of the planet.

Think for example of Steve Jobs. What are the skills or attributes that made Steve Jobs uniquely qualified to build a computer company able to compete with IBM, and a software company able to compete with Microsoft? Was it not his love of the beauty of perfection? One of the stories that demonstrate this is his insistence on including many different fonts in the Apple Computers, at a time when the font was considered irrelevant to computing, because he had recently taken a calligraphy class. This type of 'irrelevant' fixation on perfect beauty in design was what made Apple great.

So when you are considering who to model, who to DTI with, consider not only the best of the best within your field, but also talented individuals outside your field.

Lex Luther

Then there is Lex Luther, the arch nemesis of Superman. At first sight, it seems like there couldn't be much of a matchup, after all, Luther is a mere human being, while Superman is from Krypton. Luther has no special powers while Superman has more superpowers than virtually any other being in the universe.

But Lex Luther compensates for his lack of superpowers by being smarter, more cunning. His great intelligence and ambition allow him to routinely escape from incarceration, whenever Superman defeats him. In fact, and you may not know this, Lex Luther eventually becomes president of the United States and has ambitions of dominating the universe, no small achievements for a boy from a small town in the Midwest!

Is the best way of achieving my goals is to become Superman? I don't have super strength, super speed or super senses. Perhaps I could better proceed by becoming Lex Luther (absent the universal domination perhaps)?

Being able to DTI with the opposite of your role model can present you with amazing insights into what you are trying to achieve, and how to achieve it. As we get further into the DTI process we will be talking a lot more about what 'opposite' means in the context of DTI. For example, it could be someone with the opposite skills, beliefs and values, like Lex Luther to Superman. On the other hand it could be somebody who has achieved the same outcomes, but in a very different way; think perhaps Bill Gates to Steve Jobs. Finally it could be somebody who has absolutely no skills in the area in which to model, and while this sounds counterintuitive, we will be coming back to this concept for a very important reason later on.

The Instant DTI Process

So let's finally get on to the instant DTI process. We will be adding a lot more detail to the process as we go through the book, but we want to provide you with a quick and easy way to experience DTI. We will assume that you have already selected somebody to model, perhaps Steve Jobs for business creativity, or Superman for strength and moral rectitude, or...

Event Matrix

Whoever it is, we need to turn that abstract character into actual experiences into which we can associate. We do this by creating an Event Matrix.

The Event Matrix is a list of short meaningful episodes from the model's life. We will give you some examples in Chapter 15, but for now simply choose three or four events from the life of your model that you feel are significant. If you can't choose these events, then you don't know enough about the model, and you should do some more research. Fortunately it is pretty easy these days to research most people's biography using the Internet and the Great Goddess Google.

So now you have chosen three or four events you feel are significant and tell you something important about your model. Next, turn each of those events into a small movie within the theater of your mind. If it makes it easier for you, you might want to imagine you are sitting in a movie theater watching each of those scenes on a movie screen. They do not need to be long scenes; they can be measured in seconds or minutes as long as they are telling you something important about that person.

Once you are able to watch each of the scenes on the movie screen of your imagination, make sure you have the answers to the following questions:

- Where does the scene take place?

- Who else is present? What is their relationship to the model?

- What is the model doing in the scene?

- How is he or she behaving? By this we include asking, what is that physiology? What is their facial expression? What sort of gestures are they using?

- What are they saying?

- Where are they putting their attention: what are they looking at and listening to?

- Based upon this, what are they thinking, or at least what do you think they are thinking?

- Based upon this, what are they feeling, or at least what do you feel they are feeling?

- Based upon all of this, what you think is important to them? What do they believe about themselves, the world, and their place in it?

Now, watch the movies again in light of this new information. See how each scene provides a slightly different view, slightly different information about who the model is as a person.

Dream Incubation

Depending on how long this process takes (for example are you spending 10 minutes, or a number of days?), and depending upon the intensity with which you do it, you may find yourself dreaming about the model. For example, I (Shawn) am researching the history of hypnosis for a series of posts on our Blog Hypnocafe.com, and spend my nights dreaming of meeting Mesmer, Braid and other great hypnotists of the past. Such dreams are great indicators that your unconscious mind is connecting with the model and his experiences. Dreams generally serve two purposes: first, dreams are designed to integrate new learnings that we have made throughout the day; second, dreams function as our own inner therapist. Dreams can help you process and clear emotions. It is a great sign when you *begin to dream about your model*, whether the DTI is for a generative or therapeutic purpose.

The DTI Process

Now you are going to do the DTI itself. Imagine yourself back in that movie theater watching those scenes from the model's life. This time when you get to the end of the first scene, rewind it to the opening frame and float into the picture so you actually become the model. Allow the movie to run again, this time experiencing it from the inside. At the end of the first scene, allow yourself to float out of the movie and back into the seat in the movie theater.

Now allow the second scene to run from beginning to end. Once more, rewind to the opening frame of the second scene, float into the movie, into the model, and allow the second scene to replay so you experience the second scene from the inside.

Repeat this process with each of the remaining scenes, one by one.

Congratulations, you have completed your first DTI!

The Swish

In order to make the DTI useful and available to you when you need the skills of the model, you can utilize a pattern from NLP called the Swish. The Swish pattern is designed to link two pictures together, so each time you see the first picture, you will automatically see the second picture in your imagination. The first picture will be whatever you actually see in a specific context. For example, if you want to feel more confident when dealing with your boss, then the first picture might be your boss' face.

The second picture is the model, so if your model is Superman it will be a life-size, three-dimensional, big bright colorful picture of Superman. We are going to chain the two pictures together so that whenever you see your boss' face you automatically have the experience of stepping into your Superman DTI.

To run the swish, simply:

- Imagine seeing your boss in front of you.

- Take that picture of Superman and shrink it down to the size of a postage stamp and imagine sticking it on your boss' forehead.

- In a moment, but not yet, that picture of Superman will burst out from your boss' forehead and appear life-size in the space between you. So go ahead and imagine your boss's face, see the picture of Superman on his forehead, and then imagine that picture of Superman bursting out, becoming life-size between you and your boss!

- Finally, imagine stepping into Superman and having those super-skills when dealing with your boss (please bear in mind that we are talking about skills such as inner strength, patience, compassion and so on, not the ability to pick somebody up and throw them over a building!).

Repeat this process in a number of contexts in which your boss may be present, or whatever the context in which you would like the skills of the model to be available to you.

- See what you will actually see in the context

- See your model, shrink that picture down to the size of a postage stamp and place it somewhere in the context

- Imagine the picture of your model springing out, getting bigger and closer and brighter, and three-dimensional as it moves towards you

- Step into the image model and feel how good it feels to have those skills

The more frequently and vividly you imagine this, across a range of different contexts where these skills will be useful, the more deeply embedded they will become in your conscious mind. We will be coming back to the swish pattern later on and expanding upon it.

Ecology Check

Now that you have imagined being able to do this in a number of different situations so those skills are available to you, ask yourself if there is anything about your experience that appears wrong, uncomfortable, dangerous, or damaging to the people around you? If there is, then please go back to the beginning of the process. You might want to select a different model, or select a different context in which to use those skills, all to absorb a different set of skills from the model you have selected.

We will be talking a lot more about ecology and how to ensure that the DTI does not invalidate your own beliefs and values later on in the book, when we talk about the Mind Meld.

Now you're done. *Your new abilities will be available to you in the context in which you need them!*

Chapter 6: Back To The Future: Future Self DTI

One of the things we always do with clients is to have them associate into future possibilities. Take a moment to consider the HNLP Coaching Pattern: we associate the client into the problem, or present state so we can elicit the strategy and find the right place to attach the resource. We next dissociate them from the problem and ask them how they want to be different? Once they access that state we can begin to elicit the end state energy, an identity-level resource such as 'love' or 'freedom'. We may say something like, "And when you have been practicing this good feeling for so long that you barely remember that old issue, who are you being as a person?" This is a conversational future-self DTI. They have to step into the role as the 'future them' to access the answer to that question.

We can supercharge this experience using trance as described below, by building up the representation of the future self through all the sensory channels. We do this to some extent in the Coaching Pattern already, as we unconsciously suggest they make, and step into, a new self-image. However, with the future-self DTI we are creating a more explicit relationship with that future self.

Future-Self DTI

This Future-Self DTI pattern we are about to explore came out of our work with weight loss clients. One of the issues these types of clients have is their body image. It is the representations they are making in their minds about themselves. They are creating an image and running a commentary of it. They then identify with that image. They are essentially using their working memory to sabotage their weight loss endeavors. They are actually using their unconscious to maintain the issue while at the same time trying to use their conscious mind to change.

If these clients were using this type of process to create a problem, we can also use it to create a solution. In the case of weight loss, keep in mind that it isn't just the number on the scale that is the issue; it is the size and shape of the body. If a client wants to change his or her weight, they need to change the mental representations they hold of themselves and their relationship to them.

So we would begin the coaching process by having the client build up a vivid mental image of their future self; one that is happy and healthy as well as slimmer. We take time to build up both the visual representation of the future self, as well as the beliefs, values, and the end state energy of the client; how they will be as a person when they have made the change they desire and become who they want to be.

The client would next associate into that new self, experiencing the future from the inside out. We would then spend time piecing together the path they took to get there. Finally they would dissociate from that future self and associate into a version of the current self who is transformed. They associate into a new current self who is ready to take the steps to realize this goal. This way the unconscious mind has the motivation to go after that image.

The process is very easy. We do not need a formal Event Matrix because it is the modeler's future self that is the model. As such, their own life experiences will come into play and form a sort of Event Matrix as we will explain a little later.

You may also want to do a values elicitation for current self and future self. This will let you know if any secondary gain of the current un-resourceful behavior is going to be compelling enough to impede change (assuming this is a therapeutic context). As hypnotist, you may want to do a values integration piece here, if necessary.

Using Trance for the Future-Self DTI

In trance we invite the subject to make an image of his future self who has already made incredible changes. These are both the changes linked to the reason for the session, as well as all of the other generative changes that emerge from it. We help orient them to the image by calling their attention to different details of the future self's physiology—how are they standing, breathing, the expression on their face, etc. This has a two-fold effect of stabilizing the image as well as mirroring to the modeler the physiology of the desired states.

When it is time to do the DTI in trance, you can use a basic perceptual position DTI described in Chapter 13.

Future Pacing

Once you have associated the client into the future self, it is time to experience points in the future where the client uses his future skills and capabilities. The client can experience the context and trigger as his own resourceful future self. They can also have other reference experiences where they get to use those skills. For example, a client who had a fear of flying, once in the shoes of their future self, not only can enjoy flying comfortably but also relish the places they visit. They may also take that sense of calmness they now have on the plane and experience it at work, or when doing other potentially stressful activities. This reinforces the positive state and gives them a number of iterations to build up new neural connections.

The next step comes from the work of Milton Erickson. We invite the client, as his future self, to look back over this process of change, and at all of the things that happened between his session with you, and then becoming that resourceful future self. Invite the client to pay close attention to all of the steps they took to realize this transformation. This has a twofold benefit. The first, as Erickson noted, will be the client telling you the exact path to take to help them realize their goal. The second benefit is the client sees the roadmap to their success. This puts the responsibility for taking the next step in that direction solely in their hands.

For the final step you have some options. First the client dissociates from the future self and back into self. The image of the future self is left on their timeline, waiting for them in their future. This is the same principle as the outcome picture in a Swish, leaving an attractive self-image to lead the unconscious in the desired direction, so the current self has the goal to work toward. An important feature here is that the current self is also transformed. Because the client has had this experience of being in the future and seeing the pathway to success, the current self cannot stay the same. We can suggest to the self that they are, "Stepping back into the self that, in this time and place, has changed because they now know the roadmap to success." They also know on a deep unconscious level that change is in fact possible and will happen. This is the secret behind "The Secret". You make an image of the future you want, step into it and enjoy, then step back out so as to boost motivation to get there. The current self has changed because we are all changing, all the time, after all it is impossible to step back into the same river twice.

Future-Self Reverse DTI

The second option is that the client steps back into current self as the future self. This allows the future self, which has all of those transformative reference experiences to gift them to the present self. The modeler now has access to all of the resourcefulness of the future self. This idea is discussed further in the Double Reverse-DTI chapter.

Both approaches are useful and have their place. The first version is very good for creating motivation. It works well for issues around habits, as well as goal setting. The second variation is useful for those looking to generate certain states in the here and now.

In other DTI patterns you may note that we emphasize using 3rd position as a middle point for the modeler, so they don't take back unwanted aspects of the DTI (as Gilligan did when he first began associating into Erickson, and brought back a frozen arm!). In this Reverse Future-Self DTI it is less important to do that. You may want to use 3rd position at the start, before associating into the future self. Coming back, however, it is not so important to use third position. The present and future selves are both the modeler, albeit at different times, so we do not have the same concerns about carrying unwanted attributes back. In fact it may be very beneficial for the client to go from second position right back into first as this can create a blended space between present and future self.

Example: Future You as DTI Master

If you were to imagine some point in your future, when *you are absolutely masterful and can DTI with ease* with anyone you'd like to, to master any skill, what does that absolutely resourceful future you look like? Is that future you sitting or standing and what is his or her posture like? How is he or she breathing? What type of capabilities does that future you exhibit?

If you were to step into that future you, right now, what type of *possibilities are open for you for the rest of your life*, now, you can *become aware of all of the abilities you can acquire through DTI* with ease. I wonder what variety of new and pleasant states you would experience as this masterful learner. Perhaps you would *become curious* about who you are as a person at this moment, and how you are being as a person when you are this future-you.

And as you look back at the path that lead you to this point, what are the experiences you had that have helped you reach this point of being able to DTI with anyone? What are all of the key moments that lead you to be so incredibly, profoundly masterful at identifying with models and to grow in who you are as a person? How could you take all of these and continue on even further into the future?

If you were to step out of that future-you for now, you may find that it is easy to carry that knowledge with you as you *now go forward on the path to that future* and beyond. You can *find it easy to step fully and completely back into the trance-formed you* in the present moment; with that insight leading you to new learnings and wisdom, far beyond what you could possibly, consciously expect.

You can simply *go into trance* and see an image of yourself having gone through this book, having already practiced DTI so frequently that it's second nature, so if you would like to DTI with someone, you can do it quickly and easily.

Conclusion

Ultimately this approach is not dissimilar to a future pace. Traditionally in a future pace, once there has been a positive shift in physiology, we invite the client to go to the next time and place where they will be in context and see or hear the trigger, noticing how it is different, how they have changed. Next we go to another time and place in the future, followed by another, each time strengthening the change. This gives the client multiple times to practice the new state and behavior. It also pre-frames success in those future events. What we have presented here is a more formalized way of doing it that allows the modeler to fully and completely step into their future success.

If you use this pattern, as in the example above, where the modeler is stepping into the future self, masterful at DTI, you do something very important. You are collapsing dozens or even hundreds of DTI experiences into one. You are teaching the modeler how to learn. So if they have just had a number of DTI experiences within the span of one trance, their unconscious mind will generalize so that they DTI automatically at the unconscious level whenever they want to acquire new skills.

So it's not just the skills they learn, it's learning the skill of learning. It's the ability to DTI easily. So when you meet somebody in the future, a

73

teacher or somebody who has some skill, you can look at them and *you can immediately DTI with them because you've done so many DTIs before.* That's the future you that we want you to DTI with. This is the you in the future who is able to look at a teacher or model and immediately take on the characteristics of the teacher, because doing a DTI for that is your natural, automatic tendency. This is the skill of masters.

We can speak from experience. The more DTI's you do, the more automatic they become. With this type of DTI we have the ability to do in one session what could have otherwise taken many. You can take the lifetimes of many masterful coaches and fit them into the experience of one session. How much more powerful of a change worker will you become knowing that you have unconscious experiences linked to all of those life changing coaches?

Chapter 7: The Context of the DTI

In this section we will discuss the context in which you intend to use the skills you will acquire through the DTI with the model. This first step of the DTI protocol has nothing to do with the model; it has everything to do with you. Consider the following questions: Why do you want to experience the DTI? Where will you be, when will you be there, and who will you be with when you use the skills, abilities, resources and other attributes you have gained? What do you hope to get out of it? How will you use it? Is it aligned with your own values and higher purpose? Are you prepared to do what it takes to integrate the skills of the model into your own life and experience? The answers to all these questions are built upon this foundation of the context in which you want to use the skills you have gained in the DTI.

These are anything but trivial questions. Think about it this way, when you know a person and you know them well, you know them because you have a 'model' of them inside your brain, inside your own neurology. It is this model that allows you to predict how they will behave in a given situation. The closer you are to a person, and the better you know them, the more detailed and accurate this internal model becomes.

Experiencing a DTI on a deep level allows you to get to know the person you intend to model in a way that few other people will. It builds a detailed and intricate model of that person inside your own neurology. Not only that, but the protocol we will lead you through causes that model to become part of your behavioral response in certain situations. It becomes not just someone you know, but a part of who you are.

Therefore it is very important that you understand your own reasoning for experiencing the DTI. It's very important that you know exactly when and where you expect to use the skills you will acquire. It is very important that you understand and reconcile any clashes that may occur between the beliefs and values of the model, and your own beliefs and values.

Let's talk about a couple of examples. When Stephen Gilligan modeled Milton Erickson it is said that he began to develop a 'frozen arm', similar to one of Milton Erickson's physical symptoms. You see, the unconscious mind needs specific guidance to determine what to take from the model, and what to leave behind, otherwise it may take the wrong things. It is certainly nice to think that the unconscious is infinitely resourceful, that the unconscious will know exactly what to take from the model in your best interests, but as we know, the unconscious can lead us to do things that are definitely not in our best interests (just consider a smoker, or someone who is chronically overweight).

Another example of taking attributes that became problematic for the modeler involved one of our own students who modeled himself on one of his mentors within the context of marketing. The model held the strong belief that he was only prepared to help those who made the commitment, and put in sufficient effort themselves, to become successful. This is actually a pretty good belief to hold if you are a coach. In contrast, our student held the belief that he should be prepared to help everybody who asked him for help. As a result of this clash in values between model and modeler, our student found himself selling his services, but then doing way more for many of his clients than he had bargained for. The model's skills were not transferable until there was reconciliation between the values of the model and modeler.

Before you embark on a serious DTI with a particular model you should ask yourself what skills you are seeking to acquire, in what context you want them, and what you want to get out of the process. Considering these questions will help you identify a suitable model, or lead you to realize that you have been looking at the wrong model, if you have already picked one.

Specific Context for the DTI

Once you know what the context is, you can associate into that context by imagining you are back in that context, in that specific time and place, seeing what you are seeing, hearing what you are hearing, and feeling what you are feeling. Associating in this way will allow you to rebuild your own experience, and rebuild your own logical levels, in that context.

So the first question to ask is, "What is the context for the DTI? Where do I want to use the skills and abilities of the model?" The more specifically you can answer this question, the easier the rest of the process will be. Think of specific times and places when the skills and abilities of the model would be beneficial. Where are you? What are you seeing and hearing? What are you feeling? What is going on around you? How are you behaving? What is the result of your behavior?

How do I want to be different in that context?

The next question to ask your self is, "How do I want to be different in this situation? What is my outcome? What do I want to achieve? How will this interaction look at the end when I'm using the skills and abilities of the model?

These questions are very important because they provide a powerful filter for your unconscious mind, allowing you to unconsciously decide what characteristics of the model to take, and what to leave behind. For example, if Stephen Gilligan had focused on his end result in modeling Milton Erickson, it

77

is very unlikely he would have seen himself with a frozen arm!

What Are Your Values in This Context?

Before you can fully answer the question of how you want to be different in the situation, what your outcome is, and how things will look different when you have achieved that, you need to know what's truly important to you. You need to know your values in the context.

Once more, consider the context of the DTI, a specific time and place where you wish to use the skills and abilities of the model. Be as specific as possible in regards to time and place. We suggest you use a time and place from your past where the skills and abilities would have been useful for the purposes of this exercise. Go to that time and place. What are you seeing? What are you hearing? What are you feeling? As you get in touch with those feelings, ask yourself, "What is truly important to me about this?"

This form of values elicitation is not intended to be an intellectual exercise, after all a 'value' is not an abstraction, it is a real positive feeling attached to a nominalization (a nominalization is a word such as freedom or love). So allow the thoughts and related feelings to arise, and make a note of them as they do; freedom, safety, success, love, whatever they might be.

If you're working through this exercise alone you might want to use an audio recorder to record the results. Writing or typing can bring the conscious and logical mind back into the process, and break the unconscious mind's association with the context.

Once you have completed this exercise you should have a list of values, although they will not necessarily be in order of importance because you will have written them down as they occurred to you. Write the list on a piece of paper, and take a look at it. Consider if anything is missing from the list, any value which you need to add. You can also ask yourself why each of the values is important to you. "Why is this important to me? What will this do for me? What will I have, when I have this?" These questions may lead to other values you have overlooked.

When you have your final list of values take a look at them again. Begin to eliminate any duplications. For example, you may have 'freedom' and 'being my own person' as values, and you may decide that 'being my own person' is the same as 'freedom', so you can simply delete 'being my own person' from the list.

Now take the final list and rank them in order of importance. As you do this you may find that there are two values that significantly overlap; they are, 'almost the same'. You can either select the one that resonates most with you, or list them together, for example, 'relaxation and peace'.

When you have your final set of values, you can use them to help you to envisage how you want things to be different. For example, if one of your values is 'freedom' you can ask yourself the question, "If I were being free in this context, how would I be different?"

We will also need this list of your values later on to do the Mind Meld DTI, by comparing it and reconciling it with the values of the model.

What Are Your Beliefs in this Context?

We will now repeat the above exercise for your beliefs. The beliefs we are most interested in are your beliefs about yourself, the world, and your place in it, within the context where you want to use the DTI.

Again take the specific time and place where you wish to use the skills and abilities of the model. Imagine you are in that time and place; notice where you are, what you are seeing, hearing, and what you are feeling.

As you (the subject) experience yourself back in this time and place, ask yourself, "What am I believing about myself, my skills, and my abilities? What am I believing about the world around me and about other people? What am I believing about my place in the world?" Once again, you may wish to record your answers with a voice recorder rather than using a pen or a keyboard so you can remain associated into this context.

Our experience is that the beliefs of the model are often much more empowering than the beliefs of the subject. After all, this is one of the reasons the model is more successful than the subject, and why the subject might want to take on the skills of the model. If there are any limiting beliefs the subject holds that are uncovered during this process, these can be addressed using the NLP belief change process, which we discuss in Chapter 21.

Reconciling Your Outcome With Your Beliefs and Values

This is the part of the exercise when you begin to ask yourself some difficult questions.

Question 1: Is your outcome aligned with your values?

Many of us chase goals we don't really want, and wouldn't enjoy if we had them. So now is the time to take a good long look at your goals and ask yourself, "When I have achieved this goal, to what extent will I then be living my values?" For example, if one of your high values is 'freedom', and your goal is to be a successful Wall Street trader, ask yourself: "If I was a successful Wall Street trader, would I be experiencing freedom?" If the answer is yes, then all well and good. However, if the answer is no, then you may wish to rethink your goal, rethink your values, rethink both, or reconcile them so you can experience freedom by being a successful Wall Street trader.

It may be particularly important for you to reconcile your values with your goals if you are the sort of person who often finds it difficult to achieve your goals. This may indicate that your goals are not aligned with your values. If you find that you are pursuing goals not aligned with your values, you may want to explore this with a coach, adviser, or other confidante.

Question 2: To what extent are your beliefs supportive of your goals?

There are several ways in which your beliefs may not be supportive of your goals, for example you may currently believe any of the following (based on Robert Dilts' Belief Audit):

- Deep Trance Identification is not effective for learning and changing'

- Deep trance identification is effective, but I'm not a good hypnotic subject, and it probably won't work for me'

- Deep trance identification is effective, and I am a good hypnotic subject, but I don't think it will work for this particular change'

- Deep trance identification may work for this particular change, but I don't really deserve it

If you have any beliefs, such as those above, that might limit the effectiveness of the DTI, you can use the NLP belief change described in Chapter 21, or consult a qualified coach to help you through this issue.

Of course, you may believe that *DTI is a great hypnotic tool for learning new skills, and you're a great hypnotic subject, so DTI is going to work amazingly well for the change you are seeking, which is great news because you certainly deserve the best of everything in your life!*

Question 3: What are your 'modal-operators' in this context?

Modals (rather than 'models'), often referred to as modal operators, are concepts or beliefs about the possibility or impossibility, and necessity of doing something. Modals are represented by words such as:

Can
Can't
Should
Shouldn't
Must
Mustn't
Have to
Will
Won't

In our experience, models are one of the most important drivers for many DTI experiences. We often select models that have a strong drive to do something. Think of people like Thomas Edison, Steve Jobs, Superman, Milton Erickson. Each of these individuals is driven to do what they did, to pursue their dreams.

It isn't simply a matter of determination that "I will do this." Rather it was almost as if they had no choice; Thomas Edison was so determined to prove his Alternating Current superior to the Direct Current of his rival Tesla, that he suggested the Department of Corrections use Tesla's Direct Current to execute criminals in the hope of discrediting Tesla! Superman attempts to walk away from his life as a superhero but is always pulled back. Milton Erickson, weakened by his polio, nevertheless spent endless hours carrying out hypnotic experiments. Steve Jobs was driven to create the 'perfect' computer, spending millions of dollars on seemingly irrelevant details, to the point where he was driven out of his own company by his colleagues. In each case they appear almost obsessive in their drives, and it is this sense of obsession that captivates us when we choose a model.

Associate back into the context in which you want the skills. Where are you? What are you seeing? What are you hearing? What are you feeling? And as you feel yourself there; ask yourself, "What can I do, what is possible for me here and now? What can't I do, what is impossible? What can't I do? What must I do? What drives me?" This will help you to identify your own meta-programs in this context.

Chapter 8: Checking for Unconscious Alignment

What follows is a metaphor. It's not an actual description of how your brain works. As such you should *pay special attention* to it.

You have two halves of your brain, the left-brain and the right-brain. As you probably know, your left-brain uses language and logic to process thought. It is the rational part of your brain, if you will. Your right-brain uses sensory experience, pictures and feelings, to process thought. It is the part of your brain that pays attention to everything you are not rationally thinking about at the moment.

As hypnotists, we talk about the conscious mind and the unconscious mind. Now it is certainly not completely true to say that the conscious mind is the left-brain and the unconscious mind is the right-brain. At the same time this comparison does have some truth to it, and can be very useful as a metaphor.

We think things through logically using our left-brain. However, this does not mean we will follow through on these logical decisions with actions, unless our right brain has been involved in the decision-making process and is emotionally invested! For example, as hypnotists we see many people who have decided to quit smoking, and yet are finding it very difficult to do so.

Their left-brain, their conscious mind, might have made a decision to quit, but their right-brain, their unconscious mind, has not yet bought into the decision.

Now you've made a conscious decision to DTI with a certain person, to take on the skills and abilities of that person. But just because you have made a conscious decision to do so, does not mean that your unconscious mind is necessarily on board, and if it's not it will likely sabotage the process! So in this step we are going to check to see if your unconscious mind is on board with the DTI.

If not, we are going to negotiate between your conscious and unconscious minds.

Ideomotor Response

An ideomotor response is a physical response under unconscious control. Examples of ideomotor responses include unconscious gestures, twitches, blinks, and so on, as well as totally unconscious responses such as blushing and pupil dilation.

Using a Pendulum

One way of making ideomotor responses easier to see is to use a pendulum because a pendulum magnifies unconscious physical movement of the hands.

Go and find a pendulum now. If you don't have one, you can easily make one by attaching a paperclip, or some other object, to the end of a piece of string or cotton. Rest your elbow on a table, allow your wrist to *relax* and hold the pendulum between thumb and forefinger so the pendulum hangs down towards the table (but does not touch the table). If necessary, steady the free-end of the pendulum with the other hand until it is still.

Now, within your own mind begin to think 'yes'. You can say yes, or you can think of something that you completely agree with and think yes. Continue to think yes and *notice what happens* to the pendulum. The pendulum will begin swinging in one direction or another, for example it may swing forwards and backwards, or from side to side, or it may begin to swing in a circle. If the movement is small, thank your unconscious mind for participating and politely ask it if it would increase the signal until it is clearly visible.

Once you have a clear signal for 'yes', it is time to move on to 'no'. Make the pendulum still again with your other hand, and then begin to think 'no'. Again, watch the pendulum and see which way it moves. You should find it moving in a different direction, generally the opposite of way it moved for 'yes'. For example, if it moved from side to side for yes, it may move forward and backward for no. If it moved in a clockwise direction for 'yes', it may move in a counter-clockwise direction for 'no'. Again, be patient with yourself and if the movement is small, politely thank your unconscious mind and ask it to increase the signal.

You should now have a clear unconscious signal for 'yes' and another signal for 'no', and you can use the signals to check that the unconscious mind is aligned with your decision to DTI with the model you have chosen.

Obtaining the Unconscious Agreement for the DTI

Explain to your unconscious mind that you plan to DTI with the model. Because your unconscious mind is less verbal than the conscious mind, and prefers to think in pictures and other sensations, as you explain to your unconscious mind your plan to DTI with the subject, visualize this happening within your mind. If you plan to DTI and therefore absorb only a limited aspects of the model, explain and visualize that to your unconscious mind as well.

Now ask your unconscious mind if it is prepared to participate in the DTI process. Your unconscious mind can communicate with you while using the pendulum. If you receive a 'yes' signal then all is well and good. You can proceed to the next step of the protocol.

If the response from the unconscious mind is no, then you can begin to explore the objections of the unconscious mind, using the following questions as guidelines. Be careful how the questions are phrased so that the meaning of a 'yes' (or 'no') signal is clear.

- If certain aspects of the model, such as certain behaviors, feelings, beliefs or values are excluded from the modeling, and I do not absorb those aspects of the model, is my unconscious mind prepared to proceed with the DTI?

- If yes, is my unconscious mind prepared to share with my conscious mind what those aspects are?

- Is my unconscious mind totally against the DTI process with this model under any circumstances?

- If yes, is my unconscious mind prepared to suggest a better model for the DTI? And if yes, will my unconscious mind communicate that model to my conscious mind?

In the vast majority of cases, even if there is a 'no' from the unconscious mind initially, the unconscious mind will either suggest behaviors, feelings, beliefs or values of the model that should not be taken on board (and agree to the DTI as long as these are excluded), or suggest a different model.

You may also ask the unconscious mind if there is a part of it that can cancel out the negative quality; if yes would it be willing to do so and continue with the DTI, This situation came up with a DTI being done with Steve Jobs as the model. The modeler's unconscious mind did not like how Jobs treated his friends and did not want to take that on. The negotiated solution was that the part of the unconscious mind responsible for maintaining good friendships would be watchful and ensure that that aspect of Steve Job's personality was left out of the experience. If the unconscious mind says no to everything and simply refuses to cooperate, do not proceed with the DTI.

Chapter 9: Choosing a Model

In this chapter we will discuss how you can choose a model for your DTI, and what might make one model better than another.

When I (Jess) began my journey as a hypnotist I spent hours DTIing with master hypnotists like Milton Erickson. Back then I didn't know I was doing a DTI. In my mind it was just an imagination game. I would sit and wonder, "If I was Milton what would I do?" Of course, I was not satisfied by just asking the question, I had to dream myself into Erickson and find out! As a budding Ericksonian hypnotist, who else would I have chosen to DTI? With the skills of Milton Erickson I could confidently hypnotize anyone. I could feel myself the greatest hypnotist in the world!

Almost everyone who tries DTI starts off modeling the person they consider to be the 'best' exemplar for the skill they want to acquire. Raikov, the father of DTI, used this approach. For example, he had the young cellists at the Moscow Conservatory DTI with Pablo Casals, often considered the best cellist of all time. It makes perfect sense—if you want to be a great cellist, you would DTI with the greatest cellist!

But actually I might have chosen many people, not only hypnotists, but non-hypnotists as well and still brought amazing skills into my own hypnosis practice. For example, Steve Jobs created something called the Reality

Distortion Field around him, and it was said that anyone who stepped within this Field would believe anything that Steve Jobs told them! So on one level, Steve Jobs was a master hypnotist, and doing a DTI with Jobs would provide the opportunity to absorb this ability and *create your own Reality Distortion Field.*

The first question is, when you choose a model, what are you looking for, not only in terms of the model's skills, but also their other attributes? Are we simply looking for specific physical behaviors or skills, like in the case of Pablo Casals playing the cello? Or are we also looking for specific emotional skills, perhaps Superman and his sense of self-confidence or compassion? Or are we more interested in the model's beliefs and values; perhaps Steve Jobs' belief that anything was possible for him, and his love of design and craftsmanship?

A second question is, do we want to find a model that is similar to us? And if so, what does 'similar' mean, the same gender, the same physical attributes, similar beliefs and values? Or do we want a model who is very different than us, a model who will complement us in some way, make up for our own shortcomings?

Let's take a particular example; our good friend Kyle practices Wing Chun, a style of Kung Fu. He's also a great hypnotist. He wants to DTI to learn from a model how to improve his Kung Fu skills. So who should he choose as a model? Perhaps he simply says, "I want to improve my kung-fu, I've got a kung-fu instructor I'll DTI with that teacher." But what is it about his instructor that makes him a good choice? Well one obvious benefit is that he knows his teacher; he has seen him many times demonstrate the techniques he wants to improve. He has seen his model teach others and he's heard him give feedback to them. So he has a very rich sensory experience of his teacher. He has also spoken to him, and during these conversations he has consciously or unconsciously picked up on many of his teacher's beliefs and values. So creating the Event Matrix for his teacher should be relatively easy, he has plenty of events to choose from, and lots of information about his teacher's logical levels and Tree of Life (more on logical levels and Tree of Life later).

We also talked elsewhere about the importance of having rapport with the model. Kyle obviously has deep rapport with his Wing Chun teacher, so this step will be easy. Deeper rapport implies a deeper DTI.

Kyle also reports that his teacher's skill set goes beyond the physical skills, and includes wisdom that includes his beliefs and values. Kyle also values the fact that his teacher is older, in fact quite old, being an original student of Ip Man, the famous Wing Chun teacher of Bruce Lee. Because of the teacher's age, he has learned to apply his Kung Fu without relying on the source of strength and speed that only comes with youth. Because of this particular context in which his teacher is able to operate, Kyle feels confident that the insights he will get from the DTI will serve him well in the future, as he himself ages.

Choosing a Model Outside of the Field

Other people might choose a model who is outside of the field of their own skillset. This approach, this thought process, has become somewhat popular in recent times with books like 'Jesus CEO', which was followed by 'Jesus, Entrepreneur' and 'Jesus, Life Coach', each exploring how Jesus would be had he chosen a career other than Messiah (or carpenter!).

You could take this approach to DTI with anyone you respect, with any area of your life in which you would like a new approach. Imagine 'Milton Erickson, Used-Car Salesman', we'd all be driving around in rusty 1997 Pintos! Or, how about 'Leonardo da Vinci, Web-designer'? Or perhaps you have yet to consider, 'Genghis Khan, Babysitter' (don't worry we're joking about that one!).

So you can DTI with an expert in the field in which you want to apply the skills, or with somebody outside the field, bringing in a fresh perspective and a unique approach.

Building the Model

In any case, at a minimum you actually need enough information about the model to build an 'Event Matrix'. We'll be explaining how to do this later in detail, for now just understand that you need to have a number of reference experiences of your model in various situations, at various times. If you want to improve your piano playing, and decide to model a famous pianist you know nothing about, and there are no videos or recordings of him playing, no autobiography, and only the sketchiest biographical details, then you're going to find the DTI very difficult to do, because you will lack enough information.

So you have to ask, what kind of information and what quality of information is available about the model? One of the challenges with modeling Milton Erickson is that it's quite hard to get good information about him. There are plenty of audio recordings, movies or videos, but a lot of the information is controlled by the Ericksonians, who keep it very much under lock and key. Fortunately there are plenty of books about his work, both his own case studies, as well as accounts of his trainings given by his students, and other commentary. For example, 'A Teaching Seminar with Milton Erickson', by Jeffrey Zeig, takes you right inside Erickson's classroom, to experience learning from the master himself!

So, consider how much information is out there about your model? Are there videos? Is there audio? What is the quality of biographies that are there? Autobiography is much better than a biography, because in an autobiography the model will intentionally or unintentionally reveal his beliefs and values, and his meta-programs. A biography written by somebody who knew the model is good in the sense that they may describe actual events in such a way as to give insights into the model's unconscious map of the world. A biography written by somebody who didn't know the model is the weakest source of information because it describes what somebody else thinks about the model, based upon what they have read, so it's very much third hand or worse.

We will however put an important caveat on that last point. Some biographers really bring the character of their subject to life through their writing; people like Walter Isaacson who has written amazing biographies on Albert Einstein, Benjamin Franklin, and Steve Jobs. Isaacson also makes it his business to interview his subjects (if they are still alive), as well as people who know them, by examining personal writings and other sources that give insight into their personality. And although at the end of the day these biographies represent the writer's model of the subject (for example Isaacson's model of Albert Einstein rather than Albert Einstein himself), this can still provide a powerful model for the DTI, even though it is one or two steps removed from the actual model.

So in general, video is better than audio because video gives you visual cues as to how the model is behaving and their internal processing. Audio is better than the written word because audio tells you what the model was saying and also gives you auditory cues as to their internal processing, by listening to their tonality and so on. Depending on the quality of the writing, autobiography is better than biographies written by somebody who knew the model, which are better than biographies by somebody who didn't.

You can also ask the question: within this wealth of information about the person, whether it's video, audio or written word, what insight does all this information provide on the model's identity, beliefs and values, and their meta programs? If all the information simply discusses their technical abilities, you may be able to learn from this on a conscious level. However, it will be much more difficult to DTI on the unconscious level, without the higher logical levels, such as the model's beliefs, values and meta-programs.

How Much Time Do You Have?

The other thing you might want to think about is: how much time do you have? Let's say there's loads of information out there, but you don't have time to look at it all. Perhaps there are all sorts of videos you could watch, audios you could listen to, and books you could read. But you need to improve your own skill right now. You don't have weeks to read all the books and watch all videos.. In that case it might be better to pick someone who's maybe not as good as a model, but someone you know personally, or someone you have seen or read a lot about already. In practical terms, if I have an important sales call tomorrow, and there's a salesman I know who's really good, one I could model right now because I know him. Or there is another guy who is unbelievable, but I don't know anything about him and it would take weeks to research him. Maybe I should choose the first guy because the modeling will be faster and easier.

So these are the guidelines you might use to choose a model:

- Do I want to model a person within my field, such as Paolo Casals, if I'm learning the cello, or my Kung Fu teacher if I want to improve my Kung Fu? Or do I choose somebody in an unrelated field, 'Play the Cello like Picasso', or 'Sherlock Holmes' guide to Wing Chun'?

- Do I want to choose somebody who's like me in some physical way, the same age, the same sex, the same level of strength, the same intelligence? After all, will I ever be able to play basketball like Michael Jordan? Perhaps I should pick a model who is more my own size. Or should I pick somebody who's very different, my 80 year old, wizened Kung Fu teacher so that I can grow into those skills over the next 30 or 40 years?

- Do I want to pick somebody who has beliefs and values, or meta-programs that are similar to mine? These intangibles are big drivers of behavior, and if the model's beliefs and values are very different to yours, you are likely to have a lot of integration to do to make the DTI successful. On the other hand, having a successful DTI with somebody who has different beliefs and values, or different meta-programs, particularly in a context where they excel and you don't, can be hugely generative.

- How much rapport do I have with the model? Do I truly respect him? Can I truly imagine becoming him and be grateful to them for that opportunity?

- How much information do I have about them, and is it readily available?

- What is the quality of information; is it video, audio or the written word? Is there an autobiography with collected letters written by the model, biographies from people who knew him, or simply biographies?

- And finally, how much time do I have compared to how much work I need to do to prepare for the DTI?

Once you have considered these questions, you will be ready to make your final choice. If you are doing a full DTI, investing a significant amount of time then choose wisely! Don't immediately make the obvious choice, even though at the end of the day this may be the model you return to.

Chapter 10: The Counter Model

In this chapter we are going to explore an idea that may seem unusual. We are going to dive into the world of counter models, the shadow counterpart to the ideals of the model. We are going to explore four different ways of using the shadow, three of which we will describe here. The fourth will appear in the chapter pertaining to the 'Super Villain DTI' as the shadow of the Super Hero DTI.

The first approach we will examine is the counter model as a model of unconscious incompetence. Understanding what it's like to not know how to do something, but to be unaware of this 'not-knowing', allows you as the modeler to judge your own progress on a learning scale that stretches from the unconscious incompetence, "I don't know how and I don't care anyway," to unconscious mastery, "I can do it easily and naturally."

The second approach we will consider is the counter model to counter-balance the model's weaknesses. Model and counter model may each be deeply flawed as separate individuals, but together they may create a perfect whole.

The third and final approach in this chapter will be the counter-model as an alternative path or strategy to achieving your goal. Having multiple ways of achieving the same goal creates greater behavioral flexibility. In this approach, each of the two strategies, the strategy of the model and the strategy of the counter-model, will each lead to the same destination.

Counter models provide a 'three-dimensional' approach to the DTI process, the three dimensions consisting of model-modeler-counter model. Counter models allow us to think about and develop skills in ways that are no longer limited by the constraints of the model, and by our own weaknesses. Counter models give the unconscious mind a point of comparison, leading to greater flexibility and opportunities for integration, so that the modeler's learning goals are met more quickly.

Counter Model as Unconscious Incompetence

We go through four stages of learning when undergoing any learning process.

The first stage is that of 'unconscious incompetence'; not knowing something, and not knowing that you do not know it. It always reminds me (Shawn) of the old joke, "Can you play the piano?" "I don't know, I've never tried!" I enjoy this joke because my daily attempts to extract a recognizable tune from our piano makes me pine for the days when I didn't know I couldn't play! Here's another example, a month before purchasing this book you may not have known about Counter Model DTI and you didn't know that you did not know about it. It wasn't within your framework of experience, therefore there was no way to know that you did not know.

The next stage of learning is conscious incompetence. This is knowing there is something out there that is possible, and knowing that you do not yet know about it or cannot yet do it. This is the unfortunate stage when you first try something that looks easy, and realize it is anything but. Most of us have learned to ride a bicycle, and perhaps it looked easy when we watched the other kids ride theirs. But as soon as we got on our first bike and tried to pedal while steering and staying upright, we became conscious of our own incompetence. When first leading a client into DTI, you may have to check steps in the DTI process, this too is conscious incompetence; you know about the process but it is not yet at your fingertips.

The third learning stage is conscious competence. This is when a learner knows how to do a particular skill, but it still takes a great deal of conscious effort to actually do it. In this stage we like to have steps to follow. An example of this would be a musician learning his or her instrument, Shawn playing the piano perhaps. I can play a tune, however it still takes concentration. The flow is not yet established. Similarly when learning the techniques of DTI, when you have read a chapter, tried the techniques and gained some experience in DTI, you will be in the place of conscious competence.

The final learning stage is unconscious competence. At this level we do not even need to think about the skill. We do it automatically and with ease. You no longer need directions or steps, it just happens. If you've learned how to ride a bicycle, you are likely now at the point of unconscious competence; you can ride one without thinking. Even if you haven't ridden a bike in years, if you were to climb on one now you would be able to ride with ease. The concert pianist is unconsciously competent and is able to focus on musical interpretation while her body takes care of pressing the right keys at the right time. And as your DTI skills develop, *you will begin to absorb skills easily and naturally*.

Within DTI, learners will go through these four stages. It is the use of trance that allows the four stages of learning to be compressed and speeded up. This is the benefit of DTI, its whole purpose.

So the first of the counter models we will be focusing on is that of unconscious-incompetence, someone who is at step one of the stages of learning. We will deliberately choose the counter model for their unconscious incompetence. The benefit of this is to give your unconscious mind a point of comparison. The unconscious mind is able to compare wherever you are in the learning process right now, to the experience of the counter model representing the first step of the four stages of mastery. Using this first counter model allows you to consciously and unconsciously chart your progress throughout the DTI learning experience.

If you don't use such a counter model, you run the risk of always comparing yourself to the model, rather than how you were when you started the process. Let's imagine for example that you want to DTI with Walt Disney in order to expand your own creativity. You would like to tap in to Disney's ability to 'dream' ideas into realities. Modeling Disney's creativity could be quite a tall order for the average person, although by doing so you will undoubtedly become more creative than you were before you started the process. However, your conscious mind may be comparing your ability to Disney; "You're not as good as him, you never will be, who are you kidding!" The question becomes how do you, as the modeler, know that you have achieved a higher level of creativity than what you started with? You need something to gauge your progress against, not just your ultimate, ideal destination. This is where the counter model becomes very useful. You will choose a counter model that represents the opposite of creativity, by which we mean not only uncreative, but with no interest in being creative. This could be, for example, a rigidly-minded politician, a by-the-book educator, or someone else who for you represents that "This is how it's done, and there's no reason to try anything new."

For me (Shawn) the counter model for creativity is represented by SALY. In business consulting, SALY is my enemy, she stands for Same-As-Last-Year. When consulting for a business and asking why something is done a certain way, the person responsible might answer, "Well, that's how it was done last year, that's how it's always been done." Never mind if it's right or wrong. Never mind if it's the most efficient way. It's the same as last year and that's enough for SALY. So SALY, or rather the followers of SALY, are my counter models for creativity. Who or what would your counter model be for creativity?

Counter model process

The DTI process entails associating into the model so that the modeler's unconscious mind knows which direction to go, using any of the DTI techniques described in this book. The modeler first visits third position and views the model from this dissociated position, before associating into the model. Next she will dissociate from the model, in this case Disney, and back into herself (via third position). Wow, that was fantastic!

How do we utilize the counter model within this process? Well, we can lead the modeler to experience the counter model in much the same way she did the model, although likely in less detail, and utilizing fewer events. She can once again visit third position, this time to take a look at the counter model. She can then associate into the counter model, experiencing the world in a more fixed, less creative way (if modeling Disney say). "This is the way it's always been, no reason to change now!"

Now she has an experience of the model and an experience of the counter model. What do we do with these two experiences to make them meaningful within the DTI experience? What we are seeking to do is to create a mental pathway that moves from Unconscious Incompetence through Conscious Incompetence, and Conscious Competence, until we finally reach Unconscious Competence. We can create this path using perceptual position shifts.

The modeler has associated into the model, the ideal of Unconscious Competence, the end-point of the path we are creating. Now she goes back to the start of this path by associating into the counter model, the ideal of Unconscious Incompetence. She can now dissociate from the counter model by moving to the observer, or third position. From third position she can observe the counter model. This observation of the counter model represents Conscious Incompetence, because she sees the counter model from third position and realizes his Incompetence.

Staying in third position she now turns to observe the model. Observing the model represents Conscious competence, meaning she can observe the competence of the model, but is not yet able to fully access that competence without conscious effort. Finally she associates once more into the model, accessing the model's Unconscious Competence.

The experience of moving in this way begins to move her through the stages of mastery, from the Unconscious Incompetence of the counter model to the Conscious Incompetence of observing the counter model, through Conscious Competence of observing the model, to the Unconscious Competence of being the model.

As hypnotist we can begin to condition this chain of learning. Create a break-state after associating into the model and before restarting this process. Now run through the four stages by associating into the counter model, dissociating into third position and observing the counter model, from third position observing the model, and finally associating into the model. The more times

100

this process is run, the more the four stages of learning are anchored and 'chained' together.

Let's take an example. Your client wants to model Steve Jobs. Her counter model is Ken Olsen who said, "There is no reason anyone would want a computer in their home". After doing the DTI with Jobs you want to condition the learning chain for your client:

1. Associate with Olsen
2. Move the third position and observe Olsen
3. Turn and observe Jobs
4. Associate into Jobs
5. Break state by shaking off the experience.

Now repeat steps 1 through 5 to condition them.

Once the steps are conditioned, you can lead her to move from directly from counter model to model, from Olsen straight to Jobs.

By moving from counter model to model, the creativity of the model will seem much greater, much more pronounced, because the comparison will be with the counter model. My experience moving from myself into Disney is something like, "Wow, he was so creative!" But moving from SALY into Disney provides a seismic shift in experience, like moving from a sketch to a full color cartoon. The creative state feels so much stronger and more powerful.

Finally you return your client to third position, then back into herself, taking the learnings not just of the model, but of the learning process itself, with her.

In addition to anchoring in the four stages of learning, using the counter model also allows the modeler to judge her own progress as she applies the skills of the model. She may even see a timeline with the counter model in her past and the model in her future. She can then measure her progress literally by the distance between her position on this time line, and the position of the counter model (the distance she has come), or the distance between her position and that of the model (how far she has to go). With each DTI or real world experience the modeler can move step by step closer to the position of the model, moving further away from Unconscious Incompetence and closer to Unconscious Competence.

Counter Model as a Balancing Influence

The next counter model technique is to use a counter model as a means of balancing the less resourceful traits of a model. If we were to take a moment and think about the major cultural icons people will often choose to model, these figures tend to have very strong positive qualities, but also strong negative qualities. These negative qualities could cause an ecology issue for the modeler if not addressed. Using a counter model in this way allows the modeler to fully step into the positive traits of the model while also experiencing the complementary resourcefulness of the counter model.

An excellent example of this is Steve Jobs. Jobs had an amazing ability to create the impossible. He was able to bend reality so that the people at Apple were able to build a computer that provided the average person access to a home computer system that exceeded the imaginations of some of the brightest minds in the field at that time. On the negative side, this same drive and ambition caused issues in Jobs' personal life, which in many ways was not nearly as successful as his professional life. The same traits that allowed him to succeed in business, hurt him in many of his personal relationships.

When modeling Jobs, it may be useful to have a counter model who can complement Jobs' positive traits, while filling in the blanks in the areas where Jobs was lacking or had negative traits. In this case, Steve Wozniak as a potential counter model comes to mind. For those not familiar with the history of Apple, Wozniak was the creative, smart, and talented friend of Jobs and co-founder of Apple. Woznik is well respected in the industry, and in fact was technically more talented and creative than Jobs, although lacking Jobs' visionary side. However, Wozniak is also considered a 'nice-guy', a person who is able to maintain healthy and positive personal relationships, without the negative and destructive personal traits that dogged Jobs.

By DTIing with Jobs, but also with Wozniak as a counter model, you can step into the shoes of Steve Jobs to experience his ability to distort the reality of those around him, making the impossible possible. But you can also complement this experience with Wozniak's ability to maintain healthy positive relationships that in many ways Jobs lacked.

In order to absorb the best of both model and counter model you will have to integrate both experiences, the DTI with the model and the DTI with the counter model. This integration can be accomplished a number of ways including using a visual squash with both the model and counter model as presented in Chapter 15. The modeler can also practice compartmentalizing both models by anchoring the positive traits of Jobs in one specific context, while anchoring Wozniak's traits in another. For example, the modeler can experience making the impossible possible in the office as Steve Jobs, while at home experiencing the importance of family and friendship as represented by Steve Wozniak.

Counter Model as Alternate Path to the Desired Outcome

The final use of a counter model that we will explore here is that of the alternate path to the desired outcome. There is more than one way to develop a skill set. And the counter model can provide an alternate route for the modeler to achieve her goal, so that she can unconsciously choose the best route to accomplish that goal. This use of the counter model teaches the unconscious mind to be flexible by illustrating that there is more than one option available.

Once again we can consider Steve Jobs as the model. Perhaps the modeler wants to be more original and creative, for example, using Steve's experience in building the Apple II as reference for 'creating something original'. In Steve Jobs' map of the world, style was everything, and it was impossible to separate form from function. The look of the computer, the feel of the computer, and the style of the computer were intrinsic to the computer as a tool. Jobs was also a perfectionist, separating the world into the 'insanely great' (anything that he did), and everything else anyone else did, which was basically crap. And Jobs believed that hardware and software were inseparable, that the software had to fit the hardware like a hand in a glove.

Of course at the same time that Jobs is creating the Apple II, Bill Gates was also creating software in which the computer industry would come to rely. In some ways Gates and Jobs appear to be similar, they both worked extremely hard and as a result they both became enormously rich, building two of the world's leading technology companies. But if we look at how they did it, we will see a very different picture. Gates was very much about practicality, about making things work. Arguably Gates' real skill was going to market and finding a way to secure strategic business advantages for Microsoft. The form of the product had limited interest to Gates, as anyone who remembers MS-DOS will know. In MS-DOS there were no beautiful interfaces or varied fonts, just a blinking green cursor. In fact DOS was not even Microsoft's product, but one they licensed from another company to license on to IBM. It is difficult to imagine Steve Jobs ever licensing someone else's product to on-license to IBM. Unlike Jobs, Gates had such a distain for style that he suggested people who wanted a black computer didn't need to buy a Mac, instead they should buy a PC and a can of black spray paint. Of course, Apple's focus on style has ultimately forced Microsoft to massively improve its own user experience, leading Jobs to accuse Gates of stealing Apple's ideas.

Once you understand the differences between Gates and Jobs, Bill Gates becomes the counter model or counter example. He is ultimately as successful as Steve Jobs but for different reasons, following different strategies, holding different beliefs and values. Steve Jobs was a creative visionary who literally made reality bend to his will. Bill Gates took advantage of the world as it was to his own advantage.

Steve Jobs created products that he believed in, holding the belief that people would buy them if they were 'insanely great'. Bill Gates took advantage of market opportunities, such as buying DOS to on-license to IBM at a low cost, knowing that other computer manufacturers would likely follow IBM's standard and pay him to use the DOS system.

Steve Jobs was obsessed with the style of his products, but left much of the technical work to Wozniak and others. Gates didn't care about style, but did understand programs from the inside out and was hands-on in the construction of Microsoft's software. Legend has it that Gates reviewed every line of code produced by Microsoft for the first 5 years of the company's existence!

Jobs dabbled in drugs, meditation and Eastern philosophy, yet was considered impossible to get along with by many of his colleagues. Bill Gates seems so with a more prosaic life, but seems to have no difficulty getting along with others.

Both the model and counter model, Jobs and Gates, were able to accomplish amazing leaps in home computing. However, they did it in very different ways. The modeling of both teaches the unconscious mind to think outside the box and not fall into the trap of exclusive "or's". By this we mean, "I must do this the same way as Steve Jobs," or "I must use the same process as Bill Gates."

Just as in other exercises with the counter model, you can use perceptual positioning shifts to allow the modeler to associate into the model, or into the counter model whenever useful.

Conclusion

In summary, utilizing a counter model in the DTI process opens up new options to the modeler, depending on the counter model chosen. It allows you to transition from incompetence to competence. The counter model can neutralize negative traits in the model so that ecology issues are less likely to arise. And finally Counter Model DTI can help to build an internal flexibility in which the modeler recognizes there is no one exclusive way of accomplishing their goal. They can integrate the best of both worlds to not only achieve their goal, but to also experience a more well-rounded DTI.

Chapter 11: Rapport with the Model

In this chapter we are going to discuss building rapport with the model, how to generate it, and why it's crucial to do so, neurologically speaking.

Many spiritual and mystical traditions have recognized for centuries the importance of students making a commitment to the teacher. For example if you wanted to join the Shaolin Temple to become a monk and be taught the mysteries of Shaolin Kung Fu, you had to show the proper devotion. You had to sit outside the temple to show that you wished to become a student, and even then you had to wait until you were called, which could take days or weeks, or perhaps you would not be called at all. Even if you are lucky enough to be invited inside the temple, you will spend months sweeping the flagstones and carrying out other mundane tasks to further test your dedication, before you are taught any of the mysteries of the school. You then have to practice rigorous and painful physical exercises before you could be taught anything of a martial nature. On one level, this is the teacher asking, "Are you going to be a good student? Am I being wise in investing my time in teaching you?" and challenging the prospective student to demonstrate the answer.

But there is something more fundamental to this process. You see, you can only truly learn on a deep level from a teacher you truly respect. Learning is about much more than simply listening to what somebody says, after all this is the whole basis of DTI. DTI relies on your Mirror Neurons activating to give you an internal experience of the teacher's reality, and research shows that mirror neuron's only become activated when you feel a sense of 'sameness', especially when built on foundations of respect and admiration for the other person.

What we are doing by creating rapport with the model is building response potential within the DTI process. If you want to DTI with the model you have to be serious. You have to want to become like the other person, you have to want to model this person on a deep unconscious level. This is really important for the DTI to be successful.

Let's say you're a human being from 100,000 years ago, you live in a village with at least 30 people. You can't model everyone, so your brain is saying, "Who do I want to be? Who are the winners and who are the losers?" You're going to pick the winners to be your models, your unconscious mind is going to say, "Be like him, he's a winner." And without this deep rapport, deep respect for the model, you're not going to be creating the same brain states, or the same physiological activity in the body, as the model.

Of course you may be modeling somebody you know, perhaps a colleague or a friend, or a team-mate from your sports team. In this case you will probably already have rapport, and this rapport can be deepened in the context of the DTI by speaking to the model, and asking permission to do the process with them.

But even if you are doing the DTI with somebody you do not know, perhaps somebody who is no longer even alive, or even somebody who never actually existed (like a super-hero), you can still take steps to build rapport.

Building rapport by asking permission to DTI and thanking the model

One way of building rapport, before we do the actual DTI process, is to ask permission from the model to do the DTI. By this we mean going into trance and having a conversation with them, asking them for permission to associate into them, to DTI with them.

It may sound odd to be asking permission from somebody living or dead, real or fictional, to go through your own mental process using your own imagination. However, gratitude has a very deep and profound effect on the unconscious mind. Those of you who are familiar with NLP will know that patterns such as the Six-Step Reframe use 'gratitude trances' to build response potential to change. Thanking the model after you've done each portion of the process will also help to deepen this rapport.

So, whenever you begin a DTI process, ask for permission from the model. And when you conclude, thank them for their help and for the learnings they have provided. In any case it feels good to show gratitude, so why not!

And ultimately this is not really about literally thanking the person, the model, rather it's about thanking the part of yourself that is the model.

Building Rapport With Dialogue

You can also build deeper rapport between yourself and the model using the Dialogue Process discussed elsewhere in the book. The Dialogue Process allows you to verbally receive insight and instruction from the model by asking questions about how the model performs his skill, how does he know it's time to start, how he knows what to do next, and how does he know it's time to stop.

You can deepen the rapport further during this process by asking the model for advice, and by opening up your hopes and dreams within the context of the DTI.

Building Rapport With Breath

In our experience, an even more powerful way to build rapport is using breath, by matching the breathing of the model. To do this, close your eyes and imagine the model is sitting in front of you. If you haven't yet chosen a particular model, just pick somebody who you like and respect. Set your intention to learn something from this model.

As you see the model sitting in front of you, pay attention to her or his breathing, is it fast or slow? Is it deep, or shallow, from the belly or from higher in the chest? Does he breathe through the mouth or through the nose? Does he pause between their in-breath and out-breath, or is the breathing more fluid? Spend a few minutes noticing the breathing pattern in as much detail as you can. Incidentally, this exercise will also sharpen your visualization skills.

Once you have spent some time paying attention to the model's breathing, notice your own breathing. You may find that it is very closely matched with his in terms of speed, depth and so on. If not, reset your attention to learn something from him and repeat the exercise. If you are unconsciously in rapport with the model there should be a matching of breath.

Most people find that not only are they matching breaths, but the model also begins to take on the physiology and the posture of the model. In addition, the modeler is also likely to experience a change in his internal state. He will be beginning to feel something of the state, or the emotions of the model. When you feel it, you know you are moving in the right direction.

Chapter 12: Dream Incubation

Dreams have captured the imagination of cultures around the world since the dawn of humanity. They were often considered to be messages from the gods, sometimes in the form of divine inspiration, and other times appearing as dire warnings of disaster. In more recent times they have also been used within the context of therapeutic change work. Freud thought them to be repressed desires from the unconscious mind, while Carl Jung believed the dreamer to be dipping into the collective conscious.

More recently, dreams have been the subject of scientific research, which indicates they play an important part in learning and laying down long-term memories. When you sleep, you dream, and when you dream your brain is making sense of the world around you and your experiences.

We have used this framework extensively during our own DTI explorations. For example I (John) incubated and experienced a series of dreams when I was first learning hypnosis by DTIing with Milton Erickson. These dreams followed a pattern where I worked as a psychologist in a prison, under the supervision of Dr. Erickson. As you can imagine, even in a dream my clients had very difficult issues on which I had to consult Dr. Erickson, seeking guidance and advice. Learning directly from Milton Erickson in this way gave me enormous insight into therapeutic hypnosis. I also encourage my students to use dream incubation prior to, during, and after the hypnosis training where Milton Erickson was used as a model, and also in the photo reading training, where the students would typically DTI with the author of the books they were reading.

When we were writing this book, I (Shawn) used dream incubation to DTI with Konstantin Stanislavski, creator of the acting system called the 'Method' (often called method acting) mentioned earlier. These dreams took place in a small Russian village located on the side of a very steep mountain. I knew the mountain was steep because in my dreams I was typically walking up the main street with Stanislavski while he made insightful comments about the villagers we passed. Although the village was small, the street was long and very steep, I would wake exhausted in the morning!

Dream incubation and interpretation provide powerful tools for any sort of learning or change. And whether you are using DTI for yourself, or as a coach working with others, you can *utilize the power of dreams to lay the foundation for a successful DTI*, as well as to integrate the learnings of the DTI process. In this chapter we will be exploring some easy strategies you can use to incorporate the dreamwork process within DTI.

The average person may think dreams are random and fantastic images strung together in a broken plot that either holds no meaning at all, or on the other end of the spectrum, is filled with mystical knowledge. Of course, both of these perspectives hold some truth! However, we are far more interested in the usefulness of dreams as a process of learning and healing. Every night people generally spend over two hours of their sleep time dreaming. That's a lot of time interacting with your unconscious world! These two hours are spread out over a number of sleep cycles, each cycle lasting roughly 90 minutes. Each sleep cycle consists of four stages, only one of which (REM sleep) is associated with dreaming.

During these cycles we experience two types of dreams, dreams for integrating learnings, and dreams for emotional well-being. During dreams associated with emotional well-being, the mind uses the dreamscape as a safe place to work through emotional issues, and let go of previously emotionally charged events. You may have had times in the past where you went to sleep feeling bad, emotionally drained in some way, but wake up the next day feeling refreshed, and that old issue seems far behind you now. This is because while you were sleeping your unconscious was using dreams to work through those negative states. It is an opportunity to hit the emotional reset button.

The other type of dreams, those associated with learning and integration, provide the brain the opportunity to rewire itself so that new experiences are linked up with already existing neural networks. This is why infants, who naturally experience rapid brain development through learning, spend 50% of their sleep time dreaming.

It has also been discovered that dreaming impacts skills acquisition. One study showed that people who were taught a new mental skill, and then experienced REM sleep, were able to recall the skill after waking. On the other hand, those who were taught a skill but then deprived of REM-sleep, were unable to recall that skill after waking. (http://www.ninds.nih.gov/disorders/brain_basics/understanding_sleep.htm)

You may be able to *recall a time where you had a novel experience, or learned something new, and in some way it appears in your dreams* that night. For example, when I (Shawn) was learning to ski, my dreams were full of ski-runs!

Now you are learning how to deep-trance-identify, so *tonight, as you sleep and dream, you may have dreams about times when you were young; learning through pretending. Or perhaps you will have a dream where you become your model and experience the world through their eyes (like Shawn with Stanislavski). Some people dream that the model is teaching them (John with Dr. Erickson), while others find that their dreams contain pieces and fragments of the new learnings. Still other people may think they haven't dreamed at all, yet this too can be a sign of the changes taking place at the deepest unconscious level!*

Through the process of dream incubation you can use the brain's natural functioning to lay the foundations for the DTI, as well as integrating the learnings you acquire through the DTI process. This is a multilayered approach because the ability to DTI is a learned skill set whereby you are learning how to learn. Within a specific DTI experience you will learn specific skills, and integrate those skills with who you already are. These skills are the abilities, states, behaviors, and beliefs that you acquire through DTI with your model.

There is also a third learning layer, above both the specific skills you acquire, and the ability to learn through DTI. This final layer is connected with the therapeutic nature of dreams themselves; whether you are using DTI as a generative, or therapeutic, practice you cannot help but *experience other profoundly beneficial emotional shifts in your life*. Your unconscious mind can take both the specific skills of the model, and your newfound ability to learn by modeling, and begin to apply both on our unconscious basis to *make profound changes in your life*. After all, you never know how far change may go!

Someone could for example DTI with Jimi Hendrix within the context of playing guitar, then discover that the fear of public speaking has unexpectedly dissolved. Perhaps the unconscious mind has taken not only the physical guitar-playing skill of Hendrix, but also his ability to perform naturally and confidently in front of massive audiences, and generalized it in the life of the modeler. Or perhaps your unconscious mind has integrated the learning process of DTI, and unbeknownst to you decided to DTI with Martin Luther King, or some other great speaker, whilst you dreamed!

On the therapeutic side someone could DTI with the calmness and peace of the Dalai Lama as a means of letting go of some previous traumatic event, only to find as a result that they now experience more love and compassion in their day-to-day life. Perhaps the unconscious mind absorbed a lot of compassion as part of the DTI with the Dalai Lama, or perhaps the unconscious mind decided to DTI with Jesus Christ while you slept! You really never know just how far a change may go!

With dream incubation you will directionalize the modeler's dreams so they can develop their skills as a modeler, integrate learning that they made through the DTI process, and use the dream itself as another opportunity to DTI with the model from one or more of the perceptual positions (observing the model, speaking to the model, or becoming the model). The technique to do this is straightforward and is described below.

Note, that during dream incubation, we are not telling the modeler what to dream. We are simply *letting the unconscious mind know that these are the areas to explore and deeply consider while the modeler sleeps and dreams.* We are planting the seeds, and it's the unconscious mind that will grow the plant.

Using Dream Incubation With a Client/Modeler

Dream incubation is very easy when you are guiding someone through a DTI experience. They will already be in trance, which means that incubation can be done using post hypnotic suggestion. You are, after all, already speaking directly to the unconscious mind. We typically do dream incubation toward the end of the session, when we are ready to guide someone out of trance. This reminds the unconscious mind to take on the learnings from the trance experience, and use dreaming as a way of integrating it on a deep level.

We keep these suggestions very open. There are a couple of reasons for this. The first is that the unconscious mind knows how to dream in ways that are ecological for the person. We are simply inviting the unconscious to continue doing what it already does well. Their unconscious mind knows more about them, and what's needed during dreaming, than we could ever know.

The second reason for keeping the suggestions indirect and general has to do with the nature of dreams themselves. Some people may experience dreams as being nonsensical fragments without a central plot. Other people may forget their dreams and thus think they hadn't dreamed at all. If the guide sets a specific expectation around dreams, and the modeler experiences something different, they may jump to the conclusion that the process doesn't work. We are giving them every opportunity to succeed, and keeping these suggestions general and open-ended means that they cannot fail.

You can keep this short and simple by suggesting something along the lines of:

"Tonight when you sleep you will dream, and when you dream, your unconscious mind can integrate all of the learnings you've made. Now, you may remember these dreams, or you may choose to forget them. If you remember them, they will give you additional insight into your next steps, but if you choose to forget them it simply means your unconscious mind is making changes on an even deeper level."

The above suggestion is very broad and covers two main possibilities: either the client remembers the dream, or she doesn't remember the dream. The client's unconscious mind can make whatever meaning out of it she likes.

You can become a little bit more elaborate with this process, using double binds and universal quantifiers so that whatever experience the client has at night, when they wake up the next day they will be sure that the unconscious mind has gone through a process that is beneficial for them. Below is a longer example of what we like to use with students and clients.

"Throughout today you have learned many things. You've learned about dream incubation and other aspects of deep trance identification. Eventually tonight you will sleep and you will dream. Now I don't know what type of dreams you will have. Some people have exciting dreams, while others have boring and mundane dreams. Some people have Technicolor dreams and others black-and-white dreams. Some people have dreams with a cast of thousands or only a few... of you... may even think that you have not dreamed at all. And let that be a sign of the changes taking place on the deepest unconscious level."

The above suggestions let the unconscious mind choose which way it would like to integrate the learnings, and the client is left knowing that whichever way is chosen is the right way to experience change and growth. Of course the same type of suggestions can be used to create dreams in which the modeler experiences another DTI.

Self Dream Incubation

Dream incubation for yourself relies on a direct line of communication between your conscious and your unconscious minds. Self-hypnosis is the easiest path to establishing this type of communication, and if you are going to be practicing DTI by yourself, it is certainly important that you are easily able to access trance states.

The process highlighted here is in three stages. The first is to prepare the unconscious mind for dreaming. The second stage comes as you're falling asleep at night, and initiate the dream. The final stage comes in the morning as you wake and recall the dreams you had.

Stage 1: Preparing for the dream

In order to prepare for the dream you will need to set your intention, prepare your body, and prepare your mind.

To set your intention, decide that you wish to have a dream experience of your DTI model. In order to activate this intention it's important that you take specific a physical action. We suggest you write your intention down in a dream journal, which you keep for this purpose, so that the writing becomes the physical activation.

On evenings where you have set the stage for dream incubation, it is important to eat sensibly (not overeating, not under eating, not eating food that might disagree with you), as well as avoiding alcohol. This will help to prepare your body for the dream. You should also avoid activities that might over-excite your unconscious mind, such as the late-night news, and instead spend some time simply breathing and relaxing before you go to bed.

To begin to prepare your mind for the dream incubation, you should enter a hypnotic state. The induction we are about to share with you can be used for dream incubation (as well as a part of your DTI process).

Begin by finding a comfortable place where you will not be disturbed during this trance. Take a moment to get comfortable and find something in front of you, at least 3 feet away, on which you can focus your gaze. Allow your vision to narrow down to the tiniest detail and focus on that. You can notice any differences in color, variations in light and shadow, even the texture of that point. Imagine you could narrow your gaze down even more so that it's almost as if you could see the atoms and molecules that make up that point.

Next, allow your gaze to relax, and your focus to soften. Still looking at that point, let your vision expand so you can take in more of the space in front of you. The more you relax your eyes as you keep looking at that point, the more you can take in everything that is to your sides, above you and below you. You could allow your awareness to expand, and as your vision expands you can sense the distance between yourself and the walls in front of you, behind you, and to your sides. You could be aware even of the space from the top of your head to the ceiling.

As you do this, begin to notice the comfortable, relaxing feeling that is deepening in your body and mind. Allow it to spread from the top of your head to the tips of your toes. It is as if each time you exhale, it sends another wave of peace, comfort and relaxation through you. When you are ready you can close those eyes and relax even more deeply enjoying the comfort in your body and the quietness in your mind.

You should now begin a preparatory visualization. We like to do this using an Aleph point. An Aleph as a particular place, perhaps a place in nature, real or imagined, that acts as a starting point. The term Aleph was used by the writer Borges to describe a point from which all other points in the universe are visible. Choose an Aleph that is meaningful to you.

Once you are in a trance, or at least a deeply relaxed state, visualize going to your Aleph. The Aleph is the place where you meet your model during DTI, or from where you go to the place where the dream is to take place. In any case, if this is your first DTI with this model, introduce yourself, welcome your model and verbally set your intention for the dreams you would like that night. You may wish to gently suggest to your unconscious mind your intention for the dream incubation, and ask your model to take part in the process. Thank both your unconscious mind and the model for assisting you in this process.

It is time to come out of trance so allow your awareness to drift back to the outside world and enjoy the rest of your day.

Stage 2: Falling Asleep

This protocol is based upon Shawn's work with lucid dreaming and shared dreaming.

When you go to bed to sleep, once more allow your vision to expand so you can see the entire room around you (or so you could see the room if it was not dark), and then allow your eyes to close while you are in this state of expanded awareness.

Within your imagination, go back to your Aleph point and enjoy the sensory experience of being there. Pay attention to the details, see the landscape and the sky, hear the sounds around you, feel the ground under your feet, notice any scents or fragrances. When you're ready, allow your model to appear in front of you, and allow the experience to unfold in whatever way it chooses, knowing you have an amazingly resourceful unconscious mind.

If you experience this deeply enough, with all sensory involvement, all this internal journey, there is a very good chance you will begin to

118

'drift off', for a second or two. You may even fall asleep completely, but if not, you can simply repeat this process from the beginning; expanding your senses, closing your eyes if they are open, going back to the Aleph, experiencing the Aleph with all your senses, and meeting your model.

Stage 3: Recording your dreams

Once you have woken up in the morning, and before you get out of bed, begin to recall the dreams you had during the night. Simply allow those memories to come.

Thank your unconscious mind, and the model, for those dream experiences. Now record your dreams in your dream journal.

Dream analysis

Once you have accumulated a number of dreams in your dream journal, if you wish you can begin to self-analyze those dreams. Discussion of dream analysis is beyond the scope of this book, and we refer you to the excellent Dreaming Realities by John Overdurf and Julie Silverthorn.

You can use this dream incubation process as often as you like throughout your modeling project. The more you practice this, the easier DTI and dream incubation becomes, because you are programming your mind to directionalize dreams in a precise way that allows you to learn easily.

Chapter 13: Basic Perceptual Positions DTI

In this chapter we are going to be moving into our protocol, and our first official DTI modeling experience. The technique we're going to be looking at is perceptual positions. This is how Gilligan modeled Erickson, and the idea is very simple: after having interacted with your model either live, or through videos and books etc., and building the Event Matrix, you will be going into trance and, as a consciousness, observing the system from various perspectives that we'll talk about in this chapter. This may involve stepping outside of yourself, stepping into the model, observing the model, observing the system as a whole, and observing the system on a 'quantum' basis, which we will explain later in this chapter.

When I (Jess) was using DTI as my pathway to learning hypnosis I used a simple but elegant process that made it easy. What I would do was to step out of myself, and step into the hypnotist I was modeling. I had a couple of people I was modeling at that time, and I would bring the most challenging, fun client I could possibly imagine into the space. I watched the model work with the client then stepped into the model and experience it from the inside out. I would end the experience by stepping into the role of client in order to have a richer understanding of the skills before returning to me.

This was a mental exercise that allowed me to try on different situations, and different variables. And if you are starting to realize I was modeling both the Master Hypnotist and the client at the same time, you'd be right.

What ended up happening as a result was that my own skill set developed far more quickly than I had expected. I started looking at things differently and in a far more resourceful way. So perceptual positioning, dissociating from self and associating into other person, allows the mind to act 'as if' you are that person, and to experience the world as if you're the model.

To do this technique, there are four main perceptual positions that we're going to look at:

First Position

The first position is me-myself, as I am right now. I'm me, I'm in my body, right here. And being inside my own body, I can see out of my own eyes, hear out of my own ears, and being me I can look out of my own eyes and see you over there.

First position is how many of us tend to spend a good portion of our life, and it is certainly a great position to experience your own life from. This is the baseline; it's where we start from. We should point out that first position is not where everyone spends all or even most of their time; some people spend their time in second position, or third position or fourth position, as we will see.

Second Position

The next position is second position. Second position means we associate into somebody else. So if you are with somebody else, and you experience things from their perspective, looking through their eyes back at yourself, then you are in second position.

If you're not used to using perceptual positions, this may sound a little bit odd, but actually many people unconsciously experience things from second position much of the time, naturally. For example you probably know somebody who says things like, "I know you think...", or "They're going to really enjoy this...", or some other statement that implies they know what the other person is thinking or feeling. They have put themselves into another person's shoes to draw those conclusions. In short second position is stepping into someone else's point of view; someone else's perspective.

Third Position

So we have first position and second position. Now we have a transition step, represented by third position. Third position is a dissociated position; I'm looking at things from the outside. It's as if I'm a disembodied awareness, perhaps an impartial and unemotional camera viewing and recording the scene. If you imagine drifting outside of yourself, maybe to some spot on the wall, from where you can look over and see yourself over there, then you're in third position.

Just as some people spend a lot of time in second position, seeing things from another person's point of view, thinking their thoughts and feeling their feelings, other people spend a lot of time in third position. You can tell these people because they are often very logical but emotionally detached. They might say things like, "Let's look at this logically."

Integrating First, Second and Third Positions in DTI

Consider a situation where you are with another person, in this case your model. You feel yourself in your own body, looking out of your own eyes at your model. This is first position. From first position you can begin to interact with the model.

If you are modeling someone you know, you can actually sit down with them and speak to them. We do modeling projects during our NLP Master Practitioner course, and sometimes students will model one of the trainers and will ask to spend time interviewing them.

Even if you are modeling someone you do not have direct access to, you can still 'interview' them from first position. Such an unconscious interview can not only build rapport with the model, (see chapter 11), but can also provide surprising insights. One of my (John's) students was doing a DTI with an author. The student didn't know the author and did not at that stage have any biographical details about the author. The student 'interviewed' the author from a 'first position trance' and during the conversation the author provided details of his personal life. The student was quite amazed when he finally looked up the author's biography to learn that these details were extremely accurate.

In order to interview your model (assuming they are not available to you live), enter trance, see the model in front of you, build rapport with them (typically by matching their posture, breathing and so on). Now introduce yourself, thank them for taking the time to meet with you, get their permission to ask them some questions and DTI with them, thank them again, and begin the conversation. Simply allow them to respond as they respond, do not try to 'make' them say anything.

Now, if you were to imagine floating out of yourself, and becoming a detached and impartial you-as-observer of the scene, you would be in third position. From third position you-as-observer will be able to see you-as-yourself and also the model. You-as-observer will be able to impartially observe the interaction that takes place between you-as-yourself and the model. You-as-observer can observe how the model moves, speaks and behaves compared to you-as-yourself, and notice the differences between the two.

From third position you could imagine you were floating into the model, seeing out of their eyes and hearing out of their ears. You're now in second position. From second position you can look back at yourself, and seeing yourself over there you can begin to feel whatever you-as-model feels about that you-as-yourself over there.

Why Third Position is So Useful

The third position in DTI is very useful; it does a number of great things during the DTI process:

- It allows you to see that you-as-yourself, interacting with the model before you associate into the model. By noticing the differences between the model and you-as-yourself, what makes the model different to you, you can gain valuable insight into how to experience the DTI.

- Third position is a nice stepping-stone that allows you, as the subject, to fully dissociate from yourself prior to associating into the model. This allows you to have more neutral and expanded perception of the model, rather like clearing your palette before tasting a new wine.

- Third position allows you to see yourself practicing the new skills, after you have experienced 'being' the model. As you develop your skill-set to come closer to the skills of the model, you can actually see yourself progress as you observe from third position. You can step outside of yourself and see where you're at in terms of the skills, see where the model's at with those skills, and compare the two. This step will be particularly important as you refine the DTI using iteration.

- Third position allows you breathing room, after the DTI, and before you re-associate with you-as-yourself. From this neutral observer position you can decide what experiences, skills, beliefs, values and meta-programs of the model, you should take back into you-as-yourself.

In practical terms, we find that for most subjects it is also much easier to associate into the model, if the subject is associating not from his own body, but from a dissociated position.

How to step into third position

It is very important to consider what happens when you dissociate from yourself into third position. Are you dissociating from your beliefs, values, meta-programs and your own identity? Or are you just dissociating from your body, taking your personality with you?

For the purposes of DTI, what's going to happen is that when the subject is in first position, they have all of their own skills, abilities, beliefs, values and meta-programs. They are themselves and have everything that goes along with that. When they step out of themselves, as just an awareness, their beliefs, values, meta-programs and so on can stay behind, or at least stay behind enough to create the space for them to experience things afresh. In NLP we would call this a 'know-nothing' state, a sort of tableau rasa, or fresh-slate. Whether we can in fact completely dissociate from our beliefs and values is another matter, but even partially dissociating creates the space to have a new experience, to 'not-know' long enough to learn something new. After all, 'not-knowing' was Raikov's criteria for a successful trance.

We have to admit that the authors have something of a difference of opinion on this matter. Some of us lean heavily toward leaving your own attributes behind as far as possible for the reasons given above. If you don't leave behind your own beliefs, values and meta-programs during the DTI, the DTI is going to be a 'muddy' experience, combining elements of you with elements of the model.

Other writers lean toward taking their own attributes with them when associating into the model. The benefit of taking your attributes with you is that first it is easier. Second, integration of your beliefs, values and meta-programs with those of the model begins during the DTI itself, as the two personalities are forced to coexist within the DTI. Try each method, and determine which works best for you.

If you're a hypnotist, leading a client through a DTI, and you say, "See the model, you're looking at Milton Erickson over there, now float out of yourself and into Milton Erickson, and experience this event through Milton Erickson's eyes..., now float back into yourself bringing those learnings..." With this sort of DTI the subject is likely to take all his own stuff with him when associating into Milton Erickson, and will be experiencing the event with some strange hybrid of his own beliefs, values and meta-programs combined with those of Milton Erickson.

To dissociate the modeler from their own beliefs, values and meta-programs, you as the hypnotist, might say something like, "...as you're sitting in this chair now, see Milton Erickson appear life-sized in front of you... now float out of yourself, and, as pure consciousness, pure observer, float over there so you can see your body in this chair looking at Milton Erickson, and Milton Erickson looking back at the you in the chair...now as pure consciousness, float into Milton Erickson..., and as Milton Erickson, look back at your body in that chair..."

So if we want the subject to move into third position as a consciousness, not as himself, he gets to leave behind his own beliefs, values and meta-programs.

So when he associates into second position, when he steps into the model, seeing through the model's eyes, hearing with the model's ears, having the thoughts, and feelings of the model, he can also begin to experience the capabilities, beliefs, values and meta-programs of the model as well. And with this new sensory experience, these new thoughts and feelings, beliefs, values and meta-programs, he experiences the first event in the Event Matrix of the model from within the trance; acting as the model would, and creating a real-time first person reference experience as the model. Remember, the brain doesn't know the difference between something that is intensely imagined and something that exists in the outside world.

Repeating this process through a number of different life events of the model, the subject begins to build a library of reference experiences 'being' the model. This is how Gilligan acquired the hypnotic skills that he has. If you listen to Gilligan speak, you can hear Erickson come forth from a very deep level. There are things that he does that he doesn't seem to have conscious awareness of, that come out of having done this type of modeling with Milton Erickson, so that he is literally able to channel Erickson.

Fourth Position - Quantum Perceptual Positions.

There is one final position to consider, and that is fourth position.

Robert Dilts describes fourth position essentially as 'the system'. By this, we mean, what is the larger context? If I DTI with Erickson, and I take on his skills, what system am I becoming a part of? The system could be Milton Erickson and one patient working in a session. Or the system could be Milton Erickson with a classroom full of students. Or it could be Milton Erickson with his family, when he was a child. Or it could be Milton Erickson as part of the medical community. It could even be Milton Erickson within the system of global trance and hypnosis. The question is what am I becoming, that's larger than simply being Milton Erickson? What other people does the model interact with in each event? Of course it also depends on whom you're modeling; if you're modeling Milton Erickson, most of his interactions are going to be with one client, or a small class of students. But if you're modeling Steve Jobs, then the system becomes much bigger; you can't model Steve Jobs without considering the computer industry from the 1970s onward, and that means you also have to consider his effects on society.

Alternatively we can consider the system that the subject is a part of. Consider how these skills, whatever it is the subject is modeling, will fit into his life, and the groups and systems there are parts of.

And of course, we can consider the dual-system that contains both Milton Erickson's system and the subject's system, a meta-system if you will.

And there's even another way of thinking about fourth position as a system. Suppose I DTI with Milton Erickson because I have a client coming in who wants to become an expert marksman, and I want to model how Erickson worked with the US Olympic shooting team. On a wider level, my DTI isn't just about the interaction between Erickson and the Olympic team, and it isn't just about my interaction with my client. It's also about how these different experiences are fitting into an entire chain of experiences, involving every hypnotist or coach who ever taught mental skills to athlete. Thinking about it in this way can really open up your perspective.

So, by fourth position, we are talking about much more than simply a "system". Fourth position is the 'Field'. The Field comprises not just the players and objects (the 'Forms'), but also the space in-between that defines boundaries among the Forms, the space within the Forms and the relationships (spatial, temporal, and cause-effect) between the Forms.

Fourth position segues easier than one might think from third position. Ask the modeler to be a 'consciousness' aware of relationships between subject and model, relationships of matter and energy, space and time. When you go to third position and observe the space in between the model and the self (and the counter model), you will find that boundaries that appeared solid, may temporarily dissolve or re-organize themselves. They dissolve precisely because the subject is the field, and the model is the field—take your pick—on some unconscious level all is one. Experientially, and perhaps neurologically, the subject is no longer 'separate' from the model—or indeed separate from anything else that might be relevant to achieving the outcome.

Neurologically, dominant hemisphere (left-brain) functioning is slowed during this 'quantum' fourth position experience, allowing for more direct right-brain inputting and re-organization. This is a simple way to achieve integration via this right-brain neurological pathway. It is basically a gentle but rapid 'overload induction because the conscious mind (left-brain) is unable to process all possible physical, spatial, temporal and energetic relationships using its favored 'linear-processing'. Quantum fourth-position should be experienced only after second position installation (DTI) and third position installation (observing self acting as-if) processes have been completed.

So the fourth position is really an over-arching context, not specific times and places, but the whole.

How Context Creates Meaning for Others

Now, there is one caveat to all of this discussion of 'systems'. Let's imagine that one of your friends invites you around to their house, and they say, "My father lives with us in the house and he's a little bit on the bizarre side but don't be concerned about it. It's fine." And you go around to your friend's house, and you walk through the kitchen. And in the kitchen you see this old man sitting there and you look at him and he slowly raises his head and looks at you. And then he slowly lowers his head again. You think like, "I guess that's the bizarre father right?"

129

But this is actually a scene where Jeffrey Zeig, one of Erickson's students, meets Erickson for the first time, and Erickson raises his head slowly, looks Zeig in the eye and then stepwise, moves his eyes down. Zeig says that it was a brilliant trance induction, because Erickson made eye-contact, got his attention and then unconsciously instructed Zeig to go down, to go inside.

The point is that the context in which this experience takes place is absolutely fundamental to the meaning that is made from it; if you experienced this in a context where you've been told there's a senile old man in the house, who then behaves in an odd way, you say, "He's senile." If you go and meet the great Milton Erickson, and he behaves in an odd way, you assign a meaning to that, it's very different. So if you just modeled Milton Erickson's behaviors without understanding the system in which they took place, you may not get the results you want.

Let's take another example, suppose you want to DTI with Donald Trump and behave the way he does. First of all, you will not be making a lot of money, but more importantly you won't be making many friends either. Because The Donald behaves the way he does because he's The Donald; if you behave the same way, and you're not the Donald, no one is going to be buying it.

So being able to float, not only into the model, but also into the context in which the model exists and acts, is vital to successfully taking on the skills of the model. And what we are doing is training ourselves to also float into the people the model is interacting with, and see the model's behavior from their point of view. This is something which Milton Erickson fully and completely understood, he used to teach his classes in his garage where he had little school chairs with the desk in front for the students to sit in, and he would give them forms and he would tell them exactly how to fill in the form. If they made a mistake, they had to do another a form. You see, he was doing a regression, taking them back to their school days, and making sure they absolutely knew who was in charge, because he understood that any experience only had meaning within a certain frame (quantum fourth position defines all possible relationship frames).

So the question is not whether you should, or indeed can, copy the behaviors of the model. Rather it's about how do you set the context so that the other people in the system understand the meaning. To find out, step in to their shoes and look at the model. How they understand what's going on creates their meaning. If you are modeling Milton Erickson, you want your clients to see you as Milton Erickson, the world's greatest hypnotist, not a senile old man!

Marketing provides great examples of context setting. You can model the best salesman out there, but if you don't step into the shoes of your customer on some level, you'll fail. You have to be able to step into your customer's shoes and look at yourself as they see you. When I (Shawn) am doing business consulting I am very aware of how my clients are seeing me, some see me as a 'guru' and listen respectfully to my advice, while others see me as a 'technical resource', and pepper me with questions. Either way is fine with me, but if I'm not paying attention to how they are seeing me, everything gets tangled up.

Here's another example, there's a great video on YouTube about this martial artist who's an internal Chi Master, and he's fighting all his students and they're flying across the room without him even having to touch them. He puts up a prize for anyone who can defeat him, and a fighter from another school comes in for the challenge. The challenger starts off very tentatively because he's heard of the 'Chi Master' and how amazing he is. The Chi Master's reputation is the context that has created the meaning for the challenger. Then the challenger hits the Chi Master and the Chi Master falls down and bleeds, and the whole frame, the meaning, is changed and of course the challenger goes on to win the fight easily. The reason the Chi Master was unbeatable before was because every student in his class has this perception that he's the unbeatable Chi Master, they made themselves lose by unconsciously throwing themselves about. But as soon as he stepped out of this system, his own class, he got his ass kicked. So being able to step into system, perhaps by associating into the students of Dr. Erickson, is fundamental to understanding what's going on.

Chapter 14: The Classic DTI Induction...with a Twist

What I (John) will be covering in this chapter is the classic DTI induction. You'll be reading a sample script which you can use in part or in total. It is, by no means, necessary to include all the language in this script to create excellent results, but the main elements/suggestions are important.

Ultimately it will be dependent on skillful pacing and leading of subject/client in this process, and also on the set-up done before this stage.

I've provided headings for most important suggestions involved in the process along with sample language. Following each section there is a commentary which explains the rationale for that section as well as any important features.

You'll find the entire script without commentary in the back of the book, so you can get a feel for the flow of the process as a whole. You may even want to read that now to format your unconscious mind before you read this Chapter. Either way is better.

Conscious-Unconscious Dissociation Induction Combined With Previously Established Trance Anchors.

*As you listen to me, know you can do so with your conscious mind and your unconscious mind. I know that you have something that you'd like to **learn from this experience** and I'm not sure just how much your conscious mind will continue listening to me or if it will begin to wander from one thought to another...There are so many things one could think about that it's easy to lose track and simply follow whatever train of thought can **increase your curiosity** and comfort in knowing that no matter what you think you are, you're all ways more than that.*

Commentary:

Optimally, you will have done preparation work so that the client is a well-trained hypnotic subject. What you've just read will give you a flavor of how I'd begin the induction while utilizing any other trance anchors previously set.

The reason why conscious unconscious dissociation is a useful metaphor in this case, is that it allows for flexibility of communicating the conscious mind and unconscious mind as separate "entities." It will make for a cleaner amnesia of the important elements of the experience. It should be noted again, that the intent in DTI is not for the client to have conscious awareness of the process. The intent is to "model" the unconscious processing of the model.

Suggestions to Activate Associations for Dreaming to Deepen Trance and Encourage Trance Phenomena.

*Now...your unconscious can begin to trance-port you to a wonderfully natural way of being......still...relaxing comfortably knowing that what you're doing now is as natural as you're breathing...... deeper as you are... Just like after a full day of activity there comes a time when you feel the onset of sleep. It's a natural process, your unconscious mind knows how to **relax your body** and create those familiar sensations that let you know that your body's unwinding, your thoughts are* *unwinding from one thought to another while other unconscious processes take you smoothly into the rest...of your thoughts about sleep and rest...assured it's so easy to unconsciously incorporate sounds around you while you're sleeping comfortably, it takes place even without knowing that....within, you're sleeping; **peacefully dreaming** of people, places and things that make **your dreaming** new realities possible for you.*

*Now, you, the **unconscious** mind can **listen deeply** and trans-port (subject's name) anywhere because at the level of dreams one can be anywhere with anyone in a moment's notice.*

*For example, now...you're looking forward to meeting (model) and I'm not really sure where **you'll have a satisfying meeting of the minds** together exchanging ideas about how **you can (outcome)**. There are so many places you can meet (the model) that "I'm not sure just where you'll meet for an engaging **trans-for information about (outcome)**.*

Commentary:

One of the easier ways to access and deepen trance is by talking about dreaming because they are so similar. Dreaming itself is chock-full of hypnotic phenomena, so using it activates the neural pathways associated with the phenomena we'll be using later as part of the DTI.

For example, we rarely remember all of our dreams or the content in them, so amnesia is a central part of dreams. While we are dreaming and asleep, we are capable of incorporating sounds in our environment in to the experience of our dreams, much like hearing a hypnotist unconsciously while in trance.

Within dreams all we are is thought and energy, so we are not constrained by the time, space and matter. You can dream you are in Hawaii at your current age, then be in high school the next. You can meet people whom you've never met "in person" and learn from those experiences.

Other than our large striated muscles, all of our other systems, particularly emotions, are active and functioning, but without the normal consequences of our waking state. All these factors make dreaming a simple way to activate neural networks where the client has had direct experience of what we are suggesting in trance.

Additionally, if Dream Incubation had been used in the preparation and research phases of the process, it would activate these associations as well.

Note the transition from dreaming to setting up the "meeting" with the model. By introducing dreams it opens up the idea of transcending space and time, "you can be anyway with anyone in a moment's notice," which makes for smooth segue to a different location and/or time.

Suggestions for Creating a Context of Safety by Using the Metaphor of a Power Spot to Introduce the Meeting With the Model.

Because we all have places where we love to go and be where you're in your element. Now, some refer to this as a power spot, some as an Aleph point. When you're in your power spot it's a place where you're at your best, where both of you can just be.... Feeling comfortable, at ease, looking around, enjoying the surroundings and appreciating how they can enrich your experience, there's nothing like being where you love to be with someone interesting, being yourself... Because (the model) is someone you can look up to... find excellence in yourself...

Commentary:

This is a metaphor borrowed from the work of Carlos Casteneda. Think of it as using a specific context to elicit resource states which would be favorable to the process.

As Milton Erickson emphasized in his historic paper on Deep Trance, safety is a critical element to a client's ability to access deeper trance

136

states which include considerable amnesia and other more exotic hypnotic phenomena To the extent the deeper aspects of the personality know this is a safe experience, it allows the tendency for conscious vigilance to relax. The power spot is a way of establishing a "safe place" without having to raise the issue directly. There are many other ways to accomplish even the preparation, but this point cannot be emphasized enough. The main reason why people cannot access "deeper states" is because they have not addressed the intent of being consciously vigilant. For example, in doing self-hypnosis, many will report they don't go as deeply by themselves as they do when they are guided by a therapist. One of the reasons is because they have not handled the contingencies, the "what if's" in the situation. If I am at home and go into deep trance and the phone rings, am I going to answer it or not? Circumstances that are this basic can cause us to be slightly vigilant.

In the case of DTI, much of this can be addressed before this induction by eliciting a well-formed outcome and checking congruency.

Suggestions for Eliciting Universal Experiences of Rapport and DTI

*And as you find yourself in this context with (model) I'd like to ask you, the unconscious mind to **prepare (subject)** for a wonder fully trance- formative experience where you can **begin learning at a deeper level about what's really important to you**. As it prepares it can begin to activate those automatic processes that make everything proceed easily and quickly. There are so many automatic processes that you know unconsciously that make what **you're learning... what you want...** happen spontaneously and naturally...In fact often the best learning occurs when you're not focused on learning, because you're **completely absorbed** in what you are experiencing...*

Now, in the same way I know there have been times when you've been at a movie and you've been so involved in the movie you could feel exactly how that character was feeling......... Or perhaps you've driven in a car as a passenger and you couldn't *help but automatically put your foot on the brake because you identified so closely with the driver......... There may have been times in your life when you had a good friend you spent a lot of time with. I wonder if you ever noticed how easy it was when you started to use the same expressions, some of the same gestures or movements, laughed the same way...it seemed like you knew what they were even thinking...sometimes....as they were pausing for a moment in the middle of a sentence, you might have even ....that's right..... finishing the sentence, because you knew how to **intuitively***

Identify at the deepest level, unconsciously...

*I know that you know how to identify in ways that are useful for you to do......you've done it all your life and you can do it... Now..in the same way know that you'd really like to model (_____), to actually identify with (_____) in a deep way. You've been wanting to identify with (_____) for some period of time because (_____) has certain values, beliefs, abilities, behaviors, feelings, attitudes that you would really like to **model** and begin to **experience for yourself**. Now, I'm wondering what that person looks like and what you observe about them that fascinates you.*
*When they capture exactly what it is that you want to experience for yourself. It's probably not easy to **imagine all (model's) information, memories, beliefs, values and inner workings**, just yet...... because there's always so much more going on that what you think and...*

Commentary:

As with the elicitation of any hypnotic phenomena, providing the client with "universal experiences" is a way to "grease the skids" for the processes you want the client to execute. Universal experiences are those kinds of experiences that most everyone has experienced and if they haven't, it is easy to imagine how it would be. They are a form of indirect suggestion.

In this case, the examples used are to activate times when the client has unconsciously identified, or been in deep rapport with someone.

By suggesting these experiences up-front they open the door to making direct suggestions which will be more likely accepted.

Suggesting Second Position to Facilitate Identification

Go ahead and see (the model) over there.......and notice that you can easily imagine floating right over into (the model)........Now I don't know when.........you're unconscious......... will make the necessary adjustments to have you *float up as a mind as consciousness*....(Calibrate)...*that's right*... (higher pitch) *float up and over toward (the model)......until you are directly above (the model)....*

And then when you are all-ready.... leaving (client's name) over there ...float right (lower pitch) *down into (the model)*....................... (calibrate to physiological shift)............*as you (model's name) are experiencing the world Now ...knowing that at the unconscious level there's a lot more going on at the unconscious level than what you're now seeing, hearing, and feeling......being yourself (the model), Now, you, (the model) are unconsciously competent and this means you may not always be consciously aware of what makes you so competent. But communication can be transmitted and received on many levels seen and unseen heard and not heard, felt and not felt consciously. So in a moment there are some questions that (subject's name) would like to know the answers to, which you know well. I also know it's quite possible that sometimes it may be easier sometimes to demonstrate what you know to (subject) so that learning can take place on a deeper level...*

Commentary:

This is the pivotal move of the whole pattern: assuming the perceptual position of the model. Notice that the process instructions are to "float up as a mind, as consciousness," first then to float down into the model, as opposed to "to float over into model." The idea here is to increase the dissociation from the client's body and personality. In other words, the client is being invited to "de-identify" from self. (More about the utility of "de-identification" in a later chapter.)

The intent is to make the separation as clean as possible to set the stage for the client virtually "being" the model, not being him/herself while identifying with the model. You might also want to spend more time in this in-between third position to observe the model before floating down into them as discussed above.

Also important is the use juxtaposition of "you, (the model's name)." This may initially create mild confusion and temporarily blur the boundaries of self and model. At this point any reference to the self is using spatial prepositions like "that," "over there" third person, "he/him," "she/her," or by the name. So for example after "I," as mind, has floated into Erickson, the hypnotist would be saying, "...so as *you, Dr. Erickson* seeing John *over there*, notice how interested *he* is in what you know and how you do what you do...."

Suggestions to Stimulate Unconscious Association as the Model. A Nice Template for This is Neurological Levels.

(You'll find a fairly comprehensive list of other questions in the Appendix)"   "
""""¶""""
What is your Mission in life?"
How do you know you're fulfilling your mission?
What do you believe about yourself
What do you believe about your abilities (or whatever is being modeled)?
What's really important to you about (what's being modeled)?
And how do you know you're fulfilling this?
What do you believe that makes it possible for you to do (know) what you do (know) so well?
How do you know when and where to do what you do_____?
How do you_____?
How do you know you've done it well?
Now for the next few moments I'm going to be silent while any other communication can take place between the both of you.

Calibrate....allow one or two minutes of silence.

Commentary:

Remember, this is not a conscious process, so it is important that the coach has questions prepared to prevent too much conscious participation. You're not interested in engaging the subject about what questions they might have, as they will have to re-associate to self. The idea of "an interview" is just a way to set up the dissociation and a conversation. There are many other ways to do this, the simplest of which is to just invite the subject to identify with the model in the current context. I'd do this only if the client was a well-trained hypnotic subject who could easily let go of the current contextual markers. This is why setting up the power spot is useful as well: it further dissociates the client from the present time space context, thus loosening his reality testing in general.

You can also use suggestions to further insure there is less conscious participation. For example: *"You can be thinking one thing consciously and that is different distinct from the unconscious learnings which are occurring." This allows for some conscious thought, in case the subject is very aware, but opens the possibility that the "important stuff" is occurring unconsciously, outside of conscious awareness.*

The purpose of this phase is to generate questions to stimulate the thought process of the model. These can be questions that were discussed when you established the outcome. It is not important or even desirable for the model to verbally answer the questions. The questions are rather indirect suggestions to stimulate certain thought processes as the model.

Optimally, you could have the client be the model and actually interact with the current environment as the model. I've used this to train advanced students where, for example, student A identifies with the model, and, while in trance they assist student B going into trance.

Suggestions to Return to First Position, Self, With Suggestions for Ecology.

*....That's right ....so much to **learn**..........**memorize** it....... so little time to notice consciously.. what?............who's doing the learning........that's right,* (subject's name) *is learning and so are you two, aren't you?* (model's name)........ *Perhaps you'll begin to notice, not yet, but when you do,* (subject's name) *over there... being fully receptive what you know now...go ahead, and as you're ready, as a mind, as consciousness and **float up**....... seeing* (subject's name) *and* (model's name) *down there, then float above (subject's name) **now floating down into*** (your subject's name/ the body you usually call home),*yourself*...... (Calibrate) *Now, you, (**Subject's name**), can allow your unconscious mind to **safely integrate** all this experience only in a way that is compatible and honors your total personality, **all together**,* (subject's name) *you, yourself, NOW.....Take all the time you need to allow that integration to complete itself.* **(Give time to integrate.)**

Commentary:

Note the confusion at the moment of leaving the Model, just as there was mild confusion used when going into the model. The blurring of boundaries is what allows for deeper identification to occur as well as amnesia of the experience. In the above language, it was done by using a combination of punctuational, scope and phonological ambiguity: *notice consciously.. what?............who's doing the learning........that's right,* (subject's name) *is learning and so are you two (too), aren't you?* (model's name)........

After you suggest making the perceptual position shift back to first position, self, then provide suggestions for alignment and integration. The integration may take some time, particularly depending on how long the subject was "being" the model. When the subject first floats down into self, expect to see some bilateral asymmetry in the physiology. As the integration completes itself you'll usually see a pretty significant breathing shift after which the physiology should be looking symmetrical. As with the integration following any form of change work, bilateral symmetry is a good sign!

Classically, at this point, you could add any other post-hypnotic suggestions and reorient the subject. The next phase in this particular protocol is to further enhance what has already occurred, as well as allow for a greater de-identification with self, to open the field to any other information from the model or anywhere else.

The New Twist to the Classic DTI: Fourth Position, the Omni Position

To recap, Fourth Position in the HNLP model is not the same as the fourth position discussed in Dilt's model of perceptual positions. In this case, fourth position is the omni position which comes from a massive foreground background shift of perception. It is where the client assumes/imagines being the space between the self and model, then all the space between all things, and the space within all things.

From a quantum physics perspective, the "space in between" to people or things is not only the space that separates, but the space that connects all things. This space is the "stuff" of which everything is made, including us.

So, the fourth position maneuver invites the subject to relax all of our "normal" reality boundaries. At this point there is no separation from "them" and everything else. The subject has the experience of being the entire "field" as expansive as is possible. There is no separation between the subject and any other information that is out there that can be accessed. In more esoteric circles this is more of an experience that "all is one" as well as one way to "channel" information beyond just one particular model.

This is a novel way of providing yet another way to gain access to information which the subject normally considers outside him/her. Further it allows for the opportunity to access information from anywhere else (which may include sources other than the identified model.)

The utility in adding this to a classic second position DTI, is that it is a state which can be cultivated and used in real time. So imagine, if you will, that you could be observing someone in vivo, then access fourth position which dissolves the boundaries between you and the person, and all is one? Think there might be some cool learning that comes from that? Now imagine the same pattern as a meditation to help you develop the ability to access information/energy you normally think is "outside" of you. Eventually it can eliminate the need to the second position maneuver all together.

Just some ideas to consider. For now, let's take a look at the language to facilitate this type of experience after a second position DTI.

This picks-up directly after the DTI.

Suggestions for Fourth Position.

Now, as you're ready, once again go ahead and float as a mind and not a body, as consciousness; just float way up, until as a mind, as consciousness, you can observe (subject's name) down there with (model)...And as you do, now, notice the space in between them and all the space around them. As you are.... you may now begin noticing the space in between you as consciousness and them...and all the space that surrounds you all and is within you all.

(Pause to calibrate to client.)

*And as you pay attention to the space between and around them, take a deep breath (Facilitator does this at the same time) and exhale. As you then begin to inhale, just go ahead, **breath in** and **be the space in between**... and...realize the space connects you all to each other, realize the space pervades you all because **you are one** and the same and have access to the same information.*

Commentary:

As mentioned this is like a massive figure-ground shift and then some! I've found that connecting the breathing as above makes the process easier for subjects to experience: the first inhale and exhale is a pace, with the exhale proving the feeling of "letting go" then the inhale encourages breathing in the space (like air). I"m sure there are other ways to accomplish this, but this has been field-tested for over 12 years.

The other more hypnotic aspect of this maneuver is it tends to create a "null set" in being all the space that is difficult for the dominant hemisphere to access, so it can tend to check out, while the unconscious accesses and reorganizes information without the tethers of the dominant hemisphere. Of course, having an experience of boundlessness where all is one has its own perks!

(Pause)

Suggestions for Integration and Ecology

Now...begin to take form as a mind so that you can once again find yourself floating above (subject and model) there, so you can float as a mind back down into (subject's) body.....now.... to safely integrate all this information only in a way that is compatible with and honors your total personality, all together, (subject's name) you, yourself, NOW......

Take all the time you need to allow that integration to complete itself so that in a few moments you can begin once again to let your mind wander from one thought to another while your unconscious mind can continue to let things rest for a while so it can begin to organize what you've experienced in a way that supports your outcome.

Commentary:

This is the same re-integration language we discussed at the end of the class DTI move. Again, calibrating to symmetry is important here.

Suggestions for Outcome and Spontaneous Self Hypnosis

*Now, I'm not sure when you'll know that you've integrated the model into your own personality. It might be sometime soon, after you've come back outside, maybe when you'll need to use what you've learned or maybe it will be sometime when you least expect it tomorrow or a few days from now. You may not even notice it even though your unconscious mind will begin manifesting a new way of being that others will recognize that you've changed. There's really no way to know how soon this will happen. I only know that you'll find it quite natural to **go into a trance** whenever necessary to **refresh this experience** or **review what you've learned** or even when you'll **begin using your new skills** in a naturally unconscious way.*

Commentary:

These suggestions provide for a variety of ways the subject can experience the changes made. Basically, it is classic indirect suggestion. It also encourages spontaneous self-hypnotic experiences which can be triggered by the unconscious mind. In this way the subject's unconscious mind may elect trance as a way to refresh suggestions and experiences which have been occurring. Additionally it may be that the subject needs a "trance-formational" moment to attempt some of the new skills that were part of his outcome. It is not uncommon that the unconscious may have the subject whistle right through an experience; that if it were overly conscious might have precipitated some performance anxiety or hesitation. This way the first run gets done, without recognition of the usual markers that let the conscious mind realize, "Oh, here comes the hard part" and as a result...success!

Suggestions for Amnesia

*Because it's so easy to forget things you don't need to know until it's time to remember what's important. While you've been listening you haven't had to remember where you've put your car keys, but now that I mentioned it, your mind can **automatically remember the keys** if it's important to you now... otherwise **you'll remember the keys when you really need to use them.** Otherwise it's far more enjoyable to just live life and experience the opportunities* *that unfold before you. ...And appreciate that your unconscious mind can do a great many things for you outside of your awareness, whether you remember to go into a trance to **refresh this experience** or **review what you've learned**, or even when you'll **begin using your new skills** in a naturally unconscious way.*

Commentary:

Suggestions for amnesia work very well at this part of the sequence, because it is likely that any of the suggestions for spontaneous self-hypnosis triggered by the unconscious will be buried, thus insuring that self-hypnosis will be spontaneous.

As with most of the other parts of the script, there are double entendres, otherwise known as ambiguities. In this case of forgetting then remembering car keys, the other meaning is referring to the "keys or learnings from the DTI experience.

Suggestions for Self Appreciation and Re-Orientation.

*Because it's wonderful to sometimes just take a moment to appreciate that you've got a conscious mind that gets to be aware of the marvels of this life and you've got an unconscious mind that supports you behind the scenes so you can be consciously aware that it can unfold to you if you're willing to **open your eyes** to the possibilities.*

Commentary:

As a part of re-orientation, what better way to encourage the conscious mind back in in the picture by giving it something constructive to do: appreciation.

At this point the next step depends on timing and the availability of a suitable context for a test drive to trigger the results of the DTI. So, for example, if this was done later in the day or evening, you might just suggest the subject do something else to let things settle, get a good night's sleep, then do a test drive in context some time the next day.

If it's earlier in the day, client willing and there is suitable context, encourage him to do a test drive to find out what happens. As was mentioned elsewhere in the book; it's important to think of this process as life. It's a recursive process, not "once and done." So depending on the experience the subject has, he may identify other refinements to be made when he puts himself in the context where the new abilities or skills are wanted. At that point you can re-do this process or use the huge palette of other processes in this book to further develop and refine the new ways of being.

Chapter 15: The Matrix model

Once you've chosen a model, you will need to gather enough information, of the right kind, to allow you to DTI with them. The question is, how?

I (Jess) have had the experience of deciding to DTI with someone I knew something about, someone I had seen, or read about, doing whatever skill I wanted to model. I would go into trance, see them in front of me, float into them, and feel how it feels to be them. While I might've had some kind of positive experience from this type of DTI, it was never life-changing for me. You have probably had the same sort of experience.

Traditionally, DTI has involved watching the model perform the skills you're interested in, either live or on video. Or, if this is not available, reading books, preferably autobiographical, describing what they did and how they did it is all right. Once you have seen them in action, literally or figuratively as it were, you will have consciously, and more importantly unconsciously, gathered the information that will allow you to DTI with them.

Of course, there is validity in this approach. Because we all possess Mirror Neurons, we all have the ability to construct an internal model of another person's reality simply by watching their physiology, their posture, their breathing, their facial expressions and so on. So if you watch a video and see the model making a gesture, striking a certain pose, then on the level of Mirror

Neurons, this does provide information about the model's internal reality.

This was also essentially the approach taken by Raikov, although Raikov also relied heavily on the auditory sense (hearing). But you must remember, Raikov was primarily interested in subjects who were already quite expert, such as cello students from the Moscow Conservatory, modeling very specific skills of specific models, such as Pablo Casals playing the cello. The DTI was based upon the students listening to a recording of Casals playing, and because they were already experts in playing the cello, they were able to unconsciously absorb both technical skills and musical interpretation from the DTI.

Indeed, if you're looking to hone a very specific skill, in which you already have a great deal of expertise, Raikov's method is ideal. However if you are looking to model a more generative skill where you are not yet yourself highly skilled, then Raikov's approach may not be sufficient. For example if you wanted to learn to play the cello from scratch by modeling Pablo Casals, then you would need to know what drove Casals to take up the cello, what drove him to practice on a daily basis, how he approached his practice, what drove him so that he felt compelled to perform for millions of people, what internal representations (whether pictures, sounds or feelings) allowed him to play music in his own unique way, and so on. So what sort of information do you actually need to do all this? At what point in your research will the information you have be enough for your unconscious mind to build a good model?

In this chapter we will detail our Event Matrix model of DTI. The Event Matrix will allow you to build a multidimensional model for DTI, a model that will resonate with you both consciously and unconsciously. This will allow you to DTI on a much deeper and more profound level than ever before. It is especially powerful when you are seeking to learn a skill you do not already possess (rather than improve or extend a skill you do already have).

The Event Matrix requires that you 'observe' your model across a range of different times, contexts and activities, not just performing the one skill in which you are particularly interested. Again, 'observation' can include watching and interacting with the model, watching video of the model performing her skill, or being interviewed about her life, reading books about the model, particularly auto-biographies revealing her thinking style, emotional drivers, beliefs and values, as well as recounting factual episodes from their life

The reason for this is that it will provide us with not just information about how the model does this particular skill or ability, or even how he learned that skill, but it will also reveal where and how he spent his life; the people he interacted with, his emotional outlook on the world, his beliefs about themselves, the world, and his place in it, as well as his values, meta programs, and identity. For those familiar with NLP, you will realize that we are exploring their Logical Levels. Don't worry if you are unfamiliar with NLP, we will describe Logical Levels in more depth shortly.

Perhaps you want to DTI with Erickson, and say to yourself, "Oh, yes. I love the idea of being like Milton Erickson, and dropping people into trance like he did." But perhaps this vague idea is based on one or two books that you have read about him, or a couple of videos you have seen, so that your internal model of him is quite limited and one dimensional. As a result, your DTI experience is also going to be somewhat limited and one dimensional.

In our view it's really important that we consider several specific episodes from the model's life across a range of contexts, and consider what each of these episodes tell is about the model as a person. This is really how we learn.

For example, consider the Bible, the New Testament, and the life of Jesus. The New Testament is all about specific things he did, and specific things that he said. It's not just this vague story about how wonderful he was. It's filled with specific episodes from his life that demonstrated who he was on a much deeper level. This is the sort of modeling that we are looking for.

So we don't just want a general portrait of the person. Think of anyone who you have heard of who has a reputation as a 'larger than life' character. Their reputation is al-ways based upon specific episodes from their life. When I was a boy, listening to stories of daring-do, one of my favorite stories was about Lord Nelson, the British admiral in the Napoleonic war. Probably the most famous story about him occurred before he became first Lord of the Admiralty. At the time he was a junior admiral leading a British fleet under the overall command of an admiral called Sir Hyde Parker. At that time, the British were fighting against the Danish fleet at the battle of Copenhagen and Nelson had gotten himself into a very precarious position face-to-face with the Danish fleet, which was in a strong defensive position. Admiral Parker, fearing Nelson's fleet was about to be destroyed, ordered him to withdraw. The order was given using signal flags hoisted on Admiral Parker's flagship, and one of Nelson's crew pointed back telling Nelson that Admiral Parker's ships were ordering him to withdraw. Nelson, who had lost one eye fighting the French, raised his telescope to his blind eye, and in front of all his men, famously says, "Ships, I see no ships." Using this as an excuse not to retreat, Nelson continued fighting and the Danish fleet was defeated.

Somebody could have simply told me that Nelson was an aggressive and determined naval commander. But that would not have had the same impact as listening to this story. So, what do we learn from the story? Well there are several conscious lessons that we can take away:

- Nelson led from the front. He could presumably have stayed back with Admiral Parker, but instead was in the thick of the fighting against the Danish.

- Nelson was aggressive, almost to the point of recklessness (at least Admiral Parker seemed to think so, as he was sufficiently concerned about Nelson's position to order him to withdraw).

- Nelson was self-confident enough to disobey a direct order. After all, if Nelson's fleet had been defeated he could have been court-martialed, assuming he wasn't outright killed by the Danish.

- Nelson was calm enough in battle to use his quick wit and sense of humor, rather than simply disobey the order. Using his own infirmity as a reason to disobey was the sort of thing that made men followed him through the gates of hell.

However, there is much more to be learned from the story when we consider it from a more unconscious basis.

Imagine if you will, as I did listening to the story as a boy, that you are standing next to Nelson on the deck of his ship. The smoke of battle drifts over the deck and you can see the flash of gunpowder. You hear the thunder of the British and Danish cannon as the opposing fleets' fire broadsides into each other, the shouting of the gun crews, the whistle of cannonballs and musket balls firing overhead, crashing into the masts or the sides of the wooden ships, the cries of the wounded. There is the smell of gunpowder in the air as officers race around yelling orders. Nelson's adjutant is shouting in his ear, and pointing off to Admiral Parker's distant signal. And in the midst of the noise, danger and insanity of battle, Nelson calmly raises his telescope to his blind eye and jokingly says, "I see no ships.

As I imagine that now, I understand the trust and confidence his men placed in him, and how they would follow him into the jaws of battle. I can begin to appreciate who Nelson was as a person, what was important to him and what he believed, and I can better appreciate his calmness in the eye of the storm. That kind of moment in time tells you more about him than a dry description of the battle.

Now experience this from a DTI perspective: seeing Nelson dressed in his formal admiral's uniform, on the deck of his flagship, float into that experience so you are seeing out of Nelson's eyes (or rather 'eye', as you have only one). Your attention is fixed on your enemy, the Danish fleet, and your own ships in relation to that. You are focused on victory, so that nothing else matters; the sounds and the smoke around you, the flying cannonballs, and the whistle of musket balls are nothing but minor distractions compared to your goal. You feel a hand on your shoulder and look around into the face of your adjutant, fearful and confused, pointing in the opposite direction, away from the Danish fleet. For a moment you are not sure what he is trying to tell you above the thunder of the cannons, then finally you understand, he has seen the order to withdraw. Looking into his eyes you realize your response is going to create his reality, his thoughts and his emotions at this time, as well as the reality of the rest of the sailors in your fleet. Will they run or will they fight? Taking a moment, you raise your telescope to your eye, or rather to your eye patch, to your blind eye and say "Ships, I see no ships." You lower your telescope and look back at your adjutant. You see that he understands. With a slight nod of your head you turn your attention back to the battle…

This need of our unconscious minds to absorb information on a deeply personal level is why we need stories about a person to truly understand them. The stories are what really let you know who a person is, and what they've gone through that has made them who they are. It's that specific point in time that lets you understand them.

When you're speaking to the model, or watching a video of him, or when you're reading his biography or autobiography, you look out for those moments in time that encapsulates who the person is. What are the events that made him who he is?

When you're doing the DTI, these are moments that you need to go into, to experience; these moments in time that define a person. It's these moments in

154

time, these stories, these episodes that really make DTI appealing. Stories talk to the unconscious. These events, these stories are metaphors for what you want from the DTI. And you're already starting a DTI process because you're already actively involving the unconscious mind, through story.

Let's go back to the Mirror Neurons. They respond not just to what you're seeing, although that's what their name implies, but also to sounds and narrative. If you read a story of somebody who is doing some physical action, your Mirror Neurons are firing up, mirroring that particular action. If you watch a video, or even if I tell you a story about a runner, say Usain Bolt, a Jamaican sprinter in the Olympics, in the 100 meters:

He's on the blocks, settling down. He's spent the last four years training for this moment, endless hours on the track, and hours in the gym. The starter calls them, "On your mark," he rises up in the blocks, every muscle, every sinew, every nerve, poised, "Get Set..." feeling electrified, a fraction of a second slow off the blocks may lose the race, a fraction of a second too soon and disqualification is possible. The starting pistol fires and you're off...

As you read that, a part of your brain is going through the experience. But if I just tell you about the person, if I just say Usain Bolt won the 100m at the London Olympics, consciously the information may be the same, but it doesn't get the Mirror Neurons firing off, because they don't have any specific sensory description to attach to.

And this is what a lot of people don't understand when they try to DTI. They have some information about the person, the model, offering a general sense of who the model is, but not backed by events containing rich sensory data that the unconscious can attach to. And you need these specific moments in time because they are going to inform your unconscious more than any amount of data, or general information.

And as we said, Ericksonian hypnotists like to model Milton Erickson. I could say, "Milton Erickson had the expectation that his clients would go into trance." Now that doesn't tell you very much, but if I remind you of the video where:

Erickson is sitting over there, in a room full of students, and he's staring at a girl in the class and he says to the class, "Watch her go into trance."

Or the description of his Teaching Seminar, as:

Erickson turns to one of the people in the class and goes, "Who do you think is the next person in the room who will go into trance?" It doesn't matter what she says, because it could be her, or she could say it will be somebody; it may even be you, going into trance. It really doesn't make a difference; it's just Erickson's expectation, complete certainty that somebody in the room is going to go into trance!

And those events inform you about Milton Erickson on a deeper level than just reading a book about technique explaining that people cycle in and out of trance all the time, and that all Erickson had to do was wait. But reading about it is just not the same as experiencing it.

So these events demonstrate what to do and how to do it, they provide you all sorts of information about logical levels, and they put this information in a context.

Logical Levels

Robert Dilts introduced logical levels into NLP, although they predate NLP and can certainly be traced back to Maslow's hierarchy of needs, if not before. Logical levels have been criticized for being neither logical nor levels, nevertheless they provide a powerful tool for discussing and analyzing human experience. The levels are as follows:

Context: Where am I when a particular experience takes place, in what environment, and who else is around?

Behavior: What physical and verbal behaviors do I have in that context? What do I do? What do I say?

Capabilities: What emotional and physical skills do I exhibit? For example, am I confident or nervous?

Beliefs and values: What are the beliefs I hold about myself, the world, and my place in it, when I am in this context? What values do I hold in this context; what is important to me?

Meta-programs: What are the underlying behavioral and neurological patterns that drive my behavior? For example, am I moving towards a specific outcome or moving away from risk? These drivers are called meta-programs in NLP, and we will be talking about them more in a later chapter.

Identity: Considering everything else, what is my identity in this context? Am I a leader? Am I a follower? Am I exploring? Am I creating? Am I teaching? What is my role?

Beyond identity: How do I fit in with everybody else around me in this context? This could be my family, my colleagues at work, my teammates, my friends and neighbors, or whoever is part of this context. How do I fit in with the bigger picture, with God or the divine, however you perceive that to be?

By considering each of these levels separately we can *build up a rich representation of a particular experience.* Combining these levels with a number of events in the model's life can build up the Event Matrix. We will give a full example in the next chapter when we talk about Tomas Edison, the famous inventor.

Context

One day Jesus came to Milton Erickson as a client, a man with delusions, "I'm the savior, I'm Jesus Christ." Now the patient was modeling himself after Jesus, but only at the level of Identity, "I am Jesus," without any particular context. Normally the 'context' in this sort of interaction is doctor-patient; the patient says to the doctor, "I am Jesus Christ" and the doctor tells the patients that he is actually mentally ill, not Jesus Christ at all.

But Milton Erickson chose to apply different context, and he said to Jesus Christ, "Well, I've heard that you are a carpenter. The workmen outside need help building the library. Why don't you go and help them?" Jesus goes off and helps, and Jesus Christ became the handyman for the hospital. So the 'context' in which someone becomes Jesus Christ is critical; if the context is in a mental institution, then being Jesus Christ represents mental illness, but in the context of building the library, Jesus Christ brings important carpentry skills.

There are (at least) two contexts that are important, the first is the context in which the model is being observed; Superman leaps a tall building, Admiral Nelson holds his telescope up to his blind eye in the midst of a battle, Milton Erickson hypnotizes a patient.

The second context is where does the modeler want to use the skills of the model in their own life? So, I DTI with Superman so that I can use x-ray vision, super hearing, and Superman's strength and compassion when coaching my clients. I DTI with Steve Jobs to bring creativity into my business. I DTI with Horatio Nelson to bring single-minded determination to publishing a book. We talked about this second context in Chapter 7.

Behavior

The second logical level is the level of behavior: how is the model behaving in the context? Because we chose a number of contexts we will have to ask this question a number of times; because the model will be behaving differently in each context. It is this variety of behavior that gives us a richer unconscious blueprint to follow in the DTI.

Capabilities

As we move up the logical levels to capabilities, asking what the skills and capabilities are that the model uses, it becomes much more difficult to answer the question because it is more subjective. For example, if we are looking at Thomas Edison it doesn't help to say he had great skills as an inventor, because we can't simply replicate that skill. We have to break it down into things we can model and replicate, such as self-confidence, determination, collaboration, visualization and so on. We will give examples in the next chapter when we talk more specifically about Thomas Edison.

Beliefs and Values

Now we are moving even further up the logical levels, and becoming even more abstract. Not only do we have to uncover what was important to the model, and what the model believes about himself, the world, and his place in it, but we also have to identify which of these beliefs and values play an important role in driving the model's behavior.

For example, Thomas Edison became immensely rich as a result of his inventions. On the face of it we can say that money was of value for him, and that is certainly true. However, money was only of value to the extent it allowed him to spend more time inventing, to hire more super-smart people to work with, and to buy more cutting edge laboratory equipment to play with.

The money itself was a secondary consideration at best, it was certainly not a driving value for Edison in and of itself.

Consideration of the key beliefs and values of the model is an extremely subjective area. You and I may differ on what the particular beliefs and values of a particular person are and his level. This is fine because the DTI ultimately produces a blend of all the psyche of the model and the psyche of the modeler.

Identity and Beyond Identity

If we were moving into rarefied atmosphere when considering beliefs and values, we are now in totally uncharted territory. While it might be fairly easy to say that Thomas Edison was an inventor, how would we describe Steve Jobs? Visionary? Entrepreneur? Craftsman? Hypnotist? He has been described as all these things (and a lot worse besides) and they're all true when he is viewed from one direction or another.

In fact, this is the benefit of using the Event Matrix to build the DTI experience. There are many documented events in Steve Jobs' life that demonstrates his visionary leadership, his ability to see where the world was moving, irrespective of the feedback of focus groups that only told him where the world had been. There are also many events that show his business acumen, and his ability to negotiate ruthlessly with business partners. And there are also events which show him as a craftsman, for example the fact he had the signatures of all his team inscribed inside the casing of each computer, even though it would never be seen by the customers, demonstrated his pride in design to the point of obsession. He also had the ability to hypnotize those around him with his vision, and in fact people refer to Steve Jobs' Reality Distortion Field to refer to this effect.

It is only by considering a number of events from the life of the model, from the point of view of the logical levels, from context through to identity and

160

beyond, for each event in the Event Matrix. We are able to build a rich experience of the model for all unconscious minds to work with.

In the next chapter we are going to build an Event Matrix for Thomas Edison (as well as the Silver Surfer), to show how this process works in practice.

Chapter 16: Examples of the Matrix Model (Silver Surfer and Thomas Edison)

We have talked in the previous chapter about taking specific episodes from the model's life and using these as the basis of the DTI. So for example, when I (Shawn) DTI'd with the Silver Surfer, I identified specific episodes within the Silver Surfer's life, or mythology, which are illustrative of who he is.

Once more think about this is in terms of NLP logical levels, allowing us to build a richer picture of any experience based on the context in which the experience takes place, the associated behaviors, emotional states and other resources; the beliefs, the values, the identity, and everything else that is beyond identity. So that when we focus on the specific events from the Silver Surfer's life, each of those events gives us some information about the Silver Surfer's logical levels.

Logical Levels For the Silver Surfer's Adventures on the Sun

Environment or Context

The first, or lowest level is environment. This refers to where the episode takes place. So with the Silver Surfer, the first episode in the DTI took place on the surface of the sun.

Behavior

The next logical level is behavior; what is the model doing in that environment? And in this case the Silver Surfer was surfing close to the surface of the sun, moving from one side to another to avoid the solar flares.

Skills and Capabilities (Emotions)

The next level is skills and capabilities; what skills does the person have, what is he capable of? Within the framework of NLP we often equate skills and capabilities with emotional states. For example is a person capable of feeling confident, and do they actually feel confidence whilst behaving in this way, in this environment. Now the Silver Surfer is of course totally awesome and fully capable of surfing over the surface of the sun, fully capable of avoiding the solar flares. But I also have to ask myself, "What is his emotional state while he is surfing the surface of the sun?" And my take on that is not that he is confident, but rather that he is pushing his own boundaries, taking risks, daring the universe to destroy him.

And this brings up a good point, you may know where the model was, the environment, you may know what the model was doing, the behavior, but you might not know for certain how he was feeling. It is up to you as the modeler to interpret this based upon everything else you know about the model.

Beliefs, Values and Meta Programs

The next Logical Level consists of beliefs, values, and meta-programs. We will be talking about these in more depth when we discuss integration, and in particular the "Mind Meld" technique.

There is a lot of overlap between beliefs, values, and meta-programs, and also a lot of confusion as to what they are. For example, I may believe it is impolite to eat with my mouth open, but this also implies that politeness is a value to me. For now, I will simply make the following simplistic definitions:

Beliefs are my underlying assumptions, conscious or unconscious, about how the world works, and my place in the world including my ability to change the world.

Values are those things that are important to me as principles to live by. For example freedom is a value for me, while my grandfather's pocket watch is not (even though it may be valuable).

Meta-programs consist of a set of neuro drivers that govern our behaviors. Examples of these neuro drivers include: 'Toward-away', i.e. am I more motivated by achieving my dreams, or by avoiding disaster? 'Options-Procedures', i.e., do I want to do things my own way, or would I prefer to follow a checklist, a well-defined process?

One of the meta-programs that we will be focusing on is that of 'modal operators'. Modal operators are ideas like 'must', 'can', can't, 'should', i.e. things that are necessary, possible, impossible, and so on. It turns out that many of the people we choose to model have strong modal operators of necessity, meaning they have to do what they do; they are driven to do it. Even though the process may be difficult, and may have to sacrifice time or money or comfort to achieve their goals, they are driven to do so.

It is very important to consider the modal operators of the model.

Now we return to the Silver Surfer, within the context of beliefs, values and meta-programs. Again, it is impossible to know for certain what the model's beliefs, values, and meta-programs are (unless they have been specifically stated in an autobiography, or in the case of the Silver Surfer, a comic book), so the modeler is largely left to his own intuition. This is particularly difficult

164

in the case of the Silver Surfer because he is so alien to the way a human being understands the universe. However, the two forces which, at least to me, shape the Silver Surfer's existence are a value of 'exploration and adventure', blocked by an inability (modal operator of impossibility) to leave the environs of planet Earth. It is these conflicting forces that create the tragedy of the Silver Surfer's existence. His adventure, surfing over the surface of the sun, risking his own destruction, expresses his loneliness and despair resulting from this drive for adventure but inability to leave Earth.

Identity

The final logical level is identity. Who are you? Who is the model? In the case of superheroes this became a fascinating question because we have secret identities (Clark Kent) as well as super hero identities (Superman).

For example, in the case of the Silver Surfer, his original identity was Norrin Radd, a member of a humanoid alien race. His identity as the Silver Surfer was inflicted upon him by an almost godlike creature called Galacticus; against the will of Norrin Radd. Being almost immortal, the Silver Surfer has almost forgotten his original identity, but occasionally rediscovers his 'humanity'.

So as we consider the series of events from the model's life, we construct a matrix consisting of these specific events mapped to the environments in which each takes place, the behaviors of the model in each event, what each event says about the model's beliefs, values and meta-programs, and finally what that says about who they are as a person (or a super hero as the case may be!).

The purpose of doing this is to provide a fertile soil of experiences from which the unconscious mind can learn. The unconscious mind learns from experiences, not from information and data.

Event Matrix for Thomas Edison

Let's take a more comprehensive example of a modeling exercise with Thomas Edison, the greatest inventor, and perhaps the greatest engineer who has ever lived.

Let's take a look at him. He's an ordinary, plain looking person. There are stories that he would walk to his research lab without ID. He would walk to the gates of his lab in Menlo Park in New Jersey and the security guard might or might not know him. So, he might get stopped and have to wait until somebody else came in who knew him. There is nothing in how he looks to let you know externally he is a genius. If you simply did a physical identification (using the NLP New Behavior Generator for example), if you simply stepped into this slightly chubby, balding, middle-aged gentleman, very formally dressed, you probably would not have an experience of the genius that was Thomas Edison.

But if we take events from his life and we map them onto Logical Levels, where is he, what's the environment, what's he doing in the environment? What does that tell us about his state, his skills, his capabilities, his resources? What can we deduce about his beliefs, his values, his meta patterns? Who is he as a person, what's his identity, and even beyond that? Then we get a more refined picture, a deeper experience.

So for example, let's take a scene from Edison's childhood. He started work at the age of 12, but let's go back even further, to when he was a young child. He's eight years old, and he's home-schooled. And his mother adores him and has total faith and confidence in her son; that he can do anything. She encourages him to read voraciously, so here he is young Thomas Edison, only eight years old, literally devouring books. There's nothing about him, if you look at him, that lets you know his future genius. But here he is, and he steps into the kitchen to speak to his mother and he says, "Mother [because that is

166

how children spoke then], Mother, I want to build a laboratory in the basement." He's eight years old remember, and he has just told his Mother, "I want to build a laboratory in the basement of the house, and do chemistry experiments."

Most any parent would have said, "Absolutely no way, I'm not letting you set the house on fire, or blow the house up! There's no way I would let you do that." But Edison's mother is different, she has absolutely total faith in him, believes in him. She says, "All right, go and build a chemistry laboratory in the basement of the house."

Now we know the environment, we know what he did. If you step into that experience, if you float into and become the young Thomas Edison, with that total sense of confidence, approach your mother and say, "Mother, I want to build a chemistry lab in the basement of the house." What does that tell you about your state, about Thomas Edison's state at that point in time? And what does it tell you about your capabilities then? It's perhaps something like, 'I can do it. No limitations; absolute confidence'.

What about the beliefs that you, Thomas Edison, might have at that point in time, perhaps something like, 'You're going to create something… you can do whatever you want… you're going to discover something'.

And the values? It's important for you to find out, to discover, to create something. It's more than important; it's a burning unquenchable desire!

What about the meta-programs that you, Thomas Edison, are running? Let's take a look at a few that might be driving young Thomas.

Toward pleasure, or away from pain? Edison is obviously 'toward'. He wants to build the laboratory. He wants to find things out, to experiment. He's not moving away from ignorance, he's moving towards knowledge.

Internal or externally driven? He is clearly internal. It's true he's reading books, books written by other people, and the books are telling him all this stuff, all this information. But now he wants to find out for himself, in fact he needs to find out—he is driven to find out. He needs to do it himself. That's internally driven.

So just that one experience tells you a lot about your Thomas' Logical Levels, and also about his identity.

Floating into a series of those experiences gives us a much richer map of the person unconsciously. You're stepping into the physicality of a series of experiences, and all the unconscious information about Logical Levels comes along with that. This gives us a way of modeling on a very deep level. It's still a DTI because you are stepping into Thomas Edison's experiences, but now it's allowing you to get a much deeper matrix, a much richer fabric of experiences.

So as you think of each of those experiences, float into the young Thomas Edison, and experience what he experienced from the inside out. "I am going to speak to my mother. I'm eight years old. I'm going to speak to my mother about building a chemistry lab in the basement of the house. What has to be true for me right now as I'm walking up to her to ask her that…in this time and place? What am I doing at this point in time? What skills and capabilities do I have? What resources, what feelings and states do I have? What are the beliefs I have to hold, and what are the values I have to hold? What are the meta-programs that drive me to do that and what is my identity as a result?"

Let's consider another event. Now Thomas Edison is twelve years old, he goes out to work. That was normal back then. He's working on the railroad, as a sales boy. He buys supplies in one town and as the train passes through the next town, he sells them, he's trading. Maybe one town has a shop that sells denim, and the next one doesn't, so he buys denim in the first town and sells it in the second, saving everyone in the second town a journey, being able to sell it for a little bit more than he buys it for.

Then he goes up to the owner of the railroad and guess what? He says, "I want to build a lab in the train. I want to build a chemistry lab in the train." Imagine you're 12 years old, it's your first job, and you go up to the owner of the company and say, "I would like to build a chemistry laboratory in the train, to continue my experiments. Don't worry about fire or explosions I've got it all under control."

What skills and capabilities, what states do you have to have, as the 12-year-old Thomas Edison, to go to the owner of the company and say that. It's that same state of absolute confidence, absolute certainty that he had when he asked his mother if he could build a laboratory in the basement of the house. But this time he needs even more of that confidence, because this isn't his mother anymore, this is his boss, and he's only 12 years-old. You've got to be very determined, and very internally framed, because now he doesn't get to think, "I know my mother will say yes," now this is a chemistry lab in the train!

Let's go on to a third event. Young Thomas Edison decides he wants to make more money. You know what that's like, right? He's sitting there in the train between stops, and he's got fruits and vegetables or whatever he's been buying to sell. And he's thinking, "How can I make more money?" Then he has this idea, he thinks, "I've got my lab already, but what I need is a printing press. If I have a printing press, I can print a newspaper and sell it." This is a great idea because how did news travel from one place to another back then? There is no television, there's no radio, information travels with people and people travel on the train. So the train is going to be the carrier of the news. People in the towns don't need to say, "What's the news from the next town?" because Thomas Edison is going to jump onto the platform and shout, "Buy this newspaper. Here's all the news." You have a ready market.

Now he has to go to the owner of the company and say, "Thank you for letting me put the chemistry laboratory on the train, now I want to put a printing press on as well. Is that okay?" What are the skills and capabilities that he has at that moment in time as he's thinking, "How do I do make more money? I know, I'll set up a printing press on the train and print a newspaper." What beliefs does he need about himself and his place in the world? What's important to him, what values does he hold? What meta-programs is he running?

You may think he is pursuing money, and by the way, he pursued profit for his whole life. But he was thinking beyond money, he was asking himself, "What can I do with the money?" For Thomas Edison it was never about the money as an end, it was always a means to an end. Money flowed through him, he was a conduit for vast amounts of money, but it was never about the money as wealth because he spent his life in the lab. To live the life he lived, he could have gone and worked in somebody else's laboratory and experimented his entire life. So it was never about, "Oh, I need the money for a big house." How do we know this? Because you can step into Thomas Edison's experience, so you experience it too, and you'll know what it was like to do that.

Let's move things along a little bit further. Now Thomas Edison is selling his fruit and vegetables from the train. And he's producing and selling his paper. But it's the not enough for him. Imagine yourself back then in his shoes, float into him and let's find out what he's thinking. "I want to make more money. Not because it's money, but because I want to build my business. I need capital so I will have money to invest in the next venture. I'm doing well but I need more." At this time the American Civil War is raging. So Thomas Edison sits and thinks, and he thinks, "Okay, I've got my newspaper. There's a war on, which is a good thing if you own a newspaper, but how can I boost sales? How can I boost sales of my paper while I'm sitting on a train waiting to arrive in the next station?" He's got all these hours just riding on the train between stations, thinking, "How can I boost sales of the paper? I've got all this great content, and I'm the only game in town when it comes to news because nobody has any other way of getting information, but how do I boost sales?" And he sits and he thinks, and he thinks, and he thinks. And then finally the light bulb goes off (metaphorically speaking as there was no light bulb then, Thomas Edison had not gotten around to inventing it yet), but young Thomas Edison thinks, "I know, the telegraph!"

So he starts to telegraph to the towns ahead, sending something like, "Great victory!" or "Major battle fought at Gettysburg!" And when the people in the next town received the telegraph, news went around town and everyone talked about it.. "Oh, there's a victory in the war. I wonder what that's about. I wonder what happened at Gettysburg. Let's wait for the train to find out." So now when the train gets into the station, there's a thousand people on the platform clamoring for news, "Where's the paper? Give me a copy!" So now you have the young Thomas Edison, 15 years old; he's already a newspaper publisher, a journalist, and an entrepreneur. He's writing his own paper not because he wants to be a writer, but because he wants to build his business.

Let's fast forward a little. Thomas Edison is a young man, still a child by our standards. The train has stopped in a town and Thomas Edison is walking down the street, when he sees this small child step into the street, and there's carriage bearing down… Disaster looms! But Thomas Edison grabs the child and pulls it out of the way; he saves this child's life. Now the child's father is there seeing everything, expecting to see his child flattened by the carriage, but instead seeing Thomas Edison snatched the child from the jaws of death! So the father runs up, he says, "Thank you so much! You saved my child! You can have anything. I will give you anything you want. You saved my child's life."

Just imagine somebody saying that to you when you are still teenager! You

171

would probably ask for the new Xbox! But Thomas Edison thinks for a moment and says, "I want you to get me lessons in using the telegraph."

Imagine stepping into an experience, being offered anything you want, and choosing to learn a specific technical skill. What does that say about your skills and capabilities, your state, about your values? You could have anything in the world and you ask for a lesson in the most boring subject imaginable; you want to learn something so much that it is the most valuable thing in the world for you. You want to learn to use the telegraph because you understand how important it will be, how it will change the world. What does that tell you about Edison, his beliefs and values, his meta programs, and who he was, his identity?

And considering all these experiences as a sequence, you start to get this picture of who Thomas Edison was, in a much richer way than if I just told you dry facts about him.

Let's move ahead further in time. He learns how to use the telegraph and gets a full time job in the telegraph company. He becomes an expert telegrapher, and he is so valuable to the company that he's working six days a week, 12 hours a day. Fortunately, that means he has plenty of spare time to work on his inventions! He comes back from 12 hours in the office, six days a week and he thinks, "Right! Now, I can really get to work inventing!"

Imagine that; imagine floating into Thomas Edison returning from a 12- hour shift and stepping into the lab to begin work. What are you believing about yourself and the world? What has to be most important to you? Now what does that tell you about his skills and capabilities, beliefs, values, and meta programs?

Moving even further ahead in time, Edison invents an automatic voting machine. It will allow the representatives in Congress to vote and for those votes to be automatically counted, immediately. This represents an amazing leap forward in the technology of democracy! So he races to the state capitol (at this stage he's based in Boston), and says, "I've got this great invention, an automatic vote counter!" He just knows that they will embrace this! Imagine being Thomas Edison of the moment, proudly showing your awesome invention that you made in your spare time, after working six days a week, 12 hours a day.

But they say, "We don't want it! You don't understand politics. The whole point of politics is there's a vote and it takes time to count the vote, and while the vote is being counted, that's when all the lobbyists come and pay us to change our votes! Your machine is going to put us out of business; it's going to stop all the corruption, so we don't want it." Thomas Edison decides that that is the last time he is going to invent something just for the sake of inventing it. He's only going to invent something that there's a market for.

And so what does that say about his skills and capabilities, his beliefs and values and meta programs? It's important to him that people use the inventions he creates, otherwise there's no point in creating them. It's important to actually solve a real-life problem. There are a lot of inventors out there who invent all these amazing things, and everybody says, "Wow, that's so cool… but I don't want it." Thomas Edison wasn't that type of inventor.

We're not finished yet because Thomas Edison has barely gotten started. He moves to New York. Why? Because you can find money in New York, it is where all the money people are. There's no serious money in Boston. So what do you do when you're Thomas Edison, and you need capital? You move to New York. What does that tell you about him? He's not moving for the weather, that's for sure, and is not moving for the social life because he doesn't socialize. He is moving simply because it's important for his business.

So he moves to New York and opens his lab in Menlo Park, the world's first pure research lab. Only he doesn't need to ask anyone's permission this time! He gets in the brightest brains, and the latest machines. It doesn't even matter what they do, the brains or the machines, as long as they do something that's new and interesting. And because of all the smart people and wonderful machines in the lab, all the best engineers around are clamoring to come and work there. He has no idea when he's actually going to create but he believes, with complete certainty, that he will create amazing inventions. He believes he can invent anything. And he believes that if he gathers the right people, with the right values, in one place then what they can achieve together will be so much greater than what they could achieve individually.

One of the things he's working on is the light bulb. Thomas Edison thinks in pictures. He's sitting there with his notebook, drawing a filament, a certain shape. Imagine floating into him and feeling your hand draw the filament. Now you draw another one, a different shape, then another one, a different shape again, and another and another. You draw pages and pages and pages in your notebooks, diagrams and pictures of light bulbs with different shapes of filament. What does that tell you about his beliefs, values, meta programs and who he was as a person? Certainly one belief he holds is that if he tries enough times, he can create something, anything, he puts his mind to.

Let's press ahead with him inventing the light bulb. How do you make light bulb filaments? No one has any idea because the light bulb has not been invented yet. Put yourself back in Thomas Edison's shoes, he knows they need something very thin that will glow when conducting electricity, and you wonder if bamboo would work, because the fiber of bamboo grows very straight, and very strong, because each thread of the plant is a single strand of cells. But the exact quality of the bamboo fiber depends on the type of bamboo. What do you do? You find an explorer and you send him to South East Asia, to China. And you tell him, "Bring me back 100 different types and varieties of bamboo." What does that tell you about who Thomas Edison was?

174

He's not saying, "Just bring me back one that works", he says, "Bring me everything you can find, because I'm going to test them all and I'm going to use the best one."

The line that everyone remembers Thomas Edison for was when he was asked "How does it feel to have failed a thousand times?" and Edison replies, "I didn't fail thousands of times, I didn't even fail once. I found a thousand ways not to make a light bulb." When you tell people this line they think, 'oh, that's a clever line', but Edison wasn't trying to be clever he was just describing his model of the world. He truly believed there was no such thing as failure. This is absolutely aligned with who Thomas Edison was: experiment, experiment, experiment. There's no shortcut, its experiment, experiment, experiment and test, test, test. No matter how long it takes it is going to get done because there's simply no other alternative.

So Edison and his team are working on the light bulb, and they finally get it to work at 3:30 one afternoon. It's the end of the experiment and the bulb has been burning for 14 and a half hours, which means that Edison started this experiment at 1:30 in the morning; that's how hard he worked, and that's why he was unstoppable. Imagine floating into Edison as he starts the experiment at 1:30 in the morning, feel the excitement, the anticipation! You can't wait to figure out what this experiment will do, and it works for 14 and a half hours, and then it blows. You think, "That's fantastic, because if it will last that long, I can make it last a hundred hours, and if I can make it last 100 hours, it becomes commercially viable."

So for Thomas Edison the invention is not the end of the process, it's the starting point. It's the beginning of making a product which is viable, and that's only the start of the process of taking it to market. Amazingly he built the electrical grid just so he could sell his light bulbs.

As Edison is inventing his light bulb, and as he's experimenting, the bulbs are all blowing out. Some people might have thought, 'Oh, it's not working, I failed,' but of course Edison thinks, 'Isn't that interesting, I wonder what is going on, I wonder what just happened?' This is going back to this idea of the experiment: every result is giving you more information. And Edison noticed that there was a pattern to the way the filaments were blowing out, the same part of the filament was blowing out first, in a regular way. He says, "This is telling us something. I don't know what it is, but it's telling us something and I'm going to call this the Edison Effect." No ego there, right. "I don't know what it is; we have to find out what it is so let's do more experiments." So, they make all these light bulbs with all sorts of different filaments and foils so they can find out how the electricity flowed by noticing which parts of the foil gets black. And as a result of that, he invented the valve, the electrical valve. Now the valve is what was used to make a TV work, so Edison basically invented TV, or at least the technology that runs a TV. And he invented it by noticing what was going wrong. "Wow, something is going wrong. That's awesome. What does that tell us?" As we say in NLP, there is no failure only feedback.

Anyway, now he has invented the light bulb, and there's a huge growth surge, a huge explosion of business in the U.S. as a result. All sorts of other companies jump on the bandwagon. But Edison has JP Morgan as his backer, in fact JP Morgan's house was the first house to have electric light installed. JP Morgan went out and started to buy all the competing companies and roll them up into Thomas Edison's company, which is called the Edison General Electric Company. But JP Morgan decides to change the name to the General Electric Company, or GE. Now Thomas Edison gets pissed off because JP Morgan has taken Edison's name off the company so he sells out, he sells all his shares and declares, "I'm out of this business." And after he has sold his shares, the share price rockets, and the shares he just sold become infinitely more valuable; he's asked about it, "Why is it you sold your shares when you could have had so much more money if you had kept them?" And Thomas Edison replied, "But look at all the fun I had with the money." Now by 'fun' he didn't mean going to Las Vegas, or buying a yacht, he meant experimenting "Look at the experiments I was able to do with the money I got from selling the shares when I sold them. Why would I want to wait for more cash …and do nothing while I was waiting, when I can do everything I want to do right now?

Taking all these events, all these moments in time, and associating into Edison's experience, experiencing that from the inside and asking yourself, "What does this mean to me as Thomas Edison? What must I believe about myself and the world to have done this, to have said this? What was the most important to me? Who am I as a person? Explore the logical levels, the map of Edison's experience. It's these moments in time, these slices that let you build the picture in a compelling way. If I just said, 'Thomas Edison was a great inventor, and he wasn't really interested in money', that would not have created that experience.

All we're doing is giving you a method of absorbing the information in a way that is much deeper and more profound and more detailed than you'd get reading the book, or just being told about it. You need to visualize the scene, see the young Edison going on, and see his mother, then step into that and experience it from the inside.

Now it doesn't necessarily have to be based on logical levels. It could be based on the Tree of Life for example, or on some other map of reality. What is important is to step into each experience and find out what has to be true for the person, for them to do that in that way, in that time and place. Logical Levels is just one way of describing that.

This process of associating into another person's life story is natural and happens all the time. Research says if you read a novel and the novel has a scene where people are doing things and feeling emotions, your brain is firing off as if it was you in the scene, because of your Mirror Neurons. We are simply suggesting that you do it more on purpose, because then you'll get a much more profound experience, much deeper and much richer. And when you do, you can make these resources, these beliefs and values your own, if they're useful to you.

Chapter 17: Raikov's DTI

Alexander Raikov, the father of hypnotic DTI, used deep trance identification to improve the performance of students in Russia. In particular he worked with musicians in the Moscow Conservatory of Music, but also with art students and language students. In this chapter we're going to discuss his protocol in a little bit more depth, because it contains several interesting elements that have not been widely discussed, if discussed at all, in the West. We have experimented with and incorporated several of these ideas into our own protocol.

Raikov and Trance

So what was Raikov doing that was different to what we've been talking about so far? One of the things Raikov says is that the deeper you go into trance, the more effective DTI is. In fact, Raikov says that it is "the trance itself that is the creative space that allows learning and change to take place." If we compare that to many of the descriptions of 'DTI' in the West, and we are thinking in particular of NLP's 'New Behavior Generator', the trance is likely to be much lighter, and sometimes the technique is done without any discernable trance at all being induced.

But if, as Raikov says, trance itself is the state where your mind and your brain are preparing to reorganize and rewire, then we should be doing everything in our power to deepen the trance during the DTI experience. In Raikov's model, trance is the mind opening up to a new experience, literally preparing to rewire itself.

Of course, this all begs the question, "What is trance?" In fact it's much easier to say what trance is not, than what it is. What trance is not, at least according to Raikov, is anything that you already know. This idea that trance is the mind opening to something it doesn't already know, seems to be based around the idea of the 'critical factor'. In hypnosis the critical factor is that part of the mind (or the brain) that decides whether information should be accepted. The critical factor is the part of your mind that likes to hang out with people who think the same way you do, read newspapers, and watch TV news shows that share your politics and worldview, and generally seems to be comfortable when your opinions are confirmed by what you see and hear around you.

So when you are in the presence of something you already know, or something you already believe, the critical factor is not strongly activated. It is only when you are in the presence of new information, something you don't know, or something you disagree with, that the critical factor sounds the alarm, raises the drawbridge, drops the portcullis and slams the door. This is why trance is a wonderful modality when you want to make major changes in your life; trance de-potentiates the critical factor, putting the palace guard to sleep and letting in the new information.

When you're thinking about something you already know, you're not in trance, but when you're absorbing anything else, which by definition is something you don't already know, you are in trance. Trance, at least according to Raikov, is your mind saying, "I'm ready to be reorganized. I'm ready to take in new information." Now we are not trying to argue that this is the only definition of trance, or even that it is a correct definition of trance, but it is useful for thinking about DTI.

So Raikov says the deeper you go into trance, the more you are able to learn on an unconscious level; therefore the more effective DTI is. Raikov is also saying that the more novel the experience, the more the subject is likely to access trance, and the more the subject is in trance, the easier it is for them to learn. A virtuous circle: novelty leading to trance; trance leading to learning. DTI certainly provides the novelty in this process!

Obviously, if we're doing a DTI using perceptual positions, than your subject is automatically in some kind of trance. Perceptual position work involves positive hallucinations, because when you imagine seeing something that is not there, such as Superman, Thomas Edison or Steve Jobs, you are hallucinating, and positive hallucinations are trance phenomena. The more you positively hallucinate the deeper you go into trance.

Raikov and Regression

Positive hallucinations are not the only trance phenomenon used in DTI. There are plenty of other's, which tend to lead to a deeper trance. One of the ones that Raikov uses in his protocol is an age regression, taking the subject back in time, in this case back to childhood.

There is a concept in neuroscience, and indeed in educational theory, called scaffolding. Scaffolding refers to the idea that everything we know is built upon things we learned as a child. For example we talk about 'standing on your own two feet' because that's how we learn to walk, and we talk about 'looking up to someone' because when we were a small child we literally looked up to any adult. These types of metaphors describe the learning process as a process where one learning experience literally supports the next. As Robert Fulgham wrote, "All I really need to know I learned in kindergarten."

So when we take someone back to childhood, we take them back to the time when they were most open to learning, because these fundamental building blocks of experience are very fresh in childhood. Milton Erickson understood this very well, and frequently used an 'early learning set' to put his clients into a learning state.

So the protocol that Raikov uses is a deep trance induction, followed by a regression to childhood. The subjects then experience the DTI from this childhood perspective, when learning is easiest for them. These are the first important pieces of the DTI process, according to Raikov's protocol.

Raikov and Physical Action

There are a few more key elements to Raikov's DTI protocol. The first of these is converting the DTI experience into some kind of physical action. Once the subject has experienced the DTI, Raikov gets them to do a physical action to utilize those skills. While still in trance, the subject performs a physical action, a utilization of the skills he has learned from the model, so those skills become integrated into his physiology. They are engaging the motor cortex, the same part of the brain that will be active when they utilize the new skills in the outside world. This action can be directly linked with the skill set, perhaps twitching the fingers of a pianist.

This physical action does not need to be realistic, it can function more on the level of metaphor. The action activates the skills experienced in the DTI, taking those skills and embodying them physically, through motion. It is also not important for the subject to 'look good', playing the unconscious piano perfectly, because they're in trance. It is simply for them to take those abstract learnings, direct them into their motor cortex, and simply allow the experience to begin to flow through their body.

Returning to Their Current Age

Using regression has the added benefits when you bring the modeler back from childhood to his current age. Following the DTI, the modeler gets to grow through life day by day, this time being able to integrate and use the skills he learned in the DTI through each day, and each phase of his life; until he comes back to the present. Raikov grows the child back up using these skills, through each day of their life, so now they have a lifetime of experience with the skills of the model. You might say:

"Time is passing, and now you have these skills but with each day that goes past, you find you're better able to use these skills."

For example, if you had experienced a DTI with Milton Erickson, and absorbed his sensory acuity, you would have spent your life being able to observe the people around you, just as Milton Erickson did.

Putting the New Skill into Practice

Finally, Raikov would have his subjects put the new skills into practice by testing them, both before and after the DTI process, in front of an independent panel. He would put students in front of the panel who had gone through the DTI process, and other students who had not, but had simply been put into trance, but not subjected to his DTI protocol.

The students who had undergone the DTI showed significant improvement according to the views of the panel, both in terms of technical skills and artistic interpretation. No doubt this independent judgment also reinforced the change in the minds of the subjects!

Raikov's Protocol

Here is Raikov's protocol in a nutshell:

- Induce deep trance

- Regress the subject to childhood

- Do the DTI in this deep trance regression

- Embody the learnings through physical action

- Return subject to his current age, bringing the learnings back through his lifetime

- Have the subject practice the skills in real-life

Chapter 18 – Regression and Looping

In the chapter on the Raikov's protocol we talked about regressing the subject back to childhood. Now, here's the question, when you do the DTI in the modeler's childhood, who do you DTI with? Do you DTI with the model when the model
is an adult, or do you DTI with the model when the model is a child?

The answer is, it's a judgment call.

Let's suppose you wanted to DTI with Mozart. Mozart is a child protégée in music. If the subject wants to be a musician, or a composer, you can regress the subject to childhood, and have them DTI with Mozart as a child, perhaps composing musical pieces at the age of five. Then you can have both the subject and Mozart grow up a little, and DTI again, perhaps playing for Prince Maximilian III of Bavaria at the age of six in Munich. Then growing up a little more and visiting Johann Christian Bach, the son of Johann Sebastian Bach, in London when Mozart is age 8, and so on.

In contrast, suppose you wanted to DTI with Stephen Gilligan, to gain greater skills in hypnosis. Gilligan says he learned trance as a child in an abusive home Those experiences taught him to use trance states to avoid physical and emotional pain. Personally I wouldn't want to experience that in a DTI, but I would happily DTI with the grown up Stephen Gilligan. So in this case I could regress to my childhood, but as a child would only DTI with the adult Stephen Gilligan, the one who has all those that hypnosis skills, no matter when, where or how he learned them.

So the answer to the question, "Do you DTI with the model, when the model is a child, or only when the model is an adult?" is that it depends on the model, and on the model's childhood. The benefit of doing the DTI with the model, when the model is a child, is that you get to learn how the model actually learned. So you can learn the same way they learned (just much faster!).

So you could DTI either with the model as a grown up, or the model as a child growing up into an adult, depending on the context. If the model is Mozart, by all means model him as a child, but if the model is Gilligan, only use the adult, not the child.

With Milton Erickson, it would depend on your own personal ecology. As a child Erickson suffered from polio, which would be a negative thing to experience in a DTI. At the same time, while he was sick, he had the opportunity to hone his observation skills because there was literally nothing he could do other than to watch and listen closely observing others. So then it would depend on the sophistication of your client, and whether he feels able to take what he needs from the DTI and leave the rest.

In fact, you'll find that many models with whom you would like to DTI had, at best, difficult childhoods. It was these early experiences that made them who they are, in large part shaped who they became as an adult.

So bear in mind that there is something very powerful about doing the DTI from childhood and then growing up with the skills. It can completely change the subject's orientation to a lot of things, not just the context that they're working with. So it can be highly generative and is a wonderful tool. And there can be things in childhood that you would not want to experience. Ecology, ecology, ecology.

Here's another interesting thing about working with regressions that you may have experienced if you are a hypnotist or trained in NLP, and that is that when you bring memories and experience them from the perspective of 'growing up through the years', your brain takes something that seemed static, and makes it active and synthetic again. The brain can literally change memories from the past through reconsolidation, so by allowing the subject to re-experience their whole life (or someone else's life) from childhood through to the present moment, *there can be very profound changes*. In the case of DTI, 'growing up' with the skills obtained from the model, it means that you will *start creating new neural networks* that not only include those new skills, but that wire those skills in with every experience you've had in your lifetime. Not only will those experiences be changed, but the emotional content of those experiences will change as well. This can be a very generative process all by itself.

One way of doing this 'growing up' is by identifying a couple of weigh-stations a couple of specific events from the life of the subject which he can revisit consciously; while his unconscious is changing everything else. Perhaps one, two or three events from each of the decades, the 70s (if they are old enough), 80s, the 90s, 2000s, 2010's, at least one point in each one of those decades to act as a landmark for both the conscious and unconscious minds.

This may seem a little confusing, so let's give a quick example. Suppose I want to improve my musical skills by modeling Mozart. I select the first four events from Mozart's life for the Event Matrix as follows:

Age 4: playing the Clavier
Age 5: composing his first pieces of music
Age 6: playing for Prince Maximilian the Third of Bavaria
Age 14: composing his first opera

You also have the following way-stations from your own life:

Age 4: loved to dance to my mom's pop records
Age 12: receive my first guitar for Christmas and learn how to play
Age 13: put on a performance for family and friends
Age 15: form my own rock group with school friends; we begin writing songs
Age 16: my first paid gig at the village hall

At this stage I have a couple of choices, I can either zigzag between Mozart's life and my own, or I can DTI with Mozart, then bring those skills back through my life.

Option 1: Zigzag:

Regress back to:
Me Age 4: dancing to my Mom's pop records

DTI with Mozart Age 4: playing the Clavier
Mozart Age 5: composing his first pieces of music
Mozart Age 6: playing for Prince Maximilian the third of Bavaria

Return into:
Me Age 12: receive my first guitar for Christmas and learn how to play now with experience as Mozart
Me Age 13: put on a performance for family and friends now with experience as Mozart

DTI with Mozart Age 14: composes his first opera

Return to:
Me Age 15: form my own rock group with school friends; we begin writing songs
Me Age 16: my first paid gig at the village hall

…and so on.

Option 2: DTI first:

Regress to
Me Age 4: loved to dance to my Mom's pop records

DTI with:
Mozart Age 4: playing the Clavier
Mozart Age 5: composing his first pieces of music
Mozart Age 6: playing for Prince Maximilian the third of Bavaria
Mozart Age 14: composes his first opera

Reintegrate with:
Me Age 4: loved to dance to my Mom's pop records now with experience as Mozart
Me Age 12: receive my first guitar for Christmas and learn how to play now with experience as Mozart
Me Age 13: put on a performance for family and friends now with experience as Mozart
Me Age 15: form my own rock group with school friends; we begin writing songs now with experience as Mozart
Me Age 16: my first paid gig at the village hall now with experience as Mozart

Another interesting approach is the idea of iteration within a regression. This means that you regress the subject to a certain age in childhood, give them a new experience at that age, and then grow them back up to their current age. As a result of this experience they've changed, they have learnt, they have at least one more experience they can draw upon. This means that if they were to do another regression they would be able to take this new experience they have just had as a result of the first regression, so the second regression would be even better. So guess what, we regress again to the same event (or to another event). In this second regression they experience even more resources than they had before, and as a result learn even more. We can then grow them back up to their current age, where they will feel even more resourceful as a result of the second regression. And we can continue this process as many times as we want, each regression creating even more resources.

The same principle can apply with the DTI. Let's go back to the example of

Mozart. I go into a deep trance, and regress to the age of 4, and deeply identify with Mozart as he is learning the clavier. After that DTI I experience myself growing back up to my current age and fully integrate this experience.

Then, either in the same session or in a later session, I go into a deep trance and regress to the age of 5, and at the age of five I deeply identify with Mozart as he is composing his first pieces of music. After that DTI I experience myself growing back up to my current age and fully integrate this experience.

Then, either in the same session or in a later session, I go into a deep trance and regress back to the age of six and DTI with Mozart as he is performing for the Prince of Bavaria. After this experience I grow back to my current age and fully reintegrate these learnings.

When we use the Event Matrix, and combine that with Raikov's regression protocol we are going to have a very powerful way of doing DTI, especially with models where we understand how they grew up to be who they are, as a result of the events they experienced in childhood.

Chapter 19: The 'DTI Method'

Introduction to the Method

Konstantin Stanislavski was a Russian actor and acting teacher who developed a system for acting known as the Method. The Method has become the dominant system for teaching acting in the West since Stanislavski's works were translated into English in the 1920s and 1930s, hence the term 'method acting'.

What Stanislavski was doing, although he did not describe it this way, was teaching the actor to deep trance identify with the character he was playing. In considering Stanislavski's work, we will use the term the 'DTI Method' to describe how Stanislavski's ideas can be applied to DTI (and vice versa).

Stanislavski first began teaching his Method through formal lectures. But he found that actors did not like to sit through classes on theoretical concepts, so he pretty much abandoned this approach. He ultimately began writing in journal form, from the point of view of a student in an acting class. As such, he was DTIing with his own students. This is a novel perceptual position that is extremely useful for teachers to adopt, because they can begin to see how their material will be understood, or not, by their students. If you are a teacher, we thoroughly recommend this perceptual position shift in improving your own teaching style!

Much of Stanislavski's material is about the techniques of acting—techniques such as how to walk on stage, how to place the foot, how to properly use the toes for balance, how to 'keep time' when delivering lines, using an 'internal metronome'. These techniques are invaluable for anyone involved in public performance, although outside the scope of this book.

Now the spirit of Stanislavski's teachings on the Method revolves around 'becoming the character'. In fact, Stanislavski had a specific term for this, 'Ya Esm', translated as 'I am being'. Ya Esm is defined by Stanislavski as, "The state of mind when the actor's personality, and the written character, come together and subconscious creation takes place." In other words Ya Esm is the actor's experience when the actor DTI's with the character in the play.

The difference between the Method and DTI is not so much in the techniques used, or the essence of the experience, but rather in the Method. The purpose of the process is to 'become' the character, within the context of the character's existence on stage within the play. In contrast the principal purpose of DTI is to take on, or learn, certain skills of the model and bring those back to everyday life.

Having said this, many fine character actors not only play the character on stage or in movies, but also actually bring the character back with them into their everyday lives. A great example of this is Dustin Hoffman, who is notorious for 'playing his character' off-screen as well as on. For example when he was playing role of Dorothy Michaels in the movie Tootsie, he would frequently dress in women's clothing and try to fool the people on and around the set, including his co-star in the movie Midnight Cowboy, Jon Voight. Similarly, when playing the autistic savant in the movie Rainman, Hoffman delighted in adopting the behaviors and mannerisms of his character off-screen, particularly with his co-star Tom Cruise. Hoffman apparently played an internal game where he scored points by 'pushing Tom Cruise's buttons' with these behaviors.

Stanislavski's acting system, the Method, is so successful, particularly for stage actors who 'live' their character in a more or less continuous and sequential way, that mastering the Method allows a deep and unique DTI. In this chapter we will talk about several techniques within Stanislavsky's Method, primarily Ya Esm, or 'I am being', and how it is to be developed.

192

I am Being

Ya Esm, or 'I am being', within the Method involves the actor 'becoming' the character, while bringing his or her own personality into the experience. This may seem like an obvious thing to say for an actor, but in fact it is anything but intuitive. It involves an abstraction, a leap of experience, to a much higher level than is normally experienced. It involves the actor actually *experiencing the identity, beliefs, values, and emotional states of the character*, before taking on the behaviors and mannerisms of the character.

A good example of this identification comes from Stanislavski's work An Actor Prepares. The Director instructs one of the students, Maria, to act the part of a student in an acting school. In effect the Director is asking Maria to simply be herself. But the difference between Maria and the character she is asked to play is that the character can no longer afford to pay her tuition, and is at risk of being expelled from her acting school. The backstory to the scene is that a friend has offered a valuable broach to Maria so she can sell it to stay in school. Maria has refused the offer, but the friend nevertheless pins the brooch to a curtain in the common room of the house in which the character is living. (At this point the Director actually pins a real brooch onto a curtain on the stage). The friend then walks out, followed by Maria's character, who begs the friend to take the brooch back, but leaving the brooch pinned to the curtain. So much for the backstory.

In the scene Maria has to return to the room to retrieve the brooch, but cannot find it. Maria's task in the scene is simply to search the curtain for the brooch, which she does with much overacting, resulting in giggles from her fellow students. Maria enjoys her own performance so much, in fact, that she totally forgets to retrieve the real brooch from the curtain where it had been pinned by the Director.

After the scene is over, the Director asks Maria how she feels, and she replies that she feels amazing, totally excited by the experience (in fact the opposite of how she would be feeling is she had 'become' the character!). The Director now tells Maria that she must go back and find the brooch and return it to him, otherwise he will expel her from the class, which puts Maria in the actual position of the character in the sense that she is at risk of losing her position in the school! In fact, the Director has concealed the pin and it is not in the curtain at all. Maria returns and searches the curtain, this time genuinely desperate to find the brooch, but of course she cannot locate it, and finally stands dejected in front of the class. The Director of course points out that it is the second scene, involving a real search with real consequences that captivates the audience.

The Director advises the students to only act for a purpose, and only for a purpose that is truly 'honest'. In Maria's case, the purpose was to remain in acting school, and the Director cleverly aligned this purpose with both the character, and with Maria herself.

The Supertask

Stanislavski calls this 'purpose' of the character in the play the 'Supertask'. The Supertask is the single idea that drives the character's behavior throughout the entire play. It doesn't matter if the character is simply sitting in a chair; Stanislavski maintains that this sitting should be done in accordance with the Supertask. We will talk about what this means in the context of DTI in a moment. When the character's behaviors and actions are aligned with the Supertask, it is called a 'Through action', meaning the character's entire being, and emotional and physical energies are directed towards this Supertask. It is only by internalizing this Supertask that the actor can experience Ya Esm, or 'I am being'.

Let's take an example from DTI. Supposing you decide to DTI with Milton Erickson, so that you can work more effectively with your hypnosis clients. Now, a client comes into your office as you are sitting in your chair, and you rise to greet them. At some point during the interaction you trust that your inner Milton Erickson will come forward and lead the client into trance…

Using Stanislavski's Method this will simply not do. As part of the DTI process you first have to decide what Erickson's Supertask is. Perhaps you decide it is to *Free and Empower the Unconscious*. Now you are sitting in your chair with the Supertask, the intention, of Freeing and Empowering the Unconscious. According to Stanislavski this Supertask literally changes the way you sit in your chair, and the way you greet your client. This is because your 'sitting' has the intention of Freeing and Empowering the Unconscious, and your 'greeting' also has the intention of Freeing and Empowering the Unconscious as well.

This may sound like a rather theoretical distinction. However, if you know anything about Erickson's work, you'll realize that Erickson did indeed begin the induction process from the very first moment of interaction. He hypnotized his clients by the way he looked at them, and through the way he shook hands. Once you understand this, you will not need to 'do' an Ericksonian handshake induction; it will arise naturally from who you are being, and from your Supertask.

Any action or behavior, not aligned with the Supertask, takes energy away from 'I am being', and the performance falls apart entirely. Every movement, every breath, every word, every look, must be aligned with, and share energy with the Supertask.

Let's take another example, suppose you decide to model Steve Jobs. What is his Supertask? The answer to the question depends upon the context in which you are seeking to model him. Let's say you decide that your Supertask is 'To create an awesome product'. Now imagine floating into Steve Jobs at key points in his Event Matrix; suddenly his actions, which may have seemed inexplicable, or even antisocial, suddenly make sense within the context of this Supertask. If Steve Jobs is driven by the idea of creating an awesome product, and by only that idea, then of course he is going to disparage anything that is not his own awesome product (which he had a habit of doing!). In addition he is likely to deride anyone who is not, in his opinion, doing awesome work on his awesome product!

Experiencing

According to Stanislavski, 'Experiencing' is the internal, visceral, experience of becoming the character. In other words, 'experiencing' the DTI. This internal experience may include feeling the internal energy of the character, as well as 'seeing' the internal images of the character—something that Stanislavski calls the 'inner eye'.

Stanislavski is particularly interested in the inner feelings, the flow of energy, the emotions, within the character. It is this visceral feeling that flows out of the body as action. After all, the root of the word 'emotion' is literally to 'move-out'.

When you are involved in a DTI it is extremely important that you pay attention to the Experiencing. You must feel the emotions of the model, as internal sensations. You must see and hear the Internal Representations of the model, as well as the flow of energy that leads to action. Great example of this 'Experiencing' is given in accounts of Gilligan's modeling of Milton Erickson. Gilligan expected that his Experiencing of Milton Erickson would be highly energetic, and there would be many thoughts and images that appeared in Dr. Erickson's mind as he considered all the options for treating his patient. In fact, Gilligan experienced exactly the opposite, a sense of peace that allowed Dr. Erickson to absorb and reflect the energy of the client.

Paying attention to the Experiencing will allow your physical actions to arise naturally from the DTI with the model. To gain control over your Experiencing, you simply need to begin to pay attention to the feelings inside your body, particularly when you are feeling strong emotions. For example, if you feel excited or strongly motivated, then notice where in your body the feeling starts, and in which direction it moves. This is the energy you can use to complete the task you are excited about.

We will talk more about Experiencing in the section below on Representation-Appraisal and Will-Feeling.

There are a couple of additional pieces from Stanislavski's work that will be particularly useful. These are the Circle of Attention, the concept of 'If', the Will-Feeling, and the idea of physical embodiment and action.

As we will see, these ideas will dovetail perfectly with the BEAT DTI.

Circle of Attention

The Circle of Attention is that portion of the stage that the actor, or rather the character, is paying attention to at any particular point in the play. Stanislavski would train his students to notice the Circle of Attention by literally shining a spotlight on one part of the stage. Over time the students were able to create their own internal spotlight to focus their attention, and the character's attention, exactly where it should be.

Suppose once again that you are doing a DTI with Milton Erickson. What is Erickson paying attention to? Clearly a good deal of his attention goes to his client's unconscious responses; such as skin coloration, gestures and other unconscious physical movements, eye movements, tonality and so on. If you are in the coaching or therapeutic world, you will of course be very familiar with this sort of attention. The difference here, and the real value of the DTI, is in appreciating on a deep internal level, just how Milton Erickson is doing this.

In the context of the DTI question you should ask yourself here is, 'What is the model's Circle of Attention?' What are they paying attention to? You can then train yourself to move your attention around, developing your own inner spotlight to maintain your attention, within the DTI, exactly where it should be.

Creating a Circle of Attention

To train yourself to control your circle of attention, try the following exercise:

First, go into a state of peripheral vision. Start by focusing on one point, perhaps a mark on the wall in front of you. Now slowly widen out your visual field so that you can see the wall around that mark. Now widen your visual field even further, so that you can see the other walls around you, the ceiling, and the floor. Be aware of the space above you, below you, and even behind you.

Another simple way to go into peripheral vision is to hold your two hands in front of you, the fingers pointing upwards. Look between your fingers, beyond your hands to the wall beyond (or into the distance if you are outside). Now begin to wriggle your fingers and be aware that even though you are looking beyond your hands, you can still see your fingers moving. Now, as you continue to focus beyond your hands, slowly move your hands apart until your arms are straight out to the side at shoulder height. Keep your fingers pointing upwards and keep them moving. You'll notice that even though you are looking straight ahead, you can also be aware of the movement of your fingers to either side. This is peripheral vision.

Once you are in peripheral vision, while keeping your eyes looking forward at the same point on the wall, or in the distance, begin to move your attention around without moving your eyes. As you do so you will realize that your attention is not the same thing as where you are looking. You can be looking in one direction but direct your attention in another. If you find this easy, that's fantastic! If not, you can begin to direct your visual attention by naming an object within your visual field. For example, if you are wiggling your fingers out to the side while looking forward, and say to yourself, "Left hand, left hand…" your attention will be drawn toward your left hand. Now say, "Right hand, right hand…" Continue practicing in this way until you can easily shift your attention around within your visual field, without having to actually look in the direction of your attention.

Once you have control over your visual attention you can begin to experiment with your auditory attention. To do this, sit quietly in a place where there are multiple sources of sound, perhaps a coffee shop where many people are talking. Listen to one conversation (without looking in that direction), then shift your auditory attention to another conversation (again without looking in that direction). With a little practice you will find you can easily control your auditory attention as easily as your visual attention.

Stanislavski's 'If'

'If', referred to by Stanislavski as 'Esli B', means the actions you would take if the given circumstances were true. If you are familiar with NLP you'll recognize this as the 'As If' frame, meaning you act 'as if' something was true.

When you act as if something is really true within the DTI, you are able to put your whole self into the action. You're no longer 'pretending' to be the model; in truth you become the model.

Representation-Appraisal

Stanislavski advises his students to use Representation-Appraisal to create this As-If truth. Representation is what the authors are calling Thoughts (T) in the BEAT pattern, meaning the pictures or movies we are making inside our minds together with their soundtracks. The title of the movie, its meaning, is what Stanislavski refers to as its 'Appraisal'.

So for example if I am modeling Milton Erickson to improve my ability to lead people into trance, I might run a movie in my mind of people I (as Erickson) have seen drop into a spontaneous trance. And my Appraisal of that might be something like, "Trance is natural and occurs everywhere." If I hold this internal Representation and its Appraisal strongly enough; as far as my unconscious mind is concerned, it becomes the truth, and I will act as if it is indeed the truth.

The easiest way to begin to find the Representations and Appraisal within the DTI process is while building the Event Matrix. With each scene of the Event Matrix, you should be asking yourself, "What has to be true for the model, for he or she to be behaving in this way? What Representations, internal pictures, movies and soundtracks does the model need to be holding for he to behave as they do? What meanings, or Appraisals, does the model need to be holding about those internal movies for him to behave in the way he does?" When you have developed a set of Internal Representations and Appraisals that would have allowed the model to behave as he did, then when you *step into the DTI, and experience these same Internal Representations and Appraisals, you will experience the world as the model does*, or at least in a way consistent with the model's experience.

Will-Feeling

Stanislavski argues that feelings (emotions) and will are inseparable. It is the emotional state that drives the will to act. He gives as an example an actor who has fallen in love, but his lover is far away and he cannot see her, and pines for her. This is his feeling. She then writes to him and says that she misses him and wants him to come and see her. He is determined to go and visit her, and this is his will.

199

From this we can see that Representation-Appraisal and Will-Feeling are linked. Each drives the other in a virtuous cycle. The actor must make a representation of his lover, and think to himself, 'How I miss her' (his Appraisal). This generates his emotional state, which in turn generates his will to visit her. Equally we can say that the actor feels his will or desire for his lover, causing him to think of her often (making Representations), and in turn thinking, 'How I miss her.'

So Representations beget Appraisals, which beget Emotions, which beget more Representations and more Appraisals, and ultimately all beget Will.

In case you were wondering, in Stanislavski's story, before the actor gets to travel and see his lover, he is invited to play the part of Romeo in Shakespeare's Romeo and Juliet. He is able to use his own Representation-Appraisal and Will-Feeling about his own lover, to bring the role of Romeo the Lover, to life.

Physical Embodiment and Action

Stanislavsky argues that for the actor to bring the character to life, there has to be some physical embodiment, some action that arises from the Representation-Appraisal and Will-Feeling. When this action truly arises from the Representation-Appraisal and Will-Feeling of the character, then it will be authentic. It is this authenticity that will captivate the audience.

This is very similar to Raikov's idea that in order to trigger the DTI, there has to be a physical action.

Bringing Stanislavski's Method into DTI

In our experience, the most powerful way of bringing Stanislavski's Method into DTI is using the BEAT pattern.

To utilize the BEAT pattern within Stanislavski's Method, you will first identify the model's Supertask. What is it the model is seeking to achieve in his life that makes him a suitable model for you and what you want to achieve? Please bear in mind that the Supertask is yours to choose. For example if you are doing a DTI with Steve Jobs you might choose Supertasks such as:

- Creating an awesome product
- Being a Pirate
- Shaping the future

Or any number of other Supertasks. The specific choice of Supertask will provide the mold that shapes the DTI.

Next, in building the Event Matrix, you will deeply consider what has to be true for your model to have behaved the way he did in that context. This will provide you with Stanislavski's Representation-Appraisal.

When actually entering into the DTI, by associating into the model, you will begin to re-experience this Representation-Appraisal from the model's perspective. You will then also get to experience the model's feelings and emotions, what Stanislavski calls the Will-Feeling of the model.

Finally you will embody the model with some physical action or behavior. We suggest you do this using the BEAT pattern, by stepping into the physicality, the breathing, the gestures, the facial expression and so on, of the model (the Body). As you are experiencing this physicality, you will begin to re-experience the Will-Feeling (Emotions) of the model. Next you will pay Attention to what the model pays attention to, what Stanislavski refers to as the Circle of Attention (Awareness). Finally you can re-experience the Thoughts of the model, what Stanislavski refers to as Representation-Appraisal (Thoughts).

Stanislavski's Method provides a time-tested way of stepping into the model using specific tools and techniques. For those with a continuing interest in developing their DTI skills, it is well worth reading Stanislavski's works in full.

Chapter 20: Walking A Mile In Another Person's Shoes. The BEAT Pattern: Walking DTI

The BEAT Pattern, created by Shawn based on John's Mind Power for Life (among other protocols), is a holistic approach to state anchoring that takes into account the fact that a state is comprised of much more than simply an emotion or feeling. It also involves physiology, awareness, and thoughts. This pattern is focused on integrating the entirety of a state into a set of easy to use resource anchors. In this chapter we will explore how you can use this process within the scope of a DTI to install the new behavior into the subject's physiology, state, sensory awareness and thought patterns to create lasting change.

One of the characteristics that make the BEAT unique is that it utilizes spatial anchors allowing the modeler to literally walk in the shoes of the model. This is a powerful process in which the modeler will build his ideal state from the ground up through the experience of the model.

As we have mentioned before, Raikov's DTI protocol requires a physical action to be taken by the subject while in the DTI. This is a way of activating the motor cortex within the modeling trance. This is important because it gets the brain ready to act in this new way in the outside world, by 'practicing' it first within the trance experience. The BEAT is done as a walking trance, which has the same effect on the modeler's neurology as Raikov's action taking. It should be noted that the external motions do not need to be the same as actions the modeler wants in the outside world. They must be representative or symbolic however (such as Raikov getting his subjects to play 'air-cello') as we are relying on the brain to map the trance experience across and onto the outside world. This is something your brain does easily through its use of metaphors.

In the next section we will first present the traditional BEAT pattern as the foundation of the walking DTI experience. Feel free to use this pattern outside of the modeling context to *build amazing states for yourself and others*; as it is one of the most powerful anchoring patterns we know.

The BEAT Pattern

The BEAT is comprised of four steps, each with its own elicitation and each with its own spatial, kinesthetic and auditory anchor. These four steps are represented by Behavior, Emotions, Awareness, and Thoughts; the four components of any state.

To do this pattern we first begin by inviting the client to imagine four points on the floor in front of him. The client will be eventually stepping into each point, so it is easiest if he imagines the points lined up straight, as if walking down a path.

Now, the quickest way to change any state is to change your physiology. This being true, we start with the body, the physiology of the state. Invite the client to step onto the first point and take on the posture and breathing of the desired state. For example, if it is a state of confidence they are creating they may pull their shoulders back, hold their heads high, and breathe from the belly at a deeper and more active rate. If the desired state is calmness, they may relax their muscles and breathe more deeply and slowly. Once your client steps into the body of that state, watch him change his breathing and body to match it. As he experiences this, the client can anchor it kinesthetically. We typically ask them to press their thumb and index finger together, B.

The client will next step onto the second point, representing emotions. This is all about how he feels the state in his body, the physicality of the state. Emotions are, after all, physical experiences comprised of sensations. We draw the client's attention to the feelings of the state and the different sub-modalities of it. The client can be aware of its location, movement, color, and intensity. We can then use that information to help the client intensify and stabilize the emotion if needed. Once he has associated into the emotion, it is time to anchor it. This time he can set the kinesthetic anchor by pressing his thumb and middle finger together, E.

Awareness is the third point the client steps onto. This is important because our state determines what we pay attention to. What we pay attention to impacts our state. For example, someone who is in an un-resourceful state may notice all the things in the outside world that reaffirm that negativity. The same is true on the flip side; when you are in a pleasant resourceful state you easily find the experiences in the outside world that help to maintain that. At this point in the pattern we are encouraging the client to be aware of the fact and awareness of certain things. This both builds the state and gives them yet another resource; they are training their brain in this type of awareness. We may ask them what it is they are paying attention to. Or we may lead them to go into peripheral vision. The client will then anchor this by pressing the thumb and ring finger together, A.

Finally we are at the point of thoughts. This is all about the client building a resourceful thought pattern, which keeps out any negativity. There are a number of ways to do this. An easy and powerful way is to ask the client to imagine a glowing ball of light on the top of his head. As he is doing that, he can repeat in his mind a simple phrase. We like to use the Zen mantra, "I am. This brings the mind to the present moment. We use a ball of light because imagining something on the top of your head tends to straighten the spine creating a more resourceful posture. The ball of light is also a pleasant visualization to achieve this. This approach has the added bonus of filling the client's sensory channels. Visualizing the light fills the internal visual channel, which means he is not making negative pictures in his mind. The mantra "I am" fills the internal self-talk channel and stops him from saying nasty things to her or his self, T. Of course, you may replace these representations with something more specific to the model if you wish.

The client can be led through this experience enough times so that the anchors are set and the response conditioned. After this the client may choose to transfer the anchors from his hand to something in the environment. For example, a client who has to give speeches may want to see the doorway to the conference room and feel this state fully and completely as he steps through that doorway. Transferring the anchors is very easy. They can either see that doorway in the outside world, or deeply imagine it. As they do they will fire off each anchor. Again the client repeats this to condition the response until it is so automatic that when he sees the door, he walks through it, and enters the state.

Using the BEAT Pattern in DTI

The BEAT pattern is a way to create and anchor a big positive state; we will go through the four steps of the DTI BEAT pattern a little later. We find the BEAT pattern to be an excellent way to activate the DTI and bring it into the body; physically, emotionally, mentally, and using the senses. The BEAT pattern itself is incredibly generative, but when added in the process to the DTI, the modeler can now call on the resources of the model for each of the four steps in the BEAT.

The BEAT DTI process can be done as one part of a full DTI, after a more standard Quantum Perceptual Position DTI, or as a rapid DTI by itself. The DTI is itself a trance induction; we typically do not do a separate deep-trance induction if using the BEAT pattern by itself, because the modeler will be walking. It can be awkward to have the subject in a deep 'down-time' trance and then ask them to stand and walk. Also bear in mind they will automatically enter an altered state as they turn their attention toward the experience of all four steps of the BEAT.

If you are using the BEAT as part of a larger DTI process where the subject is already in trance, you can simply suggest they remain in trance while opening their eyes, standing up and going through the four steps of the BEAT.

In any case, we do suggest that you lead them through the BEAT pattern while moving, so they get the opportunity to activate the DTI through their motor cortex.

The BEAT DTI in Practice

Begin by having the modeler imagine four versions of the model in front of him. Each version of the model will represent one of the aspects of the model's state: the physical body, the emotional body, sensory awareness of the world around him, and the thoughts of the model. In addition to the four spatial anchors represented by the four images, we often use kinesthetic anchors as well. Typically we use the tips of the four fingers of one hand, pressed in turn by the thumb. So we might say the forefinger represents the embodied state (B), the middle finger represents the emotional state (E), the ring finger represents the sensory awareness (A), and the little finger represents thought (T). You'll see this technique used in the demonstration below.

Splitting up the DTI experience in this way can also help with the ecology check. After all, the specific skills of the model the subject wants to require may be largely physical, largely emotional, largely sensory, largely intellectual, or some specific mixture of these. Let's think back to Stephen Gilligan modeling Milton Erickson. Presumably Gilligan wanted to acquire Erickson's sensory acuity, his intellectual knowledge of hypnosis, and perhaps his emotional reaction to his clients. However it is very unlikely that Gilligan wanted to take on Erickson's physical attributes, in particular his disabilities brought on by two bouts of polio. By breaking the model down into these four parts, Gilligan could have more easily modeled Erickson's emotional states, sensory awareness, and intellectual abilities, but replaced Ericskon's physical persona with something else, either Gilligan's own physiology, or the physiology of an entirely different model.

The modeler will be stepping into these four versions of the model, one after another. It therefore makes sense for the images to be approximately one step apart.

First Step: B for Body and Breathing

Before asking the modeler to step forward into the first model, you should get her to strongly imagine the model standing in front of her. She should notice how the model is standing, how the model is holding her body, the model's posture, breathing, gestures, facial expression and so on. You should ask the modeler to describe these aspects of the model until you begin to see the modeler change her own physiology. So that if the modeler is describing the model as having a very upright posture, and breathing deeply, you should ask her about this until you see her own posture change and her breath deepen. Only when you see these physical changes in the modeler should you ask her to step forward into the model; this guarantees the model will actually feel the physiology of the model when she steps forward.

When the modeler is ready, invite him to step into the first version of the model. He is stepping into the body of the model.

We then orient them to the experience of having the physicality of the model. While the body of the modeler and model may be very different, the modeler is able to try on what it is like to be standing and moving with the model's body.

Second Step: E for emotional state

Now it is time to associate into the model's emotions.

Once again you should lead the modeler to describe the emotional state of the model, and how they know what that emotional state is by looking at the model, until you see a change in the physiology of the modeler herself. This is where you will note that she is beginning to feel those emotions herself. When you see this, you will know the model is ready to take the second step.

When the modeler is ready he can fully step into the feelings of the model by stepping into the second version of the model. At this point the hypnotist will spend some time helping the subject build these feelings, guiding the subject to associate more fully into the experience; feeling the state and emotions of the model. You can do this, for example, by asking where she feels those emotions in her body, and then expanding on this by asking for further details: how large is the feeling, is it moving or still, is there a color associated with feeling, and so on.

As with all the steps, breaking the DTI experience down can assist with ecology. So for example in the case where the subject wants to model only some physical ability, but not take on the emotions of the model, she can replace the emotions of the model with other, more useful, emotions.

Third Step: A for sensory Awareness

Just as in the traditional BEAT, the modeler will next step into the awareness of the model. This means she will notice what the model considers is worth paying attention to. For example, if I were to have the awareness of Steve Jobs,

I may pay close attention to aesthetics, and in a broader sense, see opportunities around me.

You can also ask the modeler how the model paid attention to the world around him. For example, does he primarily use one sense over another? Or use several senses? Does he even use senses that overlap as in a synesthesia? For example, Mozart may have primarily used his auditory sense, but at the same time, he was able to see pieces of music in his mind as if they were already written, showing he had a close connection between auditory and visual senses.

The modeler can also consider how the model uses any particular sense. For example, does the model focus in on some detail of the world around him? Thomas Edison certainly seemed to have the ability to focus on one detail to the practical exclusion of everything else, such as when he was developing the filament for the light-bulb, gathering and testing thousands of samples of different bamboo fibers. Or, does the model look at the bigger picture? Again in the case of Thomas Edison, he was able to switch perspective to see how his inventions would fit into the social and economic world in which he lived. How was he able to switch between these two views, the finest detail to the widest panorama?

Fourth Step: T for Thoughts

Finally, we have the thoughts of the model. This can be the most interesting part of the DTI experience because very often the thoughts of the model experienced in the DTI are different from those the modeler was expecting, prior to the DTI. When Stephen Gilligan was modeling Milton Erickson, Gilligan was very surprised at the stillness and calm he experienced within his mind during the DTI, rather than the waterfall of thoughts and ideas he had been expecting.

If the BEAT is being done as part of a larger DTI experience, then the modeler will already know what to expect in terms of the thoughts of the model. If the BEAT is being done as an instant DTI experience, then the

209

thoughts of the model may be as surprising to the modeler as the thoughts of Milton Erickson were to Stephen Gilligan.

In any case, the modeler can now be invited to step fully into the thoughts of the model at his most resourceful. This means fully experiencing the internal representations (pictures or movies, sounds, self-talk and so on), that lead the model to exhibit the desired capabilities. With our Steve Jobs example, this could include making internal movies about things that don't yet exist, such as iPhones or iPads, and adding the commentary that it will exist in the future, and you will be the one to create it.

Conditioning the BEAT

Just as with the standard BEAT we will now condition the anchors by having the subject step through the four points a number of times. Each time to be done slightly faster, so that each of the four points, and the four anchors, begin to run into each other, creating a seamless flow of experience from physical to emotional, to sensory to thoughts.

After we have conditioned the anchors, we will future pace by having the modeler imagine being in the environment where he wants to be like the model, or actually go to that place, and fire off the BEAT anchors. They can literally step into the model's state whenever it is appropriate.

Below you will find a demonstration of the BEAT for DTI, taken from a recent course. One interesting thing about this demonstration is that the subject is going to use Bruce Lee, the famous Kung Fu master and movie star, as a model in an entirely different context, that of sales.

> Coach: What is the specific time and place you would
> like to be more like Bruce Lee?

Modeler: When I'm making a sale.

Coach: And what is it about Bruce Lee that makes him your ideal model in sales?

Modeler: It's about how he is able to read the other person's move before they do it. He also has this type of calmness and certainty.

Coach: And those are wonderful traits to have in a sales interaction.

Modeler: Yes.

Coach: What I'd like for you to do is just come stand over here. That's right. Now see Bruce Lee standing in front of you, because in a moment something amazing is going to happen. When you and Mr. Lee are ready, you can see Bruce multiply himself, so there are four versions of him lined up in front of you. Each of these Bruces is a reflection of one of the elements of that ideal state.

The first Bruce Lee represents his body and physiology when he is able to read others and act with calm certainty.

The second embodies his emotions and how it feels to be calm and certain.

The third is the Bruce Lee who has extraordinary awareness, tracking everything that is important in

211

that moment, and able to read others with ease.

Finally we have the Bruce Lee who represents the thoughts experienced when he is in this state.

Now in a moment, but not yet I'm going to ask you to step into that first Bruce Lee, feeling what it is like to have his body; calm certainty, able to react to others with ease. And as you step into that now; you can feel your posture change as your breathing shifts. Touch your thumb and index finger together. That's right. Be aware of how your breathing flows in the present moment.

That's right. When you are ready it will be time to step fully into the emotions of the experience. Stepping forward now and feeling the calmness and a certainty as you touch your thumb and middle finger. What does it feel like when you are in this way?

(…modeler is in trance by this point)

As you pay attention to those emotions you can enjoy the experience as they move through your body in whichever way they do now. In a moment you will step into awareness, carrying the body and emotions, allowing them to direct your attention as you step into and experience Bruce Lee's awareness.

What is it you are paying attention to? Is it the sounds around you, the changes in my physiology and the movements of others in the room, the space around you, or something else beyond that? You can be certain that with this calm awareness you can see and hear far more than you were consciously aware of before now. Look around and notice how easily your vision takes in the environment around you. There is a softness to the gaze and you are able to see the tiniest movements through your peripheral vision. That's right. Anchor that by touching your thumb and ring finger.

Finally you can step into the thoughts of Bruce Lee and as you do that now, you can comfortably notice what your inner experience is and what it is you are believing about yourself now. And as you do that, touch your thumb to your little finger. That's it.

Now let's do this a little bit faster. We are going to go back to the beginning, that first Bruce Lee, the body. [Coach leads modeler to walk to the side of the path he just walked so he is not going backward through the spatial anchors]

Now step into that first point. Touch your thumb and index fingers together and feel the breathing, the physiology, and the strength of Bruce Lee. I wonder what it's like to feel that strength now.

Step forward now into those emotions while touching that thumb and middle finger. Allow those emotions to grow, and you can certainly feel good experiencing that calm feeling, as you get ready to step into the awareness now.

And as you touch your thumb and ring finger, you can notice all of those important things in your awareness now. As you experience the body, emotions, and awareness that is calm certainty, now you can step into thoughts. Enjoy that inner experience and all of the beliefs that come with it. Touching that little finger and thumb.

That's right. Now when you're ready you can step out of Bruce Lee being you, completely transformed with your new skills, emotions, attention, and thoughts that lead you to success.

Great job! How was that?

Modeler: Really good!

Coach: Fantastic! Now go ahead and think about the next time and place you will be closing a sale. Do you have any sales meetings planned this week?

Modeler: Yes on Monday.

Coach: Imagine being there now. You can see the prospect and hear the conversation. And when you're ready, go ahead and press your thumb to the index finger and then fire off each anchor now. That's right! [modeler's physiology shifts] And what's happening now?

Modeler: It feels really good.

Coach: That's right and you can think of another sales meeting coming up and fire off those anchors again. That's right, each and every time the experience can become fuller and more certain. In fact, if you were to think of another time and place you may find that the more you do this the easier it becomes to just know there is a sales meeting coming up, and those anchors fire off all on their own. You could look at your calendar and see a meeting scheduled and automatically feel that calm certainty. You could go to the meeting or on a sales call and just set the intention and have those feelings now.

Additional Comments

At the end of the walking portion of the BEAT, we had the modeler step off the pathway, and hence out of the model. This is similar to the Quantum Perceptual Positions DTI where the modeler moves back into 'third-position'. This 'clears the slate' so the modeler is ready to test the anchors he has set on his hands.

In the above example you will notice that we tied the BEAT DTI into a specific context and experience of the modeler. If you are familiar with the Meta Pattern, this is the collapse of the resource into the present state. You can also make the change more generative by attaching the resources into more contexts, wider contexts.

We spent a little bit of time here as well implying that a transition can happen, so the modeler no longer needs the anchors set on the fingers, but instead has the knowledge of the upcoming meeting and the anchors will fire. This allows for a fuller unconscious integration of the skills into the modeler. The positive effects are now automatic, they do not need an external trigger, and the model becomes part of who the modeler is.

The Symbolic BEAT

You can do a symbolic variation of the BEAT pattern. In the beginning when the model multiplies, some people prefer to see symbolic representations of the different aspects of the model in place of four versions of the model. For example, they may see a diamond for the body, a heart for emotions, and so on. Either way is better and it just depends on the modeler's own preferences and how his unconscious mind creates the experience.

Integrating the BEAT DTI into the Perceptual Position DTI

The BEAT can be used to physically install the DTI after a more standard Perceptual Position and/or Event Matrix DTI. To do this:

- The hypnotist leads the subject through the perceptual positions and the Event Matrix DTI.

- Keeping the subject in trance, the hypnotist instructs the subject to open her eyes, and stand up.

- The hypnotist then leads the subject through the BEAT DTI as described above, while the subject is in an open-eye trance.

- After the BEAT DTI the hypnotist leads the subject back into a deep down-time (eyes-closed) trance, then re-emerges the subject back into normal waking consciousness.

The BEAT DTI is a fast and wonderful modality for DTI, using movement as a bridge through the different aspects of experience. It also utilizes spatial, kinesthetic, auditory, and visual anchors. In the example above these were the points on the floor, the thumb and fingers, the words used by the subject to describe the experience of the model such as "calm certainty," and seeing the representation of the model. The hypnotist is filling the modeler's sensory channels and crafting a modeling session where the unconscious mind can truly play with all of the different aspects of the model's experience.

Chapter 21: The Hypnotic Mind Meld

In the TV series Star Trek (and we're talking about the original masterpiece from the 1970s), the science officer of the Starship Enterprise was a Vulkan named Mr. Spock. Well actually, Mr. Spock was half Vulcan and half human, which gave him an interesting range of emotional issues to work with as he careened around the universe with his shipmates. Anyway, Mr. Spock has several unique and wonderful skills such as the ability to knock people out simply by squeezing their shoulder, or to solve complex four dimensional trigometric calculations in his head.

However, he had another skill that he only demonstrated occasionally, and that was the Vulcan Mind Meld. This Mind Meld allowed him to merge his mind with the mind of another sentient being, resulting in the ability not only to read minds, but also to permanently take on a part of that other being, just as they took on a part of him. Perhaps you can imagine seeing Mr. Spock in front of you, doing a Mind Meld with Captain Kirk, now imagine stepping or floating into Mr. Spock and experiencing the Mind Meld from the inside…

It is in honor of Mr. Spock that the following technique is named, '*the Hypnotic Mind Meld*'.

Congratulations, you have experienced a DTI with your model. *Your unconscious mind has literally constructed a model of the other person inside your brain.* This model contains an image of the person together with his physical traits such as gestures and facial expressions, and physical skills and abilities, emotional states, beliefs, values, and his meta-programs; the whole identity modeled inside his brain.

So what happens when their beliefs are inconsistent with yours? What happens when their values clash with yours? The following technique, the Hypnotic Mind Meld, will allow you to reconcile different beliefs and values and different meta-programs that may arise during the DTI.

It is very important to understand that changing someone's beliefs, values or meta-programs can have deep and long-lasting consequences for them, consequences that cannot be fully foreseen on a conscious level at the time these changes are made. Therefore using the Hypnotic Mind Meld should be preceded by a full ecology check to ensure that the unconscious mind is on board with any changes made.

Outline of the Hypnotic Mind Meld

In outline, the Hypnotic Mind Meld first splits the experience of the subject prior to the DTI into logical levels (as an alternative, the Tree of Life model can be used instead of logical levels if preferred). This is done as part of the preparation for the DTI.

Next, the experience of the model is split into logical levels (or Tree of Life if the Tree of Life is being used instead). This is done during the creation of the Event Matrix, which is another great reason to use this approach.

Finally, the logical levels of the subject are compared with those of the model, and any differences are reconciled or integrated within the context in which the modeler wants the model's abilities, using one of the approaches outlined below.

Problems with Values

For those familiar with NLP and values elicitation, you'll know there are two main types of issues that a client can have related to values.

The first of these issues is where there is a clash of values; the client values two different things that clash in a certain context. For example, a person who values close relationships, and also values novelty, could find himself with dating issues if the love of novelty causes him to serially cheat on his current girlfriend!

Now, because the model may have an entirely different set of values than the subject, it is very common to get a clash of values between those of the model and those of the subject. Unless these values are reconciled, the full benefits of the DTI may not be available to the subject.

The second type of issue can occur when a client has a value that is very important to him, more important than almost anything else, and that value is an 'away-from' value, meaning it moves him away from something he doesn't want, rather than towards something he does. Consider our poor unfortunate dating client. This time suppose his highest value is "not being alone," a value that moves him away-from being alone, rather than toward a satisfying relationship. This could cause him relationship issues if he is focused on his partner at the start of relationship, possibly overwhelming his partner by constantly seeking to be with them (because he doesn't like being alone). However, as soon as he is in the relationship, he neglects it because he's no longer alone, and his motivating value is missing. His problem arises from the fact that he has no value that actually moves him towards a fulfilling and satisfying relationship.

We see the second type of values issue in DTI, especially when the subject has an away-from issue in the context in which he wants to change. You will notice this when the modeler says things like, "I don't want to be that way anymore," so that he is moving away-from his current situation. Contrast this to the subject when he says, "I want to be like Steve Jobs," where he is moving towards his outcome. It is very unusual in our experience to have a DTI where the subject selects a model and the model has strong 'away-from' values. It's not impossible, and can be addressed if necessary, but we do not discuss it further here because it is, in our experience, so uncommon.

Clash of Values in the DTI

Let's take the first type of issue, where there is a clash of values between one or more of the values of the subject, and one or more of the values of the model.

To take a real-life example one of my (Shawn) students, Andrew, is heavily into Internet marketing for his products and services, and to improve his business he did a DTI with a master Internet marketer he knew well. Following the DTI, Andrew experienced a number of problems with his colleagues: first of all he found himself spending all his time helping them, with no time to grow his own area of the business. Then after a while he felt overwhelmed, and he started cutting them out of his business, and his life, including friends he had known for a number of years. When Andrew came in for a coaching session, he and I spent some time eliciting both his values and the values of the model. While the values were well aligned for the most part, there was one important difference; Andrew placed a high value on helping his friends, while the model would only help those he considered worthy of his help. As a result of the DTI, Andrew had gained a lot more skills, but was still operating with the value of 'help everybody', which resulted in him spending time growing everybody's business except his own! Once Andrew realized what he was doing, he adopted the value of the model, 'only help those who are worthy of your help, because they are helping themselves'. He expressed this by letting others know he expected them to help themselves before he would offer them assistance. I lead him through the Mind Meld (we actually used symbolic modeling as well) to reconcile the two values. I'll tell you what happened a little later.

One technique we have found very effective for dealing with clashing values is to find an event from the life of the model in which the model apparently demonstrated both values (the model's and the modeler's) at the same time. This may sound a little contradictory but actually it's not. Let's think back to our serial dater, who values close relationships and novelty. By bringing novelty into his current relationship, he can satisfy both values easily by expressing both through one behavior. The question that would identify an appropriate event in this case would be something like, "Think of a time when your model built a strong relationship using novelty..." i.e. the question that includes both values at same time.

Once this event has been identified, the subject can be asked to consider what higher value the model is demonstrating when both the 'clashing' values are shown at the same time. So in our example, the higher value, which includes both close relationships and novelty, might be "building an exciting relationship," so excitement would be a value that includes both closeness, and novelty. Once this higher-value is been identified and adopted by the subject, the clash disappears and his own value and the value of the model are incorporated.

Dealing With 'Away-From' Values

We have found that an effective way for dealing with away-from values in the subject is to find an event in the life of the model, where the model clearly shows an 'away-from' value, but 'does it anyway—where the behavior was actually motivated by a higher 'toward' value.

Let's return to my Internet marketer to see how these techniques might work in practice. Remember that he has a value of helping everybody, while the model has value of helping those who deserve help. Having initially spent his time helping everybody except himself, according to his own value, Andrew then switched entirely into the model's value, but interprets this as 'don't help someone who doesn't deserve help', i.e. an away-from value. As a result he cuts his friends from his life, resulting in personal problems!

A little questioning revealed that even though the model only helps those who are 'worthy' of his help, he actually offers his help to everybody. The worthiness comes, not from his judgment, but simply from whoever accepts the help that is offered. This very small shift in emphasis from helping everyone, to offering help to everyone, was sufficient to reframe the issue entirely. At the same time the away-from value of 'don't help those who are unworthy of help' is reframed as 'this person is not ready to be helped, yet' backed up by experiences where the model helped somebody later on, when that person became ready to accept the help.

With these reframes and values integration in place, we used Clean Language to construct a more empowering metaphor. That metaphor was a DTI with a bridge builder, who builds bridges that allow people to cross the river, but does not force them to cross. This was much more useful as a metaphor and avoided both the need to 'help everyone', as well as 'rejection of the unworthy'; those worthy of help crossed the bridge by themselves.

Reconciling Values Using the Visual Squash

Sometimes it is not possible to find events from the life of the model that allow integration of the values of subject and model in the ways described above. This is especially true when there is a big divergence between the personality of the subject and the personality of the model, so the values of each seem to be very different. The following technique can be used in any situation to reconcile and integrate the values of the subject and the model.

The first step in this technique, as before, is to carry out a values elicitation on both subject and model. When eliciting the values of the subject, the process should not only include elicitation, but also their ranking by importance. If appropriate, any cleanup work to make the values of the subject mutually supportive, and 'toward', at least for the top two or three values. Aligning values and clearing 'away-from' values is beyond the scope of this book. You can find information on aligning and clearing values in any standard NLP Master Practitioner course.

Now we elicit the values of the model. When eliciting the model's values, the subject should first be associated into the model and whilst associated, asked what is important to her as the model. Once this is completed, the subject is re-associated into herself.

The hypnotist next leads the subject to discover the highest positive intention (i.e. the highest value) associated with actually doing the DTI. In order to elicit this value, the modeler should be associated into the context in which she wants the change to occur; i.e. the context in which she wants to have access to the model's, skills, but this time in the state of the model.. This highest positive intention should be abstract. For example, if the subject is modeling somebody who is very organized with paperwork, because she wants to be able to do her taxes more easily, the highest positive intention for doing the DTI should be something abstract like 'freedom' rather than something less abstract such as "So I will have my taxes done." The reason for this is that this highest positive intention of the DTI needs to be abstract enough to include the highest values of both the subject and the model. Returning to our example, if the highest positive intention is 'freedom' then this is abstract enough to include 'freedom from my taxes' for the subject, as well as 'freedom from paperwork' for the model.

The hypnotist then leads the subject through an NLP Visual Squash (see The

Visual Squash by Jess Marion and Shawn Carson for more on this pattern, available at Amazon.com). In this case, one of the images or concepts will be the highest value of the subject, and the other will be the highest value of the model. The highest positive intention for doing the DTI will act as an attractor toward the highest shared positive intention for both subject and model. In fact, the highest intention for doing the DTI will, often become the highest shared positive intention of subject and model.

Integrating Beliefs of Subject and Model

In the context of DTI, beliefs are normally much easier to deal with than values. This is because usually the model has more empowering beliefs than the subject, and it is often possible to simply install the model's beliefs into the subject using one of the many NLP techniques available. We will briefly discuss how to use a 'submodality map-across' to install the model's beliefs in this context.

Belief Change Using Submodalities

When the model has more empowering beliefs than the subject, and the subject wants to take on these beliefs, the hypnotist can lead the subject through the following steps:

As always, as part of the preparation for the DTI, the model will explore her own beliefs in the context in which she wants to change, the context in which she wants to have access to the skills of the model.

Now we elicit the beliefs of the model. If we are using the Events Matrix we will already have these beliefs. Otherwise, associate the subject into the model. While associated into the model the subject is asked, "What are you believing about yourself? What do you believe about world? What are you believing about your role in the world and your capabilities?" Because the subject is

225

associated into the model and has taken on the model's identity including their beliefs, the beliefs solicited are likely to be highly empowering. "Anything is possible," "I can do this."

The hypnotist then asks the subject what image she sees in her mind that lets her know her beliefs are true, that anything is possible, and that she can do it.

Once these images have been identified, the hypnotist elicits the sub-modalities of the empowering belief images, meaning where the image appears to be: is it on the left, on the right or in the center? Is it at eye level, higher, lower? How far away is the picture? Is the picture in black-and-white or in color? Is it bright or dim? Do you see yourself (the model) in the picture, or is it like you are looking out of the model's own eyes? Is there a soundtrack associated with the picture? Is the picture framed, unframed, panoramic?

When this has been done, bring the subject back from the association with the model. The hypnotist can ask (or remind) the subject about her own beliefs, what she believes about herself, the world, and her place in the world? The hypnotist then asks the subject about pictures she is seeing when she thinks of these beliefs, and the sub-modalities of those pictures using the questions listed above.

If there is a significant difference between the beliefs of the subject, and the beliefs of the subject-as-model, then there will also be significant differences in one or more of the sub-modalities associated with the pictures. For example, if the subject has a limiting belief about her own ability to be creative, but when associated into the model, let's say it's Thomas Edison, she has total belief in her own creativity, then the pictures which are linked to these beliefs will also have different sub-modalities. For example, the subject might see herself failing to be creative, say getting frustrated at her computer, in a picture on the left hand side. But while associated into Thomas Edison, believing in her own creativity, she actually sees out of the eyes of Thomas Edison, looking at an experiment in his laboratory, and the picture is on the right side. Therefore, in this case there is a difference both in the location of the picture, and in the fact that the subject's picture is dissociated, because she sees herself in the picture while the Thomas Edison picture is associated because she is seeing out of Thomas Edison's eyes.

Once the beliefs, and sub-modalities of those beliefs, of both the subject-as-modeler and subject-as-model, have been elicited you can ask the subject to think about his old beliefs, and map them onto the sub-modalities of something that used to be true for them, but isn't any more. A good example we use is that the subject used to have some childhood toy, perhaps a pacifier, but doesn't anymore; this generally ensures that the sub-modalities of this are dim and distant, far into the past, perhaps to their left (if they are 'normally organized'), or behind them. This map across is done by thinking about the picture associated with the limiting belief, sending it off far into the distance, and bringing it back into the position on the 'used to be true' belief.

The subject is now asked to construct an image of himself as he wants to be, one that is similar to the image held by the model, and mapped onto the sub-modalities of the belief of the model.

Let's go back to our example of the subject modeling Thomas Edison. This subject used to own a tricycle as a small child, and when she thinks about that, the image is down on the ground on the left-hand side, about 12 feet away. The subject makes the image of herself failing to be creative at her computer on her left. She takes that picture and sends it off into the distance, and when it comes back it lands in the place where that old tricycle picture is kept. The subject is instructed to blank the screen and repeat the pattern several times, blanking the screen in between each; seeing herself failing to be creative at her computer -> send that picture into the distance -> bringing that picture back in the place where the tricycle is located.

Now she is asked to imagine seeing out of her own eyes, being creative in the context in which she wants to change. That picture is then sent off into the distance, and when she comes back, it comes back in the location where she saw the picture of Thomas Edison's lab. Again this pattern is repeated several times, blanking the screen in between each. This will install the new positive belief in the subject, regarding her own creativity.

Reconciling Meta-Programs

Please remember that changing somebody's meta-programs can have far reaching and unpredictable effects. Such changes should be made in a very specific context, after fully exploring the ecology, if at all.

Meta-programs are the preferred ways in which each individual takes in information, processes that information, and deals with the world around him. In the context of a DTI, one of the most important meta-programs is related to possibility, impossibility, and necessity. These meta-programs are revealed by word choices, such as, "I can," "I can't," "I must," "I mustn't," "I should," "I shouldn't," and so on.

Other meta-programs that are often important in DTI include 'toward' outcomes (rather than 'away-from' problems - most subjects select models who have *toward* meta-programs), options versus procedures, internal versus external frame (i.e. how do I know I've done a good job, is it because I feel I have, or because someone else tells me?), and self-interest versus concern for others. Of course, many more meta-programs exist and might be important in the context of any particular DTI. The meta programs which are most important for the model are those which drive the model's behavior. The meta programs which are most important to the modeler include those that cause the most limitations or problems.

When the driving meta programs of the model and subject are very different, then the hypnotist should pay special attention to meta-programs during the DTI process. If conflicting meta programs are not reconciled, there is every chance the DTI will have limited benefits at best.

The DTI process itself contains everything required to allow the subject to experience the meta-programs of the model within the specific context in which he wants to experience change, in which he wants to take on skills of the model. In order to change a meta-program, if there is a clash between the meta-programs of subject and model, it's necessary that:

- The subject has a congruent reason for the change within a specific context

- The subject has a reference experience for the new meta-program

- The subject is able to future pace a new behavior or feeling using the new meta-program

Each of these requirements is already satisfied in the DTI process. As part of the preparation the hypnotist will have ensured that the subject does indeed have a reason to make the change, and that reason is congruent on both a conscious and unconscious level.

By virtue of the DTI into a model, who has the new meta-program, the subject will have had an experience of that meta-program.

Finally, future pacing using the skills of the model within the context will automatically provide a future pace of the new meta-program.

Therefore, if the DTI is done using the Event Matrix approach there is every likelihood that the meta-programs of the model will be taken on by the subject. Reconciling these with the meta programs of the modeler is still vital of course!

Chapter 22: Stepping Into The Future

In this chapter we are going to explore ways in which you can integrate the DTI experience into your life beyond the session. We will be covering issues of ecology, as well as how to install the learnings from the DTI as a strategy for success whenever you need it. The processes laid out in this chapter are a useful way of closing the DTI session. They take into account your client as a whole person, who has meaningful relationships in his or her life and who is ready to integrate the new skills acquired during the DTI process.

We have already described how we can use the Mind Meld to integrate modeler and model. In this chapter we will be going further. We will:

- Integrate the modeler with his or her wider community (family, friends, colleagues, team-mates and so on, whoever may be impacted by the change he is seeking), once again using the visual squash pattern.

- Integrate the model's new states and behaviors into the contexts in which they are required, using the swish pattern.

- Make minor adjustments to the new strategies to make them more elegant.

Making the DTI Ecological for Others

When a person makes an important change in his life, this change has ramifications not only for his future, but for other people in his life as well. It is important as a DTI facilitator, and a change worker in general, to recognize that it is an essential part of our job to ensure that the change a client makes is integrated into who he is as a person, taking into full account that when he changes, others in his life may change as well.

Up to this point in the process you will have ensured that the modeling experience is one that is ecological for the modeler. This is covered when you establish unconscious permission for the DTI to occur, when you elicit the values of elicitation for the modeler and model, and when you integrate modeler and model using the Mind Meld. Now it is time to consider how the DTI experience can impact the modeler's community in ecological ways. By community we are referring to the people involved in the specific context in which the modeler is changing. This could include family, friends, coworkers, and anyone else with whom the modeler has a relationship in the specific context.

To do this we are going to use a version of the Visual Squash that will allow us to integrate both personal and community values. You may choose to do this as a traditional Visual Squash, or as an abbreviated version. We will first outline the steps of a traditional Squash in the context of DTI (for more in-depth information about the Squash please refer to The Visual Squash, by Jess Marion and Shawn Carson, in our NLP mastery series available from Amazon.com).

The first step to the Squash is to assign parts; in this case the first part is the modeler, and second the modeler's community.

A key feature of this pattern is the use of catalepsy as the metaphor for integration. Therefore, gently lift both of the modeler's hands and induce catalepsy. The easiest way to do this is to use 'ambiguous touch' while drawing the modeler's attention to the visual component of this pattern. As you lift the hands you can ask the modeler, "Which hand represents you, and which hand represents your community, your family, friends, co-workers or whoever may be affected by this change?"

Next we will create a level of dissociation by suggesting that a symbol can appear in the palm of each hand, to represent that part, one symbol for them and one for their community. In hypnotic terms, the appearance of the symbols is a 'positive hallucination' that fills the visual channel and makes it easier for the modeler to get in touch with the values associated with each part.

Beginning with the symbol representing them, we are going to be looking for the positive intention behind them doing the DTI, and behind the new skills and behaviors they have developed generated via the DTI.

Each time the modeler identifies a positive intention, you can invite him to 'chunk up' on that positive intention by asking, "And when you have that, what does that do for you?" For example, supposing the model wishes to identify with Mozart to improve his ability to compose music. He identifies his right hand with this positive intention, and the image he sees is a piano releasing musical notes. You can ask for the positive intention behind that by asking, "What is the positive intention of the piano releasing musical notes, what does it do for you when you can do music?" And the modeler says, "It allows me to express myself." So, you ask, "And when you are able to express yourself, what does that do for you?" And he replies, "It allows me to connect with others." "And when you connect with others, what does that do for you?" "I become free!"

You will know you have reached a strong value when you see a physiological shift in the modeler. Continue this process as long as you are getting a strong physiological shift with each higher value.

Once you have found a strong, high-level value on the first symbol for the modeler, his purpose for the DTI and the specific changes he wants to make, it is time to begin chunking up on the 'community' side. In this case we are looking for the values of the modeler within the community, as well as the values of the community itself. As you chunk up on the community side, you will eventually find values that are congruent with those on the first hand. Therefore the values of the modeler and the values of the community will be the same, or at least very similar.

After establishing the highest value for each side, it is time to allow the modeler and the community to complement each other in this context. By complement we mean that both the individual and the community have certain skills and resources they can, and should, share. The modeler has skills that the community both needs and will value, and likewise the community has certain skill sets as well that the modeler will need and benefit from.

A simple way of doing this is simply to ask, "What can this part, you as the modeler, learn from that part, the community? And what can be community learn from you as the modeler?" In this way the *skills and values of each part begin to be integrated into the whole.* As you go through this process of gifting skills, resources and values from, and to, each side you can indirectly suggest the hands are coming together by very gently tapping the outsides of them. You can next suggest that when the hands do in fact touch, a new symbol will appear representing the integration of the individual (with his new skills) into the community, and the integration of the community with the individual (with new skills).

When the new symbol (representing the integrated whole) appears, you can invite the modeler to bring that symbol into her or his self. This could represent the modeler coming to a new understanding of how to be as a person in this context, and also to the community in a way that is ecological to both.

Conversational Integration

You may also wish to do this integration process more conversationally by associating the modeler into the specific context where he will be using new skill sets and doing another values elicitation. This is done by asking the modeler, "And as you are here, experiencing these new states and behaviors, what is most important to you about this?" Just as with the traditional Squash, you should be looking for the value that has the strongest energy behind it, the one that elicits a physiological shift.

Now using perceptual positions, associate the modeler into a member of the community. You can suggest that this individual represents the entirety of the community in this context. They can serve as a spokes-person. Once associated into this other person, conduct another value solicitation; this time from the perspective of the community. The modeler is effectively doing a DTI with the community, or at least with a representative of the community.

Now it's time to associate back into the modeler. Ask the modeler what new skills and resources he offers the community as a result of the DTI. And likewise, what does the community offer to the modeler that she or he could not accept before, but now can really use. At this point you can suggest that the modeler and community can work together to achieve their common value.

The Double Swish

The purpose of DTI is to make skills and abilities available to the modeler whenever she needs them. It is not always desirable or even possible to do a DTI each and every time the modeler is in the specific context she wants to change, and so we need to create a 'short-cut' in the modeler's neurology that links external triggers in the context where she wants the change to the state and behaviors of the model. To accomplish this we will be using a version of the NLP Swish pattern that links the context to the model, and links the model to the modeler's future self. Just as with the Visual Squash, we will not go through all of the ins and outs of the Swish here. If you are new to the Swish we recommend you consult, "The Swish" a part of our NLP Mastery Series.

The Double Swish is a highly effective way of conditioning new states and behaviors. It allows for an automatic and instant DTI that is triggered by the context in which the DTI skills are needed, and the associated trigger.

- The first step of the Double Swish is to associate the modeler into the context where she wants the skills of the model to be available to them.

- When they see the specific trigger or triggers, letting them know it is time to 'become' the model, tell them to place a postage-stamp-sized picture of their model onto that trigger.

- Now whenever they see the trigger, that picture of their model will expand out and appear in front of them life-sized.

For example we can imagine a modeler who has a fear of public speaking and wants to be relaxed in front of groups. Her trigger picture is seeing the audience's eyes. She has chosen Oprah Winfrey as her model.

- So the modeler will see the audience's eyes and in the center of that picture, perhaps in the center of the forehead of each member of the audience, she will embed s postage-stamp-sized picture of Oprah.

- These pictures will expand out into a life-sized Oprah between speaker and audience.

- Next, the modeler can now step into the model, taking on her state, and taking on the DTI once more. This is especially effective if the BEAT has been used to condition the DTI. After all, this step is essentially the first step of the BEAT pattern.

- Now, as the model they will see the trigger again, but this time the modeler will embed in it a postage-stamp-sized image of a future version of herself, one who is completely resourceful in this context.

- The modeler-as-model will now swish this picture so it expands out, becoming a life-sized picture of her future-self.

- The modeler can now step into that future self, carrying the resourcefulness of the model with them. This is the Double Reverse DTI.

Using the example above, as Oprah, the modeler will now see the audience's eyes while feeling all of Oprah's confidence and resourcefulness. She will next embed a postage-stamp-sized image of her own future self, a version of her who has practiced feeling relaxed and confident in front of groups for quite a long time. This is the person she wants to become. Again the modeler will swish the picture so it expands out into the life-sized image of her future self. She will step into that, associating into her own future self, taking the resources of Oprah, and feeling good. She can even see the audience's eyes as she feels relaxed and confident.

Just as with the traditional Swish, we will guide the modeler through this experience a number of times, calibrating to their unconscious response.

Remember to blank the screen between each iteration of the Swish, so that the

236

chain of pictures and feelings always goes in the same order, Trigger -> Model and Trigger -> future-self. We then invite the modeler to do this at least five times internally. The end result will be that when the modeler is next in the context and sees the trigger picture and the chain of experiences is automatically triggered. Our modeler see the audience's eyes and automatically she associates into Oprah, and then into her future self. This will happen so rapidly that the modeler will sees the trigger and feel the resource state of her future self, containing all the resources of Oprah.

Future Pacing An Elegant Strategy

Up to now we have presented future pacing as going into contexts in the future and trying on new states and behaviors. This in itself is a highly valuable process, one in which the modeler will have the experience of future successes experienced in the present moment.

In a typical piece of change work there may be many contexts (and many triggers within those contexts), in which the client wants to feel or behave differently. When the client wants to feel or behave in one specific way, across a range of contexts, then the change can be generalized by associating the client into that state and future pacing her through each of those contexts in turn.

Sometimes, however, the context may be so different that a different state and behavior is required for each. This is the time when the Matrix Model of DTI is really valuable, because the model brings a range of emotional and behavioral responses across a range of different contexts. Supposing you wanted to model Steve Jobs because you want to be more creative; in some contexts 'creativity' might require the single-minded focus of Steve Jobs, in other contexts it might require the persuasiveness of Steve Jobs (often called Steve Jobs' Reality Distortion Field), and in still other contexts it might require Steve Jobs' dedication to aesthetic perfection. Once you have experienced the DTI with Steve Jobs and the DTI has been fully installed, each of the states and behaviors will be available to you during the process of 'creativity.' The

DTI bundles a number of complementary emotional and behavioral resources, and provides them as a package deal.

The disadvantage in bundling resources in this way is that the end result may not be 'elegant' (as the word is used in NLP). But we can refine this approach so that the strategies installed as a result of the DTI become more elegant. Once the more elegant strategy is conditioned, the unconscious mind takes over and the new behaviors can be initiated automatically. Note that 'elegance,' in the sense we are using it here, means finding the simplest and shortest route to experiencing new states and behaviors.

We do this by first associating the modeler into a specific context after the DTI model has been installed and walking them through the model's particular strategy as it applies in that context. Not only are we testing to see if the strategy elicits the desired state and behavior within the context, but also whether there are steps that can be left out to streamline the experience.

If necessary, we can then associate the modeler into a second context, one that logically follows the first. Again, we are trying to determine whether the context automatically triggers the desired state and behavior, and again whether any steps in the install strategy can be eliminated to make it more elegant.

You may note that many of the approaches we have detailed in this book have this aspect built into them already. For example, let's imagine you are using the BEAT DTI to install the physical behaviors, emotional states, sensory awareness and focus, and thought patterns of Jack Welch in order to 'be more confident' at work. After you have gone through the entire process, you imagine seeing your office. Do you need to fire off each of the four anchors in the BEAT? Or can you simply see the door and act, feel, sense and think with confidence? Do you even need to see the door, or can you feel confident on the train to work? Have you generalized that confidence out far enough that now you are feeling relaxed and happy when you merely think about work? Each of these is more elegant that the one before.

If the modeler is already at the last stage, then that is fantastic! If not, we can condition the response so that we are able to narrow it down to the fewest steps possible. In other words, our modeler merely needs to see her office to feel good. As with any piece of change work, we condition the response so that the neural network is strengthened.

Chapter 23: Dreaming Into You: Reverse-DTI and Double Reverse-DTI

I (Shawn) incubate a dream in which I will experience a particular type of DTI experience. After falling asleep I find myself in a strange landscape, dark and gloomy, inhabited by an indigenous people. Steep hills dot the landscape, each with a ruined structure, perhaps an abandoned villa or even a tomb, on its top. My guide leads me to one of these structures, and inside we find a class studying the rites of ancient gods. I am told that I should not be there because I do not yet have the power or experience to understand these rites. I feel powerless and unsure. Suddenly, I feel a change inside myself, a flow of power arising from being possessed by the gods themselves…

The Reverse-DTI

The defining feature of the Reverse-DTI, compared to a standard DTI, is that it is the model who associates into the modeler, rather than the modeler associating into the model. This Reverse-DTI has been in existence for thousands of years in many traditional cultures around the world, often thought of as 'spirit possession', a subject that I (Jess) have studied as an anthropologist. As Christianity, particularly Catholicism, spread through Europe, there was a transition in culture, and the practice of spirit possession became highly taboo. As a result, 'possession' by a god or spirit became 'pathologized,' and the 'possessed' lost the honored position within society that they would have previously enjoyed.

Let's revisit a couple of historical examples in which spirit possession was viewed quite differently than we originally discussed in the earlier chapter on the history of DTI.

In ancient Greece it was believed that writers, musicians, and other artists were successful because they had 'daemons' who lived in the walls of their homes. A daemon is not the malevolent spirit of modern myth, but rather a creative spirit that acted through the artist. These daemons would 'possess' the artist and it was this possession that generated the artist's creativity.

One of the ways of understanding this is through the lens of deep trance identification. Instead of a person 'possessing' the model to absorb and learn the model's skills, the model 'possesses' the modeler in order to manifest and use those skills.

With the rise of the church, daemons became demons, and 'possession' became subject to exorcisms. But outside this Western view of possession, being the work of 'demons', there is a rich and therapeutic tradition related to possession. In many non-Western cultures, Spirit possession is still linked with gods, goddesses and spirits that are summoned to heal individuals and entire communities. Possession becomes a means through which the human is transformed and has direct experience of the divine. In these traditions, which remain alive and well in many cultures, the possessed becomes a conduit of change for the entire community. The deity inside of the individual is able to solve the individual's problems and concerns, and is also able to give advice to the community.

Consider the Tamil festival of Thaipusam in Malaysia, as an example of this in contemporary experience.. Each year devotees of the Hindu god, Murugan, participate in a three-day festival that culminates in the 'possession' of several devotees by the god. During this time, Murugan can act through the devotees, giving them the ability to withstand intense pain, to heal issues in the devotee's life, and to provide blessings for the community.

I had initially looked at the Thaipusam festival from an academic perspective. From this western academic perspective, the intense religiosity of devotees causes them to experience an altered state of consciousness, one in which they

241

believe themselves to be gods. But when I looked at this from the point of view of a hypnotist, I thought, "Wow! This is deep trance identification in reverse," rather than the human associating into the god, the god associates into the human. Academia did not have the language or frames of reference to fully understand this process.

Modern Western Example of Reverse-DTI

When you look at advertisements for weight loss supplements or programs, they often show 'before' and 'after' photos. The 'before' photo shows a chubby or fat person, while the 'after' is a slimmer, perhaps even a super-fit, person. In fact, many of these pictures actually depict people who were initially super-fit, but then had some kind of injury or other issue that caused a lapse in their training regimen. No longer able to exercise, but, continuing to eat their usual diet, resulted in them becoming overweight. This is the putative 'before' photograph. As soon as they recover from their injuries, these people are able to lose weight really fast, because their body, their metabolism, their emotional states, their perspectives on food and exercise, their self-image, and their thoughts are those of a slim and healthy person. As soon as they go back to their normal exercise routine they very quickly shed the excess pounds, revealing the muscular person underneath, the 'after' photo!

Therefore what you have is an athletic, muscular person temporarily caught in a fat body! This is a naturally occurring double Reverse-DTI. It's like the statue of David; the story goes that when Michelangelo carved the statue he believed David was already present in the block of marble. Michelangelo's only job was to reveal the David within the marble.

Future-Self DTI as a Reverse-DTI

A study was published in 2013 that looked at the success stories of people who lost weight, and the coaches, hypnotists, and doctors who helped them achieve their goals. What they found was that the factor most often associated with success was a specific type of future pace in which clients would imagine becoming their future self having achieved their goals. As this future self, they experienced the habits and life of someone who was more slender and healthy, and maintained a healthy lifestyle. They then took that experience back with them as they reassociated back into themselves.

This technique (or variations of it) has been one of the most successful mental tools in weight loss. You will see that it is a 'future-self' DTI but it can also be thought of as being 'possessed' by your own future self.

Parts Installation

A distilled version of the Reverse-DTI can take place in the context of hypnosis (or NLP), when 'installing' a new part. For a more complete discussion of 'parts' and 'parts installation' you can read Richard Bandler's excellent book on the subject, *Reframing*. It is not clear to the authors why 'parts installation' never became as popular in hypnosis or NLP as Reimprinting or the Six Step Reframe (a form of Parts Reframing). It's relative disuse might be attributable to the perceived perception that the technique had the potential to fragment risk of fragmenting personalities.

Parts Installation is not Multiple Personalities

Whatever attraction Parts Installation might have held to hypnotists, interest in the technique waned, possibly as a result of psychiatric interest in multiple personalities. Called Multiple Personality Disorder, then later Dissociative Identity Disorder (DID), multiple personality diagnoses sky-rocketed from the 1970's into the 1980's and '90's, from 100 or so to tens of thousands.

This unprecedented increase in cases almost certainly resulted from the publication of the book *Sybil* in 1974. The book and subsequent movie describes a woman afflicted with DID. The book and movie offered both psychiatrists and their patients a pre-packaged experience of DID that they could (and DID) model.

Clearly, installing a new 'part' is very different from installing a new identity. A part is a specific way of thinking, feeling and acting in a particular context. These thoughts, feelings and behaviors may, and usually are, supported by an appropriate set of beliefs and values. In fact, it is fair to say that classical hypnosis often seeks to 'install' a new 'part', for example a 'non-smoker part' that engages in more positive and productive thinking patterns, feelings and behaviors than the 'smoking part'. In addition, the non-smoking part will be supported by healthy values and empowering beliefs about the client's ability to quit. There should, at the same time, also be no inappropriate 'separation' between the installed part and the rest of the individual. In fact, the hypnotist should go to great lengths to integrate the new part into the client, and into the client's overall personality.

Reverse-DTI as Parts Installation

Installing a new part (for example, the non-smoking part), using deep trance and direct suggestion, is a great way of creating change, and also very interesting when considered from the frame of a Reverse-DTI. Think about the typical client who comes into the hypnotist's office. Many clients come with the idea that in hypnosis, they will 'go to sleep' and their feelings and behaviors will change automatically. They do not expect to have to 'work' for it. The classical approach of deep trance and direct suggestion can be very powerful, especially for clients who are very 'externally framed, meaning clients who look to others to validate their experiences and actions. In this case the hypnotist's suggestions result in the installation of a new non-smoking 'part', and the hypnotist 'possesses' the client at least long enough for the 'part' to be installed. This type of classical hypnosis thus becomes a type of Reverse-DTI, in an expanded sense of the term.

Just as in any DTI, the new part is, in reality, already a part of the client. It is a representation of aspects to which the client wants more conscious access. Whether using deep trance and direct suggestion, or DTI techniques, we are simply better defining the part, and then integrating that part into the client-as-a-whole-person.

The Double Reverse-DTI

As we have seen, within an appropriate cultural context, and with well-prescribed and ecologically sound expectations, the 'possession' of the individual by a god or muse (the Reverse-DTI) can have very beneficial results, just as a careful and ecological parts installation and integration can also produce positive change.

However, without an appropriate cultural context a Reverse-DTI installing of a new 'personality' could be far from ecological, especially from a Western perspective. This is one reason why we developed the Double Reverse-DTI, where the client first associates into the model, then the client-as-model associates into the client (rather than the model associating directly into the client). The process itself is very easy. We will lay out a full protocol at the end of the chapter, but the essence of using Double Reverse-DTI entails the following considerations:

- Establish the specific context in which the modeler would like to feel and act differently.

- After inducing trance, the modeler is introduced to the model and asks for permission to DTI.

- The modeler dissociates from herself, and moves into third position.

- The modeler now associates into the model and experiences acting as the model, taking on the model's beliefs, values and skills. As usual, the hypnotist only leads the modeler into experiencing values, beliefs and skills that are appropriate, ecological and complementary to the modeler, based on full ecology checks. The hypnotist also resolves any conflicts using the visual squash or Mind to resolve the conflict.

- Now, staying as the model, the modeler is going to associate back into himself or herself, without returning to third position in between. The modeler will step back into 'you', but this time as the model.

For example, suppose I (Jess) am the modeler, and I'm going to DTI with the superhero Wolverine. I've checked ecology at the conscious and unconscious level, and made sure my values are aligned with those of Wolverine. I have a specific context in which I want to experience change and use Wolverine's abilities. I have one or more representations of Wolverine (an Event Matrix), and I have in mind everything that I would like to get from being Wolverine.

I now dissociate from myself (Jess) and then associate into Wolverine. I have the experience of acting and feeling as Wolverine. Now staying as Wolverine I step back into me, Jess. I will not go to third position this time, but step as Wolverine back into Jess.

Next I will step into the context in which I want the change, but this time as Wolverine, in Jess's body. I will experience a blending of physical capabilities, resources, values and beliefs, Wolverine-as-Jess, as well as the changes in thoughts and behaviors that come with that. Jess-as-Wolverine has associated into me and now I will enter the context and feel and act as Wolverine acting through Jess. The lines between Wolverine and Jess become blended so that the resourceful states and behaviors can express themselves and be integrated, along with values and beliefs.

As we have said before, DTI has a tremendously generative component, which means we can do this process to build skills without necessarily 'addressing a problem.' Say I (Jess) would like more confidence public speaking; I'm not afraid of speaking in public, but I feel I could use a little more confidence.

In this case I would go to the context of public speaking, maybe sitting in a training room with a class in front of me. Next I'm going to DTI into Wolverine, and experience the feelings, states, and values that are going to be useful and that are in alignment with my own.

Now, as Wolverine I'm not going to go back to third position; I'm going to stay associated into Wolverine and as Wolverine I'm going to step right back into Jess. Now I'm going to experience teaching the class in this way, Jess-as-Wolverine becoming Jess.

To conclude the Double Reverse-DTI we are going to go through a number of future paces, allowing for multiple iterations of the resource process. We invite the modeler to go to a number of different times and places where the context and trigger are present, so that they can practice acting as the blending of themselves and the model. We may invite them to go to the 'next time and place' where they will need these skills and experience having them, then to go to another time and place. We do this a number of times as it gives the modeler's neurology a number of opportunities to practice in this new way.

Finally, complete integration takes place as I realize Wolverine was always a part of me, and always will be. After all, whether we are speaking about Jess or Wolverine, it is really all 'me' at the end of the day. I have now integrated that part of me that is represented by Wolverine.

One of the useful things to keep in mind in this form of DTI is that it takes away any physical advantages the model has. If I associate into Wolverine, and into the physicality of Wolverine, then I have the strength of Wolverine and the claws of Wolverine, and so on. I would have all the things that you could say are sources, or even 'crutches', for his sense of confidence. When I as Wolverine associate back into Jess, I no longer have that physical strength and the claws. Wolverine has to adapt to the physical qualities of being Jess, as well as to the cultural behaviors of being Jess.

In other DTI methods the client is stepping into the experience of the model. This means they take on the physical traits and responses of the model as well as all of the other beliefs, values, and so on. If I were to step into Wolverine and then go give a speech, I would unconsciously also be taking on the physicality of Wolverine for better or worse. But in the Double Reverse-DTI, Wolverine has to play by my physical rules, and I can become curious about how my states and behaviors would be interpreted by Wolverine, instead of me stepping into Wolverine and interpreting his states and behaviors.

This is all about where one places emphasis in the DTI frame.

To review the process: the modeler chooses the specific model and specific context. We next use perceptual positions to guide the modeler in dissociating from himself, and associating into the model. The modeler will now experience the specific context as the model. Then, instead of dissociating again, the subject as model associates back into himself or herself. She or he will now experience the same context as the model associated into the modeler, interacting with the world in ways that conform to the modeler's physicality and sensitivities. In this way, full integration takes place.

Double Reverse-DTI for Healing

This approach can be applied in many different types of healing, as well as in generative contexts. For example, when a patient is sick, he can go into trance and find a future version of himself who has healed and is living a healthy life. He can then associate into that self and then associate back into the current self as the future, healthy self. Just think of all of the information and learnings that future self is introducing to the present self. The unconscious mind knows how to heal, and it knows how to learn how to heal. This pattern allows for that deeper part of the patient to begin piecing together the best states and behaviors to help the current self heal more quickly. The indirect implication here is that the patient is healing and there will be a time in the near future when they are once again healthy.

Another approach is to do the Double Reverse-DTI using as the model someone who has recovered from the illness.

(Obviously any hypnosis for healing should only be done by a medical professional or by a qualified hypnotist with appropriate medical referral and subject to the legal regulations of the appropriate jurisdiction.)

'BIG' DTI

Doing DTI in this way also provides some fascinating opportunities for "self" DTIs. In another chapter we have talked about the process of DTI with the future you.

But you can also use the double Reverse-DTI with the younger you as the model. For some people, their younger self represents a far more resourceful version of themselves than their current self. Occasionally we get a client who wants to be their childhood self. This isn't because of external factors, such as being looked after, so much as it does the desire to reconnect with 'childlike' qualities such as curiosity, creativity, relaxation, and so on.

This type of client wishes they had access now to the same resources they had as a child. In truth we know that they absolutely do. The problem arises because such a client loses the connection with that state. They forget how to activate that neural pathway.

Like in the Tom Hanks movie 'Big', this type of DTI allows one to reconnect with those states by using the metaphor they have brought with them, their child self.

The steps of the BIG DTI are as follows:

- DTI with the younger self as the model, in the usual way.

- Once associated into his younger self, the modeler now reassociates into his current self (without dissociating from the younger self).

- The modeler-as-younger-self now gets to experience being his current age, but this time with the retention of his childlike wonder and curiosity.

- Integration takes place.

Obviously, you should not do this DTI process with anyone who had an emotionally difficult childhood unless you are doing this as a part of a larger therapeutic reimprinting, and you feel it is appropriate to reintegrate the child into the adult client.

Conclusion

The Double Reverse-DTI creates a profound integration experience for the client. It affords the client easier access to the capabilities they desire because it has been externalized in the hypnotic state before being internalized in a new way. Think of how confident a client will feel when the context and trigger for the old problem becomes a trigger for the generative skill of the model – and they know that they have that model inside them.

The steps of the double Reverse-DTI are very easy.

You will first complete all of the preliminary work including selecting the context and model, and the completion of a full unconscious ecology check. An Event Matrix can be created for the model, eliciting the model's values.

Next, in trance, you will see the model and ask for permission for the DTI, building unconscious rapport.

You will then dissociate from self into third position, followed by associating into the model. As model you can relive the model's Event Matrix, in order to build a complete and robust experience as the model.

You can now have the experience of being the model within the specific context in which you want the change to occur.

Most important, when it is time to associate back into self, unlike other DTI patterns, you-as-model are going to step back inside you. This means the you-as-model has to play by the rules of your own (modeler's) physicality and culturally appropriate behaviors. Once again, you experience the context in which you want the change, this time being self-as-model.

Finally, full integration takes place as you can realize the model is and always will be simply a part of you.

Chapter 24: Becoming Your Own Best Coach

One of the greatest learning experiences I (Shawn) have had as a coach is to attend John's Garage course. John's Garage is modeled on Milton Erickson's famous classes that took place in his converted garage (as does John's). It's a supervision course where one student plays the role of coach, another the role of client (using a real issue), and John 'coaches the coach.'

This experience took place in the early days of my coaching. When it was my turn to be the 'coach,' my 'client' brought forth a truly deep and heart-rending issue to work through. I was deeply touched that she trusted me enough to share this issue with me as coach, but I was, for a moment, panicked by the thought, "Can I help her through this? What if I don't know what to do?" Then I realized John was by my side, and I relaxed, knowing that if I got stuck John was there to help me help my client.

Before we begin this chapter, consider what it would be like if *you can be coached by the greatest hypnotist of all time, whenever you wanted or needed it*? How amazing would it be to know that Erickson, Elman, Tony Robbins – , or whoever comes to mind for you – is waiting patiently to coach you through anything you wanted? How easily would emotional turmoil fall away when you have the world's greatest coach by your side? I wonder what type of amazing future lies ahead of you when you have this coach guiding you along the way, showing you how to step fully into your true, authentic self.

In this chapter we will be exploring how you can use DTI to build resiliency into your neurology. If you are doing this for yourself you are developing a tremendously valuable skill set. If you are a hypnotist, teaching this resiliency to a client, you can feel confident knowing that you are teaching your clients how to succeed well beyond the scope of the session.

When a new client comes in to see a coach or hypnotist for the first time, it is common for them to ask, "What if this doesn't work?" Even if they don't express this question at some level they may be thinking it. Occasionally the hypnotist may wonder this as well. While this is not a resourceful thought loop for a hypnotist, the truth is that sometimes clients experience change in the short term, but that the old pattern reappears.

The good news is we can teach our clients skills so she is resilient. What would it be like if you were to experience a positive change, and also know going forward that whatever circumstances came your way, you had the skills and flexibility to think, feel, and act resourcefully? Resiliency training is one of the most valuable skills we can give to our clients or to ourselves.

The pattern we will be presenting in this chapter utilizes DTI in a new and powerful way. This pattern gives your clients the opportunity to truly become their own coach. You will be able to use this experience to reinforce the work you've done together, and to reinforce other positive changes your client's experience. We hold the belief in NLP, that you have all of the resources you need. This pattern allows the client to develop those resources naturally. It also gives them the opportunity to experience on a deep level just how resourceful they are when it comes to resolving any issue, future as well as current.

When a person is stuck in a problem state it becomes difficult for them to see the forest for the trees. While in the problem they may not feel particularly resourceful and may end up blocking their own ability to change. This is why in the meta-pattern (see *NLP Mastery: The Meta Pattern* by Sarah and Shawn Carson for a full discussion of this pattern, available at Amazon.com), we dissociate from the problem state before associating to the resource.

The pattern we describe in this chapter allows clients to dissociate naturally from their problems and immediately step into a position from which they have full access to all of their resources.

The pattern is as follows.

- In trance associate into a specific time and place where you are experiencing a problem.

- Invite into that space the model of your choosing. This can be anyone who could help you through the problematic experience; it does not need to be a formal coach, although of course it could be. If you could choose anyone to coach you into a better state, who would it be?

- As with any DTI ask for permission from the model, making the purpose of the DTI clear before proceeding.

- Next, as a consciousness, drift outside of yourself and into third position. You can see that you, down there, in that situation. And you can see the model by your side. In third position notice the model's physiology, noticing the model's breathing and posture. You will see your own physiology, the physiology of the 'you' down there, beginning to mirror your model.

- When you're ready, drift into the model. Take a few moments to orient yourself by continuing to be aware of your posture, your breathing, and what it's like to see through these eyes, and hear through these ears. Become aware of your emotions: what are you feeling when you are this person? Notice all of the things you're aware of as the model. What do you believe about yourself and the world when you are this person? What is important to you?

- As the model, observe that other self ('you') in this specific context. See with the eyes of your model the behavior and the emotions the real you is expressing. What can you-as-model notice about you-as-you that is valuable in the problematic situation? What new things can you discern?

- As the model, this totally resourceful person, you can help that 'you' over there to change her thoughts, feelings, and behavior. Perhaps you-as-model can remind you-as-you of all of the tools you have, perhaps leading you-as-you through a piece of change work. Please note when you're using this pattern with the client you can instruct the client-as-model on how to coach the client-as-client. Consider reminding the model of the effective techniques you use, and suggest the client-as-model use them on the client.

- As the model, notice how the situation has now changed. You are most interested in how that other has changed. Look for the change in physiology that lets you know that other self has changed in a beneficial way. You are waiting to see their physiology mirror your own as model.

- Once this shift has taken place, you could go to another time and place when the self experienced the same problem, and as the model begin the coaching process again. Repeat this as many times as necessary based on what feels right.

- Now it is time to become your own best future coach. There will be a time in the future when that self may need the best coach in the world. And you-as-model can be there waiting to guide you through that context. And of course there may be another specific time and place in the future when that self could use a friendly coach. And there you-as-model are, ready with the perfect approach to help them change. If there are any other times in the future when this will be useful you-as-model can practice now coaching that future self.

- When you are ready, return to that first time and place and dissociate from the model. Drifting back into yourself, back into first position, take a moment to feel how things are now different. And as you feel that thank your model for all of the wonderful coaching they've given you.

- As your coach already knows, there may be times in the future where you could really use some coaching. As yourself, go to one of those times in the future, now, and experience receiving that coaching. Your coach knows exactly how to make this different for you so that you are left feeling confident in your natural ability to bounce back and be feeling exactly the right states.

- Once you have finished the future pacing, return fully and completely to the here and now.

Future Pacing as Model and as Self

The future pace as both the model and self is an important aspect of this pattern because we are installing in the client a resiliency strategy. In fact, the client may find, after a few experiences of self-coaching, that their unconscious mind automatically brings out the resources they need in the specific context. We are conditioning resilient resourcefulness in the client's unconscious mind.

To summarize the process:

- As yourself, go to a specific context where the coaching is useful. And invite the model to join you

- Dissociate from self, to third position, and observe the model. Take on the model's posture and breathing.

- Associate into the model and become fully oriented to their physiology, emotions, awareness, and thoughts/beliefs.

- Observe that self (use client's name) in the context and notice how it looks from the model's point of view.

- As model, coach that self through that situation until you notice their physiology shift, and they enter a more resourceful state.

- Repeat for several other times and places.

- Future-pace coaching that self.

- Dissociate from the model and associate back into self, thanking the model for the work they have done.

- Go back to various contexts and feel how it has changed.

- Future pace the coaching experience as self (so that the client has the opportunity to experience the coaching from the perspective of self).

- Thank the model for the coaching and reorient to the here and now ending the trance.

Enjoy using this technique to install your own best coach in yourself. You know going forward that you have all the resources you need, and that these resources can express themselves in such wonderful ways such as being coached by your ideal model.

When using this pattern with clients you are creating an incredibly empowering experience for them. They can know going forward that any time they need a coach it is only a matter of going into trance and enjoying the highly transformative experience of working with their own best coach.

Chapter 25: Planting Strong Roots: Tree Of Life DTI

What is the Tree of Life

The Tree of Life is a complete model of human experience. It originates in the Jewish mystical tradition of Kabbalah. According to this tradition at the dawn of creation, the Big-Bang, God expanded into the known universe. The Divine flows down starting at the point of God's entry into the universe, down through the potential of creation, archetypes (material creation), the energy of creation, the rules of existence, the true unconscious, emotions, thoughts, map of the world, and physical reality. The mystics believe that just as God flows down into creation humans can also travel up the Tree to reach the source, i.e. return to God.

In terms of DTI this map of experience gives us the ability to fully associate into a model from the point of physical reality all the way up to the highest spiritual energy, and experience what is beyond self for both the model and modeler. This approach allows the modeler to fully connect with the model on a deep level. For those who have a deeper metaphysical view, *this approach gives a pathway to the collective unconscious and a universal experience beyond self and other.*

In our approach to the Tree of Life we are interested in its implications for coaching. While the mystical components are up to the individual, as a coaching paradigm the Tree of Life offers us a wonderful map of the client's experience.

Outline of the Tree of Life

The Tree of Life consists of ten points or nodes, called Sephirot, joined by 22 pathways. It should be noted that our version of the Tree will look reversed from the traditional Tree of Life because we like to consider the Tree from the point of view of the client (in effect we are seeing the client's Tree, while the traditional view is to look at your own Tree). As we go up the Tree we will be using a specific path known as the lightning path, which you will be able to track by consulting the illustration in Appendix 3.

Physical World - Malcut

At the foundation of the Tree of Life we have the physical world. This is the world of matter. This is the world of physics, where objects exist without judgment. This is the part of experience that is governed by natural processes such as chemical reactions, physiological activity, and so on. At this level there is a physical object, comprised of molecules, that has a specific shape, size, color, and weight. There is no labeling, such as 'chair', and no sense of meaning 'that is used for sitting'. It just is. In the context of coaching this is going to be the place in which the change needs to occur. If you take the (H)NLP approach this is the specific time and place, context and trigger, in which change happens.

Map of the World - Yesod

The next step up on the Tree, directly above the world, is the map an individual has of the world. One of the classic NLP presuppositions, that the map is not the territory, is absolutely correct from the Kabbalistic point of view. The map is a collection of ideas, meanings and filters that we place on the physical world. Contained within the map are all the points of the Tree above it, which come together to create the specific map an individual has about their experience of the physical world. This is the point where meanings are made, such as, "My boss is making that face, which means he's annoyed at me." This is the interpretation the brain makes of the sensory information that the eyes take in as light, color, and movement. The brain translates that into a visual impression, and as this happens a series of neural associations are triggered. In this case one of them is connected to a complex equivalence relationship in the person's mind, 'that face = annoyed at me'. A client who is in a problem state will mistake the map for the world itself. Of course, on the generative side a client can utilize their map to create a positive experience.

Thoughts - Hod

On our path up the Tree, we will next visit thoughts. We place this on the individual's left side (on your right, if you are looking at their Tree), placing it in the location where NLP eye accessing suggests verbal thoughts are located. Thoughts can include self-talk, sounds, and images an individual creates in his mind. In terms of neuroscience we can place working memory here (see *Keeping the Brain in Mind* by Shawn Carson and Melissa Tiers). In a therapeutic context in NLP we may do meaning reframes and sub-modality shifts, at the level of thoughts, as well as altering the messages the client is saying to themselves about the particular state or issue.

Emotions - Netzach

Parallel to thoughts, on the opposite side of the Tree, the person's right (corresponding to 'kinesthetic' eye accessing), is the point of emotions. By emotions we mean emotions as felt in the body, rather than thoughts about emotions. So, on the generative side, you can build very strong states through kinesthetic awareness, i.e., spinning emotions more quickly or slowly depending on the state, as well as building up a visual representation of the emotion such as linking it to a color and moving the color throughout the body.

True Unconscious - Tifferet

We now return to the center column of the Tree. The traditional Mystic view is that this is where the soul is expressed. We think of this point as being the true unconscious. By true unconscious we mean the wise and resourceful unconscious mind described by Milton Erickson. In terms of the Tree, it is also that part of you, the one experiencing all of the other points on the Tree. The other points on the Tree are aspects of the true unconscious's experience of life.

Rules - Gevurah

Passing through the true unconscious our next stop is on the opposite, left side of the Tree. This is the point of rules. In the traditional context these were rules of morality and religious laws. For our purposes we can think of them as the beliefs and modal operator rules ('I must, I should'). The language someone uses to create possibilities and impossibilities in their lives is important. These include words such as: should, should not, can, must, must not, have to. These words may arise from rules the client has set for himself, or from rules he believes society or nature has imposed on him.

As coaches it is our job to help a client switch the modals they use from necessity and impossibility, to possibility and positive necessity. For example, "can't" becomes, "can". Similarly, necessity changes the limiting, "I must not challenge myself," to the more empowering, "I must explore new opportunities." The rules may be consciously expressed by the client, or they may be just under the surface of the particular issue the client is expressing. As a change worker you will be familiar with the types of patterns associated with the rules that a client brings to the session.

Energy - Chesed

Directly across from rules, back on the right side, we have the point connected with energy. We consider it in terms of the energy that exists in the world, much like the Qi energy talked about in the martial arts, or someone's usual energy in terms of the dominant state they and others attribute to self. For example they could be a happy, supportive, or kind person. This can also be the flow of energy in an interaction, or the energy underlying a particular state. In HNLP we call this End State Energy, which is a high level value or level, typically represented by nominalization such as freedom, love, and so on. Helping a client to become aware of the relationship between themselves, their states and their internal energy can help them to step outside the normal boundaries they've set for themselves, therefore stepping outside of the presenting issue.

In the West we are not used to considering the flow of energy that is such a valuable part of the human experience. To direct the client's awareness to this aspect gives them a greater level of control over their state. After all, if you change the flow of energy you also change state. You can do this kinesthetically through traditional means such as energy exercise, perhaps something from tai chi or reiki. We can also do this by inviting the client to become aware of that energy and begin to manipulate it through their thoughts, becoming aware of which type of thoughts increase that type of energy, and which type of thoughts change the energy.

Archetypes - Binah

Next we find the point associated with archetypes. This point is located on the left side of the Tree above rules. At the moment of creation, archetypes are the forms that emerged. Archetypes are modeled forms, for example a deer has archetypical characteristics that make it recognizable as a deer, rather than, say, a rabbit.

On a wider level, archetypes include the universal models that each of us have in our lives. When you are being the type of person you enjoy being the most who are you? These archetypes include heroes, teachers, healers, and the list can go on. Your hypnosis clients will bring their own archetypes into the office.

From the perspective of DTI, the model serves as the archetypical experience which the client is seeking. Your clients are bringing with them in a very explicit way this part of the Tree.

The Void - Chochmah

The void is the next point on the Tree, once more on the right. This is the realm of infinite possibilities. This is the space from which material creation emerges. Anything can come out of this space. This is the connection point between the Divine and form or archetype.

If you are aware of the Attention Shifting Coaching paradigm of HNLP you will recognize this as being the space in which the client's mind is open to finding new possibilities.

The final point on the Tree is connected with the Divine. In Kabbalah this is the entry point of God into the universe. If we are to think of the logical levels this is the aspect of experience that is beyond identity. You can also think of it as being the truest experience of being unlimited by time and space. In our model of coaching this is an important aspect of the human experience and one that is often overlooked.

The majority of people on the planet Earth hold some sort of spiritual conviction and a sense of spiritual identity. In the course of change work connecting with that aspect of their experience can create a tremendous amount of leverage in effecting change. Think of it this way: if a client gets to the top of the Tree and identifies themselves as a child of God, how is it possible for them to maintain the problem they are experiencing? It becomes very difficult as they are appealing to a higher authority, which is there to protect them, love them, and help them reach their full potential. If a client considers himself as one with God, then how can he experience a problem in the same old way?

Even for a client who does not hold a particular spiritual conviction, this point in the Tree can be linked to their identity as part of the universe. They are the result of countless successful genetic generations. If their ancestors were not successful people, if they failed to gather, or they weren't very good at finding mates because they were wrapped up in emotional problems, the client wouldn't be sitting in your office right now! The fact that they are is a sign that they come from a long line of ancestral success, and we know that success breeds success. The client is also a part of the magnificence that is the known universe. Out of all the planets in the solar system there is life only on earth, and they are here part of that system. Their existence alone is a rare gem that beats statistical odds.

Using the Tree of Life in Coaching

When we use the Tree of Life as a coaching modality, whether it's therapeutic or generative, we can consider each point on the Tree as a space in which change can happen. For example, we can see the problem state as being an imbalance at one or more points on the Tree, and treat them individually, maybe doing a belief change here and a state change there. Alternatively, we can take the Tree as a whole, and build on creating a new Tree.

Something to consider as well, the Kabbalah tradition contends that, while each of us has a Tree that is the sum total of our experience, we do not have just one Tree. In fact there are Trees stacked on top of Trees, based on contexts, energy flows, and other variables. The possibilities are truly limitless.

Using Lower Branches of the Tree of Life

If you think of traditional coaching, NLP and similar modalities, the techniques are focused mainly on the bottom third of the Tree, working with the client's map of the world, thoughts, feelings, and the physical world itself.

Let's look, for example, at someone who has a phobia of a particular object. The object exists as a physical thing in the material world. It is composed of molecules that exist in a particular space at a specific time. For a client the phobic reaction most likely starts with seeing the object. Because they have had a number of reference experiences of feeling fear, their map of the world says that the object is dangerous and they will say, "I have a fear of…". They see the object and instantaneously the neural networks associated with fearful experiences of the object fire off, communicating danger. At this point the amygdala takes control, and the client once more feels fear. At this point the client may also be running commentary about the experience, saying unpleasant things and drawing unpleasant mental pictures.

A traditional piece of NLP change work may involve a 'V-K dissociation' in which the client uses his thoughts to change his feelings, thus changing his map of the world. This means that when he experiences the trigger, the physical object, in the future, his map is different. With his new map, whenever he sees the object, he thinks, "I'm no longer afraid of this," showing that his feelings and thoughts have changed as well.

While something like a V-K dissociation or a collapsing anchors approach will change the client's neurology so that the amygdala no longer overrides the frontal cortex, there is much more to the client than just a stimulus-response.

263

The client could, for example, have also been running commentary on the fact that he had a phobia. This could include rules about how he should not have this issue, "I can't believe I'm feeling this, why me?". It could also include ideas about his identity as someone who is afraid. In doing so, he is actually creating a problem that is 'meta' to the phobia. This has the potential of limiting the client in terms of the range of his responses as well as his sense of identity, thus undermining the stability of the change.

Using Higher Branches on the Tree of Life

Of course, more skilled practitioners will also integrate changes in beliefs, values, and other components of the client's logical levels. The Tree of Life gives us a systematic approach to doing this. This nuance will create a vast amount of leverage to lock change into place. You may be curious at this point as to how exactly we use the Tree of Life within the coaching context. When you understand it as a coaching modality it makes the DTI process very simple, so let's take a few moments here to introduce you to the principles of Tree of Life coaching.

We can use the Tree of Life to change any aspect of the client's experience as a whole person. For example, we can address the rules the client has set for herself and her experience of the emotional energy connected with a particular state. We can then chunk up to archetypes that she can use to tap into the Void of infinite possibilities, we can generate a tremendous amount of leverage that is greater than the issue the client presents. This has the benefit of both overwriting any problems that may be connected with the particular issue as well as creating a strong connection with experience that is beyond the lower portion of the Tree. In traditional NLP terms you can think of this as being an easy to use roadmap to logical levels.

Tree of Life and DTI

Now that the model is laid out, we can explore some ways in which you can use this approach as a means of deep trance identification.

Within the Tree of Life itself we already have the idea of archetypes. This system lends itself to DTI and makes it easy to create a holistic experience for the modeler both in therapeutic as well as generative contexts. The pattern that we will be presenting here walks you, as hypnotist, through associating the modeler into all ten aspects of the Tree, as well as showing you how to use the Tree of Life as a therapeutic DTI and a generative DTI.

For this pattern we will be creating a blended internal space in which the modeler and the model will be sharing a blended Tree. The modeler will experience the model's Tree and begin to apply it to the specific context in which the modeler wants to be more like the model. This will begin to cause a shift in the modeler's Tree within that specific experience.

To do a Tree of life DTI you may choose to use the various DTI processes laid out in previous chapters. This pattern also will work quite well as an instant DTI. Before doing the overt trance version, we will introduce one extra step that will actually allow you to install a DTI covertly while also planting unconscious seeds for the DTI experience.

NLP The New Behavior Generator (NBG)

Before presenting this technique we would like to introduce you to the classic NLP modeling technique, the New Behavior Generator. This is a very easy pattern that can be used to trigger a rapid DTI experience. One premise of this technique is that you can use any gesture or other physiological cue as a starting point for a modeling experience. After all, we know that the quickest way to change the state is to change the physiology. The NBG allows you to use this physiological shift to begin the process of association. It is also easy to do and is a very rapid process.

Begin by imagining the model in front of you. Notice her or his physiology, facial expression, posture, and gestures. When you're ready, physically step into the shoes of that imagined model. Take on his physiology, posture, facial expression, breathing, and gestures. Feel what it is like to truly be in his shoes.

Become aware of what it is like to see the world through the model's eyes. Notice your state and how it has changed. Enjoy the experience of being the model.

When you're ready, step back out of the model and back into you (first position) once again. As you do so, leave behind anything that isn't useful to you. Importantly, be sure to take with you any new learnings and capabilities that complement who you are as a person.

This, then, is the NLP New Behavior Generator.

Tree of Life DTI

The first step in the process of exploring the model's Tree of Life, is to consider a very specific context. This is the time and place where the modeler would like to have the capabilities of the model, represented by their Tree. Some modelers, just like some coaching clients, may say they want the model's capabilities 'all the time'. But this is not particularly ecological for the individual. After all, they still have the same relationships, job, hobbies, and lifestyle of the modeler, so to adopt completely the model's Tree could be disruptive.

It is easier and more ecological for the modeler to access resources by putting this type of DTI within the framework of a particular context and trigger. This is about integrating Trees in a way that allows the modeler to grow as a person, at a speed that is appropriate for him or her.

Next, we use the New Behavior Generator to guide the modeler in associating into the model. The NBG is at the base of the Tree, the real world. At this point we have not done a formal induction however you will be correct in noticing trance signals in the modeler. We are using the NBG as a means of eliciting the model's Tree (at least as seen by the modeler).

Once the modeler has adopted some gesture or physiology of the model, we can begin to ask questions that will provide verbal anchors for the formal DTI experience.

In this state we can go up the Tree using the Lightning Path. We begin by asking about the model's map of the world. What is it that they know to be true about their reality? What 'causes' lead to what effects? And what is the meaning of sensory information that they see and hear?

As the modeler moves up the Tree, she can become aware of the model's thoughts. What is the model saying to herself, and what type of pictures and movies is she making in her mind?

Across from thoughts are emotions. What emotions is the model experiencing?

Moving on to the point of "rules," ask the model what she believes about herself and the world around her. Ask her what she must do and avoid doing. Ask what is possible and what is impossible. Once again we are eliciting the model's modals.

Energy allows us to tap into the energetic values (End State Energy) of the model, into freedom, peace and love. What is most important to the model about this experience?

At the level of archetypes, the modeler can explore such archetypical energies as the identity level characteristics such as 'healer', 'warrior,' and so on.

We will leave the void and the God point for later. In the next portion of the pattern the modeler will have an overt experience that will allow her to tap into a deeper level of learning that is beyond both modeler and model.

Example – Steve Jobs's Tree of Life

A modeler might want to model Steve Jobs' creativity in the workplace. The modeler will begin by seeing Steve Jobs expressing that creativity. The modeler will notice something specific about Job's physiology that lets him know he is embodying the state, capabilities, beliefs, and identity of Steve Jobs when he is being creative. For example, the modeler may notice the intensity in Job's eyes and the speed of his breathing. Whatever the modeler notices about Jobs's physiology will work, because it serves as a signpost that lets the modeler know he is accessing the correct state.

We now move up to the level of the map of the world. At this stage we invite the modeler to consider what it means for Jobs to be acting in this creative way. What is the significance of the environment and how does it relate to Jobs and his creative process? What does it mean for Jobs to be working in this environment? What causes Jobs's creativity?

At this point it is useful for you to shift pronouns when addressing the modeler so that the modeler is forced to step fully into the model. For example, you might ask, "As Steve Jobs, what has to be happening around **you** to allow you to be creative?" Using the pronoun 'you' rather than 'he' puts the modeler into the 'skin' of Jobs.

You also have the option of asking the modeler specific questions and waiting for verbal responses. You could ask the modeler, "What has to be true for something to occur," or you could simply draw his attention to some aspect of the experience by saying something like, "Notice what is true here."

Next step up on the model's Tree to the point of thoughts. This level is all about the internal representations of the model's experiences. Studies have shown that people who are successful in a given field have particular sets of internal representations with which they engage. These representations are tied to success. For example, world-class athletes not only picture themselves being victorious but, more importantly, mentally rehearse their sport. A study of three groups of basketball players was recently published. The first group actually practiced making basketball shots every day, the second group did the same thing however they only practiced shooting in their mind, and the third group did neither. It was discovered that the first group increased in skill level significantly. Somewhat surprisingly, however, the study also showed an increase in skill levels in the second group of a comparable magnitude. This shows the power of internal representation.

At this stage we ask the modeler to experience the pictures, sounds, and words that the model experiences internally. We can ask him questions like, "What are you saying to yourself? What pictures do you see in your mind's eye?" In the case of the Steve Jobs example, it may be that he is seeing pictures of a technology that does not yet exist. If he has internal dialogue the modeler may experience it as, "This will be awesome!"

268

Parallel to thoughts, we have the emotions. When you are the model, how are you feeling, what are the emotions you-as-model most readily accesses to accomplish everything that you do? We can then intensify that emotion by further associating the modeler into them and utilizing the sub modalities of the emotion. For example, if we were to ask the modeler, "When you are Steve Jobs, what are you feeling?" They may answer with something like, "I am certain, focused, and I can feel that things are going to go the way I had imagined them." The coach can help build the states of certainty and focus by asking questions like, "When you are feeling this way, where do you feel that…in your body? If you are to make that feeling of certainty move even more pronounced, what would it feel like?"

Keep in mind that states drive behaviors. Therefore you want to spend some time building up a strong positive state that builds for the rest of the session, as well as anchoring that state, so that state can be available going forward within the modeler's specific context.

Moving further up we pass through the true unconscious, and reach the level associated with rules. This part of the Tree is all about the rules by which the model lives. These will most likely be different from the rules of the modeler. If both the model and the modeler had the same unconscious rule sets, then their states thoughts and maps of the world would be similar.

At this point we are asking about the model's values and beliefs, and we are listening for what the models say they use. It is useful for the modeler to associate into the model's beliefs about themselves and the world around them For example in the case of Steve jobs, the modeler will experience what it's like to truly believe that anything is possible. Steve Jobs had this amazing ability to distort reality around him just enough to make the things that other people believed impossible, possible.

At this point you may have already done a values elicitation (and possibly a values integration) as a part of the Event Matrix, so this part will be easy for the modeler to experience. Take some time to allow the modeler space in order to experience the values of the model; things that are most important to the model. In our example of Steve Jobs, the modeler may experience the power of the importance of aesthetics, or the importance of making ideas realities.

It is at this point in the Tree where we will shift any modals of impossibility to those of possibility. As Steve Jobs said, "Don't tell me what can't be done." He did not live by a set of limitations. In fact the only limitations he ever experienced were those enforced by others, and even then it was a very rare occasion.

Now it is time to consider the energy of the model as well as the environment in which the model acts. This is connected first with the energy behind states. If you think about what it's like to be nervous, beyond the feeling itself, you can be aware of the energy. This is often either in a spinning motion, or an up and out motion. This is in comparison to calmness or relaxation, which tends to be a slower energy that moves downward. But the idea of energy is much more than just emotions, it includes the energy existing in creation.

When Steve Jobs was being innovative, creating, knowing reality will bend to meet his vision, what was the experience of energy in the body? Also, how does the energy around Steve Jobs flow and interact with his actions and thoughts. To some readers this may seem at first a bit unusual, however. Eliciting the energy is a powerful way of experiencing the model, because it encourages the modeler's experience to stretch beyond what the conscious mind thinks is possible, and is used to conceptualize the world. This begins to take the modeler out of his conscious frame of reference and into a wonderful world of unconscious experience.

Next we guide the modeler to the level of archetypes. This is one of the most useful points in the Tree because this is the point of true accessibility for the modeler. By this we mean that the modeler will be chunking up beyond the individual identity of the model, to the type of person the model represents. Meaning, in the future the archetype can serve as the reference point for all of the positive qualities found in the model. Instead of thinking about Steve Jobs, in the future the modeler can look at what he represents. The archetype gives us a way of tapping into the aspects of Steve Jobs that is most useful.

To enter the point of archetypes, we can invite the modeler to consider, "When you are being Steve Jobs, who is it that you are truly being?" This is chunking up to the level of identity. We are inviting the modeler to become aware of the form that is Steve Jobs, not just the individual. Steve Jobs could be the dreamer, the builder, a creator, etc. At this level the modeler has opened up a new realm of possibilities. For himself he has created a marker point in his own Tree. We will come back to this on the way back down the Tree.

During this process of ascending the Tree, the modeler will provide the guide with information for each point. For example, when asked about rules, the modeler, speaking as Jobs, may state that she must get her ideas out into the world. She may believe that reality is flexible and she can change it. And form and functionality are important when creating new ideas, products, or services. For each of the points she, or he, will give you the specific words to use when you move onto the next part.

Associating into the model's Tree

After you have discovered the model's Tree of Life modeler you may use whichever DTI process you prefer to induce trance.

Again we will invite the modeler to notice something specific within the model's physiology that will let the modeler know she is expressing the specific capability the modeler desires. When this happens we will use a basic perceptual positioning shift so that we create a clear delineation between the modeler as her or she, and the model. By leading, the modeler will drift into third position before stepping into second position, taking on the model's physiology.

As the guide, you are looking to see a shift in the modeler's physiology that lets you know he has associated with model. You are now ready to build the Tree.

Guide the modeler up the model's Tree by using the information you gathered during the previous exercise. For example, with Steve Jobs we may guide the modeler through a map of the world in which binary options are the only choice for Steve Jobs. There was no middle ground; things were either amazing and life-changing, or complete shit. This map of the world kept Jobs from being distracted by too many ideas.

Lead the modeler to experience each part of the Tree, up to the level of archetypes. We are calibrating the modeler's states as he continues up the Tree. The further up the Tree he goes, the more fully associated he should be at the end state of the model.

Once you move past the level of archetypes, you should begin to integrate model and modeler, using the Quantum fourth position. This perceptual position contains a tremendous amount of leverage beyond the level of identity. At this point the modeler's consciousness is split, part of him will be in the model while the other part will remain him, the modeler. By continuing the journey up the Tree, the modeler's consciousness is invited to move beyond concepts of model and modeler as separate entities, and even the archetypical identity. They are going to the Void and beyond, to the God point of the Tree. From the God point, they can have a true perspective on what it means to be a person acting in an unlimited system in which any mental, emotional, and spiritual resource is available to them. This is the territory of mystical experiences. The modeler gains a deeper understanding in the connection between themselves and the model, and this allows them to begin the process of carrying the model's capabilities back into the modeler's reality in a way that is ecological for the modeler.

As hypnotist you can now guide the modeler back down the Tree using the Lightening Path. However, it is not necessary. You can simply remind the modeler about expressing the desired capability in the specific context represented by her own world, jumping straight back to the lowest part of the Tree of Life. An example of this could be, "And you can find yourself in the office feeling the flow of thoughts as you generate new ideas and know that you must excel"

It is now time to dissociate from the model into third position. He or she can leave behind anything that is not useful. Now, taking only useful, newly-learned skills and abilities step back into first position.

From here you may want to do some future pacing, into a number of different contexts, where you can practice using the new skills.

The Tree of Life DTI is a comprehensive and powerful way of associating fully into a chosen model. As we mentioned at the beginning of this chapter, this particular approach is most powerful when incorporated into a complete DTI project, including an Events Matrix, values elicitation, Quantum Perceptual Positions, and Mind Meld Integration as necessary.

Enjoy exploring the ways in which the Tree of Life can help to construct an empowered sense of self and a new approach to the world around you. Your Tree and your model's Tree are always changing and growing. You have Trees within Trees, within Trees, so you really are so much more than you can possibly imagine. Every time you make a change at one point on your Tree, all of your Trees grow in new and wonderful ways.

Chapter 26: Metaphor Magic - Symbolic Modeling DTI

What is Symbolic Modeling?

Symbolic modeling is a powerful coaching modality that utilizes the client's personal metaphors to create lasting change. It was developed by James Lawley and Penny Tomkins based on the work of David Grove.

At its heart, Symbolic modeling keeps the coach's judgments out of the client's metaphorical map of experience, using a series of so-called 'clean' questions. During a coaching session using Symbolic modeling, the coach uses only these clean questions so as to provide the greatest amount of space for the client to create change.

The process may look like this:

> Coach: What do you want to work through today?
>
> Client: I have so much stress it feels like a vice.
>
> Coach: And when it feels like a vice, where is vice?
>
> Client: It feels like it's right here (motions to chest).
>
> Coach: Is that inside or outside?

Client: Inside.

Coach: And when vice that is inside, what type of vice is that?

Client: It's tight.

Coach: And when vice is inside, and tight, is there anything else about that?

Client: No.

Coach: And what needs to happen to vice?

Client: It needs to fall away.

Coach: And can that happen?

Client: No.

Coach: What needs to happen for vice to fall away?

Client: The screws need to come loose.

Coach: What needs to happen for screws to come loose?

Client: I need to relax.

Coach: And when you relax, where is relax?

Client: It is all over.

Coach: And when relax that is all over, what kind of relax is that?

Client: It is peaceful.

Coach: And when you have relaxed that is all over and it is peaceful, what happens to vice?.

Client: It is gone.

This is a brief example of a classic Symbolic Modeling coaching session. This type of coaching can be incredibly powerful, although it can be a somewhat lengthy process. As you can see from the above segment, the coach's only job is to walk the client through his own metaphoric experience by asking open questions. Later in this chapter we will learn how to use this same approach as the means of Deep Trance Identification. This type of language is a profound method of building states and internal landscapes.

Metaphors

Metaphors are an important part of life. We learn through metaphors and communicate through metaphors. A large part of the human experience is connected to metaphors. This is more than evident when a new client comes into the office. He will talk about problems using phrases like: "I'm stuck," or, "I have a barrier in my way."

Clients will also use metaphors in their gestures. Next time you are speaking with someone about a problem, or a resourceful state, pay attention to the gestures he uses for a problem, verses his gestures for the resource. You will notice some very interesting things. Although he may not describe the precise metaphor his unconscious mind is using, he will show it to you in gestures.

Even problems are metaphors. Think about nominalizations, ideas that are mistakenly made into nouns, as if we could push a wheelbarrow of anxiety or even happiness around the office. Words like anxiety are types of metaphor.

Clients will create stories around those metaphors. For example, I (Jess) had a client recently gesture, as if he was holding a box, each time he described his problem. Each and every time he would speak about the problem he made the same exact gesture in the same space. It was as if he was physically holding on to the existence of the problem.

One of the ways a client keeps a problem in place is through the creation of his 'story'. By this we mean the client finds it important to tell his story around the problem, and the causes of the problem. A client affected by a trauma may be using the story of his survival as a means of holding a specific issue in place For example, a client who had been in a car accident may now feel tremendous anxiety over driving. He tells his story of survival over and over again, refusing to give up the feelings associated with it, as if he fears he will lose the story. Each time he tells the story, he is strengthening the neural networks associated with anxiety. As you can see, the use of metaphors in a story is vital to experiencing problems. Transforming these metaphors is vital to finding event solutions. to them.

If clients can use these metaphors to hold problems in place, we can use new metaphors to begin dissociating them from the issue, and transforming the problem. In fact, you can think of deep trance identification as being the construction of a new solution oriented metaphor that the client can experience from the inside out. For example, in the chapter on superheroes we explored how those particular metaphors can be used, knowing any model the client chooses can become a resourceful metaphor for him.

Clean Questions

In the traditional approach to Symbolic modeling, these metaphors are brought out through a series of questions. These questions allow for the maximum amount of space so the client can explore the issue in a metaphoric environment or context. Symbolic modeling itself creates a dissociation, wherein the client is able to interact with different pieces of the issue in an imaginative landscape, where he can interact with his metaphors, and his various metaphors can interact with each other.

In a clean session a coach will use the following 'clean' questions (as well as other, less common questions):

And when X, that is X like… what?

And when X, what kind of X is that?
And when X, where is X?
Is there anything else about X?
What happens next?
What happens just before?
What is the relationship between X and Y?
What do you want to have happen?
What needs to happen?
Can that happen?

How Symbolic Modeling Works

The opening question, "That's...like what?" invites the unconscious mind to begin to construct a metaphor that dissociates the client from the problem. Saying one thing is 'like' another invites a metaphor to be created. It is an invitation to the unconscious mind to come out and play.

During this type of coaching session the coach elicits the metaphors for the problem, as well as the metaphors for the resource, solution or outcome, and then begins to piece them together.

Linking problem and resource in Symbolic Modeling is done by asking about relationships, about what needs to happen, and whether that necessary metaphoric event can indeed happen. These questions connect the problem state with the solution state through symbolic steps and processes; so that change can happen easily. Once the problem and resource, or solution, is linked within the metaphor, the unconscious mind has a roadmap for change.

Symbolic Modeling and Therapeutic DTI

We can use Symbolic Modeling as a means of Deep Trance Identification in a way that creates a uniquely therapeutic experience for the modeler. If you're using DTI for therapeutic change this allows a unique type of dissociation.

Having chosen the model as the resource needed for changing the problem, the problem and model are already linked within the modeler's unconscious. Then all that is required is to build the metaphor linking the two. Through the use of the main questions listed above, the modeler will use his model as the metaphoric representation to counter the problem. In other words they can associate into the resource (the model) before even interacting with the metaphor for the problem, within the metaphoric landscape.

Using clean questions, the hypnotist can help the client build a highly detailed sensory environment in which the client becomes responsible for the metaphoric change, which then maps across onto real life.

In a traditional Symbolic Modeling session the client's unconscious mind may create metaphors that have subtle resources attached to them. For example, a client could describe the resource as being like a blue cloud. A blue cloud could mean many things to the client. In terms of therapeutic value, clouds are soft, amorphous, can fly high above, and can bring life through the rain that falls from them. Combining DTI with Symbolic modeling allows for a much more obvious yet unconsciously powerful metaphor. The client's model will have resources linked specifically to him. What's more, the fact that the client has chosen this model means that at some level the unconscious mind has identified skill sets useful in achieving this change.

Symbolic Modeling and Generative DTI

If we are doing a more generative DTI, clean questions offer the widest range of possibilities to the subject, in terms of experience, because the hypnotist is not leading. The modeler's unconscious mind is encouraged to fully engage with the process, by creating all of the details of the sensory experience. The unconscious mind designs everything from the landscape, to the sounds, to the emotions, the feelings, the values, and everything else the modeler experiences as the model. This also increases the enjoyment of the modeling process because the modeler can fully associate into the model and simply relish the experience!

The Symbolic Modeling approach uses the modeler's unconscious mind for the greatest amount of flexibility in terms of experience. As hypnotist, you will guide the subject with a particular set of questions, however your primary role is to lead him to engage more fully with the metaphoric environment he is constructing.

This approach may be done as part of an in-depth modeling project, utilizing the protocol highlighted in this book. In this case, the Symbolic modeling portion is carried out when the modeler is inside each of the events of the Event Matrix.

It can also be used as part of a rapid DTI by jumping right into a Symbolic Modeling exercise. In the next section we'll present you with a transcript of a DTI with Spiderman, utilizing the Symbolic modeling approach. There is no formal trance induction needed. Symbolic Modeling tends to create deep trances automatically, because it requires the modeler to associate deeply into the experience in order to answer the questions.

The example below is an excerpt from a DTI session in which the modeler is using DTI as a means of therapeutic change. His desired outcome is to feel more resourceful in speaking to an audience. The modeler—being adept at deep trance—decided to keep the content private, trusting the unconscious mind would create the desired change.

> Coach: So who are we modeling?
>
> Modeler: Spiderman.
>
> Coach: Spiderman. And when you are Spiderman what kind of man is Spiderman?
>
> Modeler: Flexible.
>
> Coach: He's flexible. And when you are Spiderman what kind of man are you?
>
> Modeler: Flexible.
>
> Coach: Flexible. And when you're flexible what kind of flexible is that?

Modeler: It is a type of flexibility that gives greater freedom.

Coach: And where is flexibility, when it gives greater freedom?

Modeler: It is inside.

Coach: It's inside, and whereabouts inside is flexibility that gives greater freedom?

Modeler: It's both physical and mental.

Coach: And when it's physical and mental, where is physical flexibility?

Modeler: All over.

Coach: All over. And when there's flexibility inside and it's mental, where is mental flexibility?

Modeler: It is like space in my mind

Coach: It's like space in your mind. And when there's space in your mind whereabouts is space in your mind?

Modeler: In the center.

Coach: In the center. So there's physical flexibility, which is all over inside, and there's mental flexibility which is a space in your mind in the center. And when there's Spiderman and flexibility is there anything else about Spiderman?

Modeler: Courage

Coach: Courage. So there's Spiderman and physical flexibility that's inside everywhere, and mental flexibility at the space in the center of your mind. And there's courage, and when there's courage what kind of courage is that?

Modeler: It is the kind that...Trusts.... that when Spiderman jumps off the building he is going to have a web to swing from.

Coach: Its courage that trusts...That when Spidey jumps off the building, he has a web to swing from. And when it's courage that trusts, where is courage that trusts?

Modeler: It is inside

Coach: Courage is inside and when it's inside whereabouts inside?

Modeler: It is in the head and the heart.

Coach: And when it is in the head and the heart, what is the relationship between courage that's in the head, and flexibility that's in the head?

Modeler: If I have one, I have the other.

Coach: If you have one then you have the other. So if you have flexibility that is the space in the center, then you have the courage to trust, and when you have the courage to trust you have the flexibility that's the space in the center.

When you have the courage to trust, that's right (modeler closes eyes and dropped deeper into trance) in the heart. whereabouts in the heart?

Modeler: It's in the center.

Coach: It's in the center and when it's in the heart and it's in the center, is there a size or shape of courage in the heart?

Modeler: It's like a seed.

Coach: A seed. Is there a color of the seed?

Modeler: Gold

Coach: It's like a seed in your heart in the center and it's gold...

For brevity we have excluded the rest of the transcript as it continues for some time. Symbolic Modeling, as a therapeutic strategy, may take a full session or even multiple sessions. Although not as rapid as some other approaches, it can create a tremendously powerful, life-changing experience for the client. The rest of this particular session resulted in the symbol for the problem; being completely absent from the metaphoric landscape where the client builds a tremendous resource state.

In a traditional approach to Symbolic modeling, the coach may wait for the client to unconsciously provide the metaphor for the problem or desired state. Or we may begin the process by asking the question: "And (state) is like...what?" The same holds true for its use in DTI. The client may give you the model as a metaphor. For example, they could say something like, "I want to be confident like James Bond." A statement like this is an excellent spring-board into an instant DTI. This is also a wonderful strategy as part of a long-term modeling project. If the client has the model in Mind, as in the example above, then you can begin immediately with the clean questions listed above.

The thing to keep in mind here is that the questions lead the client's unconscious mind to build the landscape. We are creating a neural network from the resource back to the issue.

As you will notice in the transcript above, the hypnotist continuously repeats back to the client the chain of symbols the client provides. This may sound odd, but it helps tremendously to stabilize the experience and keep it active in the resourceful neural network. In fact the number of repetitions actually used has been edited down for brevity. As you go through the process of DTI, remember to always repeat the client's symbolic word-chain before each new question. As you do this the client will associate more fully into the experience. It also makes it easier for you as the hypnotist to remember and track where the client is in the process.

Unlike most of the other DTI processes, Symbolic modeling DTI does not contain a step-by-step process. Instead it relies on your curiosity and intuition as a coach. Through the process you can continuously loop through the various questions to build the metaphoric landscape and help the modeler create new neural networks.

If you're using this as a therapeutic tool you'll begin with the resource and build the chain back to the problem state. If you're using this as a generative process, you can build the experience and then use the same questions to make links to specific contexts in which the modeler wants to be more like the model.

Conclusion

When we use Symbolic modeling in coaching sessions, whether it's for DTI or other purposes, we may not always go through the entire process. The clean questions themselves are useful tools in helping a client dissociate from problem states, and associate into resource states. Feel free to use these questions in any way if they can help the modeler associate more fully into the model. For some sessions this may mean that the entire session consists of this approach. Or it may be that at some time, while working with the modeler, these questions and the metaphoric approach became a valuable tool to quickly and easily anchor a state or experience.

Chapter 27: Fly A Mile In Another Person's Cape: Superhero DTI

The Superhero DTI

The traditional approach to DTI works with a model who is a real person. The modeler chooses someone who is either alive now, or who lived in the past, to serve as the metaphoric means through which the modeler can gain skills and capabilities.

There is another form of DTI we have all experienced, consciously or unconsciously. Perhaps you've experienced watching a movie and feeling the same emotions as the character. Because of your Mirror Neurons, you are automatically identifying with that character. This type of experience has tremendous value because it allows us to experience a wide range of emotions in a safe environment.

We can take this idea and begin to use it strategically to create and transform experiences for our clients, and ourselves, by taking on the role of a fictional character. The type of model we are going to explore using this approach is the superhero. Superheroes in our culture are tremendously resourceful beings They represent the physical traits people dream of having; such as the ability to fly, super-strength, invincibility, the ability to run faster than anything else on the planet, and so on. They also represent strong emotional traits such as independence, a deep desire to do good, and the ability to overcome hardships

Superheroes are the characters of a modern mythology where each of us becomes a participant.

Superhero DTI as a Regression

So why consider superheroes for DTI? Well, aside from it being a very enjoyable experience, there are profoundly therapeutic implications. Firstly we can consider the superhero as a trigger for a spontaneous regression. Most of us have grown up with superheroes. For those who are fans, their love of a particular hero begins at some point in childhood. If you go to any superhero movie you can see a theater transformed from a mix of adults and children, to all children aged from 7 to 70, laughing with excitement, responding to the action on screen, and applauding the hero for his or her victory at the end.

In the world of hypnosis we know that working with children can be very easy, because children naturally interact at a more unconscious level. They are more open to daydreaming, pretending, and learning new things. These are all vastly resourceful traits when it comes to doing generative or therapeutic change work. Doing a superhero DTI implies an indirect suggestion to go back to childhood. The modeler can experience significant changes when she returns to adulthood. Within trance logic, she will have had a lifetime of practicing the particular skill sets she acquires.

This is why Milton Erickson often used the "Early Learning Set" in which he spoke to his clients about the time when they learned to read and write. Going back to this point activates childhood learning strategies, which are highly effective in integrating new information and behaviors. To put it simply, the activation of the neural networks built during childhood can be tremendously useful to the adult now.

Bending the Laws of Reality

The second reason this is a powerful modality for change is that it creates a parallel reality. Parallel realities are experiences in the hypnotic state that mirror, in some metaphorical sense, the particular issue the client is working through. Consciously this reality appears to have no connection with the particular issue, but unconsciously there are connections being made, and hence learnings are occurring. As a result, what happens in the parallel reality also happens in the reality of the issue. This is what occurs when we use hypnotic metaphors. We create a safe space in which the client can try on new ways of being, as her unconscious mind applies these same skills to a context that acts as a metaphor; for the context in which she actually wants to charge.

The superhero reality is an incredibly compelling one for many people. At one level this is related to the regression that is created. On another level this speaks to the dreams, values, and deeply held desires of the client. The superhero reality is a space in which magic can occur. The normal rules of physics no longer apply, and this idea alone is a very powerful metaphor. You see when a client comes for a session, he often has a very defined reality with its own set of rules. The rules have been created by the client, but as far as the client is concerned are as concrete as the laws of physics, as certain as gravity. Those rules hold problems in place in a therapeutic context, and limit a client within the generative frame. Their reality is fixed.

The law of requisite variety states that the most flexible part in any system will hold the greatest amount of influence. The reality of the superhero is one of the most flexible realities one can construct. This is a landscape in which ordinary people can be transformed into incredible heroes. This is a world where the line between physical limitation and extraordinary gifts is completely blurred. This is a place where rules become flexible and even the laws of nature can be transcended. The superhero reality is a space of unlimited possibilities.

To invite the modeler into this place is to have him step outside of his ordinary boundaries and limitations. The superhero DTI not only constructs a parallel reality, but creates one that is more flexible. It holds more possibilities than anything in the modeler's current framework of the world. This superhero landscape indirectly moves the modeler into the role of flexibility. When he is in this state, his neurology is open to change and growth.

Superheroes as Archetypes

The third reason this form of DTI is so powerful is that it utilizes archetypes. This is useful because archetypes are powerful unconscious symbols of the skills, capabilities, beliefs and values we aspire to. This means the archetype has a tremendous amount of leverage in creating change. The archetype is a source of tremendous influence for the client. To step into the shoes of an archetype is to take on that emotional strength and become a symbol for self and others.

As the archetype of the superhero, the modeler can interact in the metaphoric environment in ways that he may not believe is possible in the outside world. He has access to the physical traits and personal qualities of that archetype, thus creating a number of new reference experiences in that parallel reality.

Fun, fun, fun!

Finally we recommend the superhero DTI for the first reason cited. It's just plain fun! It adds a new charm to therapeutic and generative change. It engages the modeler's creativity and imagination as being; either unconscious of the past, or as an experience he never suspected he would experience in the coaching setting.

Remember, novelty causes the release of dopamine in the brain. The release of dopamine leads to learning and new memory encoding. The more fun you can have in a session, the easier it is for the client to learn and grow. So have fun with this and deeply enjoy the experience of becoming your favorite superhero; whether you're experiencing this as the modeler or as the coach. Either way you will experience it on a deep, unconscious level.

The Mechanics of the Superhero DTI

The superhero DTI is very easy to do and by now the process will sound familiar.

Once the desired change and context for it is identified, as with any DTI, you will select the superhero model and review aspects of the character's life to create an Event Matrix, including details about his specific beliefs, values and abilities of the superhero. If you are doing a full DTI you will want to spend some time constructing the Event Matrix.

Of course, this type of DTI can also be done spontaneously, focusing on one scene involving the super hero, or by allowing the unconscious mind to construct the scenario, should this be more appropriate for you and the modeler. If you are doing a more spontaneous DTI, and haven't spent time developing the Event Matrix, you can begin by setting the context, or reason for the DTI. You may however, still want to do a values elicitation for the modeler, as well as the hero, to allow for better integration.

Once the context has been set and the preliminary work done, induce trance in any way that is appropriate for you and the client. Once trance is induced you can jump right into this DTI. As usual the perceptual positions method may be easiest for this process. However, you can *rest assured knowing you have the ability to be flexible* with how you lead your client to associate into the model. In the example below we will use a perceptual positions DTI, although you could also use other strategies, including the Tree of Life and Symbolic modeling approaches (as with the Spiderman DTI above).

Once the modeler has associated into the superhero, it's time to actually begin the process of change. At this point we begin to construct the parallel reality for the modeler. Because he will have discussed his generative goals or therapeutic change before doing this DTI—that part of his neurology will already be activated to some extent.

At this point we can invite the modeler to play with the reality of the superhero. We may want to use a specific setting in which the superhero is using his skills and powers, (if we have an Event Matrix) or we can suggest the modeler's unconscious mind create specific experiences in which the modeler will have particular experiences and adventures as the superhero. This allows us to integrate the use of embedded suggestions and metaphors in the modeler's trance.

If we take the latter approach, allowing the subject's unconscious to construct the scenario, we do not necessarily give much input into the storyline. The subject's unconscious mind can do the heavy lifting to create a metaphoric landscape in which change happens. After all, this is what the unconscious mind does every night when you sleep and dream. Your dreams are landscapes for the mind to assimilate new learnings, creating new neural pathways, as well as process and transform emotions.

When it is time to end the DTI, the client will dissociate from the model. If you are using perceptual positions, the client will move back into third position to decide what learnings to take back with him. Finally they will associate back into self, bringing these specific skills and abilities with them.

Example of a Superhero DTI

In the following transcript you will find an example of a DTI with Wolverine in which the modeler does not disclose the issue, and is in fact not even consciously aware of the specific details, beyond the fact that he wants to feel different from how he currently feels.

The hypnotist has already induced a state of trance in the subject, and is relying on ideomotor signals, as well as verbal answers, to calibrate the subject's responses.

> Hypnotist: Let me ask you this, does your unconscious mind have a context in which the powers of Wolverine would be useful: the power to heal physically and mentally, great physical strength, the ability to cut through things, literally and metaphorically, and to be physically and mentally indestructible, to have the ability to impose your will on any situation in whatever ways are appropriate?

> (Modeler's finger twitches indicating a yes signal)

> Okay, and is there a specific situation in which you are unconscious mind would like to practice these skills literally or metaphorically?

(Modeler's finger twitches yes)

Thank you. So what I would like you to do is just to take a look at Wolverine (client is cataleptically holding a Wolverine figurine) and become aware that you are sitting in this chair and looking at Wolverine. You are, aren't you?

Modeler: Yes.

Hypnotist: That's right. You can see Wolverine there, ask him if he will share this deep trance identification with you. There you go...(unconscious yes signal)

So now I'd like for you to float out of the chair, just floating out of yourself to some position that is very comfortable. See yourself, your own body, relaxing here in the chair, looking at Wolverine in front of you. That's right. Just notice what that looks like. And that body is comfortable in the chair. You can see that body there, deeply in trance.

You can know my voice will go with you wherever you go. And as you look at that you in the chair looking at Wolverine you can see your perspective is beginning to change because Wolverine is there and that self is looking at him as you are looking at that self, that Wolverine is growing, becoming bigger, becoming larger, becoming life-size. He is big and powerful and strong. And you see that body in the chair drifting off into trance looking at the life-size Wolverine. Do you see that?

Modeler: (yes finger twitches)

Hypnotist: That's right. And that self that's going into trance in the chair has a special purpose, and that purpose involves a Deep Trance Identification. And from this position, watching that body sink deeper into trance, you as a pure consciousness can float into Wolverine, the two becoming one. That's right. The two of you merging, becoming Wolverine. As you step into Wolverine you have the power of Wolverine, the energy of Wolverine. You can take your attention inside and feel your bones, because your bones are immensely strong and unbreakable. Feel the bones in your arms and legs. Move your attention around inside any part of your body that needs healing. You can feel the power of Wolverine and any parts of your body that need healing can heal quickly.

Now bring your attention to your forearms, there is an immensely strong bones, lying along those bones are three blades, sharp, powerful, indestructible, able to cut through anything.

You can simply think those blades out of your hands and they can appear ready to cut through anything. And you can feel them and those arms can begin to move (both hands are now cataleptic). That's right. These blades had cut through anything literally and metaphorically.

And in a moment but not yet you are going to go on a journey. Now I don't know exactly where you will go to, but you can go with the power of Wolverine. I don't know if this will be a situation in your life where those powers might be useful. Or whether it will be a situation in Wolverine's life, somewhere where Wolverine can show his full strength, his full power. I don't know if you'll need the ability to use Wolverine's powers to totally focus his energy and his will on the outcome he wants, so nothing can stop him, nothing can get his way. Wherever you find yourself, look around you, see what you see, hear what you hear, feel what you feel. Notice your surroundings and any people around you and what they represent. You may or may not be aware of the problems or issues they may represent, and how the power of Wolverine allows you to deal with these situations easily, to cut through any obstacles you may face.

You can focus the intensity of your power completely on your outcome, so nothing can stop you. That unstoppable power of total focus, total energy, the strength of Wolverine with the sharpness of his claws that can cut through anything. That's right. You can know you're safe and protected, your skeleton unbreakable. And know if you get hurt you can heal yourself.

Now I don't know where your unconscious mind is taking you, and how many scenes you are experiencing. I don't know how many problems you are cutting through. You are learning to use that energy in ways that leave you totally focused so you can achieve anything.

…

That's right. Now it's time to journey back. You, as Wolverine, can come back to the office and see that self deeply in trance sitting in the chair. That's right. Now as a consciousness you can float out of Wolverine bringing with you anything positive and powerful for you, while leaving with Wolverine anything that isn't appropriate for you, and you can see the you in the chair, and Wolverine standing nearby.

It's now time to drift back into that you, that body, here in this chair, bringing only those things that will serve you. That's right. In a moment it will be time to come out of trance...One, feeling your body in the chair... Two more aware of the room around you and coming all the way back... And three, eyes open feeling amazing!

In the example above we used a perceptual positions strategy for associating into the superhero. This creates a nice buffer, using third position, making it easy for the modeler to associate into the model at the start. This also gives space at the end so the modeler's unconscious has the chance to pick and choose which elements of the experience would be useful to integrate, and which are better left in the model.

The next thing you will notice is that the parallel reality is constructed at the suggestion of the hypnotist, but by the modeler's unconscious mind. Throughout the process he refers to the specific context the unconscious had in mind, without knowing the exact details. The nature of the superhero reality is left to the modeler's unconscious. The modeler is given the freedom to create the environment in which the change will take place.

At the end of this session the modeler reported that she had created an intricate plot where Wolverine had to face specific physical obstacles and needed to negotiate with others, in a way only Wolverine could. The modeler described the experience as being as though they were caught up in a fantastic dream where they were Wolverine acting in the world.

Neither the hypnotist nor modeler had any idea what the unconscious mind was working through with the plot. The modeler exhibited a distinct shift in physiology and expressed her enjoyment with her new state.

Example 2:

This example involved Shawn as the modeler, and the Silver surfer as the model.

Hypnotist: Ah, the Silver Surfer, he's traveled quite a long way to be here.

Shawn: Across space.

Hypnotist: That's right. And before we get started would you like to talk a little bit about your specific goal?

Shawn: I would like to develop a greater ability to switch contexts throughout my day. For example, I handle a number of different projects on any given day and I would like to build a greater sense of fluidity.

Hypnotist: Now you have chosen a fantastic model for this. As you know the Silver Surfer is masterful in adapting to new situations and thriving.

When you are ready to change this context with ease, moving from a conscious context to an unconscious one, you can close your eyes and drift deeply down. (Hypnotist uses previously established trance anchor)

That's right. Now as you sit there comfortably you can hear the sounds around you… The sounds of the traffic drifting by in the streets below. I'm not sure which sounds will gently take you even deeper now but you can be curious about what those sounds have to do with your deep trance… That's right.

To help you go even deeper now I'm going to ask you in a moment to open your eyes and close them again. Each time you close those eyes you can go ten times as deep as you were before. That's right… Now opening those eyes. And close them all the way… That's right deeper and deeper. Opening those eyes again... And closing them all the way down. There you go... And opening... And closing... All the way.

In this comfortable state you can find the Silver Surfer standing there in front of you. Now I know you have a special purpose for this experience. Take a moment and ask the Silver Surfer if he will share with you this state of fluidity in different contexts... That's right.

In this comfortable state you can drift outside of yourself and be aware of what it's like, to see you going even deeper into trance. That's right. And you can see the Silver Surfer there. Now something unique is going to happen because the Silver Surfer can reach out and touch that hand of that you in the chair. That's right and as he does, his sliver physiology can transfer to that hand, moving up that arm and through that body. There you go. And as that silver spreads, that you in the chair is transforming completely into the Silver Surfer.

The you who is pure awareness watching this process can drift into the Silver Surfer resting in the chair. That's right. And as you become him, you take on his abilities, memories, thoughts, and skills because it's time to leave the office and go on a journey that starts on another world, your home world. In this place you're given a role, offered to a god as a servant. In this context you fulfill your duties. Eventually the context shifts and you become a scout. You're given the role of surfing across the span of space, visiting galaxies and new worlds. That old god wants to destroy the planets you discover. He is stuck in one mode of thinking. While you, the surfer, meet hundreds of new people and creatures. Each new planet is new opportunity to grow, a new place to use your natural ability to adapt and excel. That's right.

I don't know at which point you find the Milky Way, as you do though, what is it like to surf fluidly across the surface of sun... to see the beauty of millions of stars sparkling in the distance? That's it (hypnotist sees modeler's legs twitching). And there is the Earth, a shining blue ball pulling your attention, a new context in which you get to expand your possibilities. That's right. You, the Silver Surfer, are a master at changing, adapting, and growing. Each opportunity on that planet, a chance to discover your potential. When you are effortlessly moving between contexts, between worlds, who are you being as a person? That's right...

Now of course when you surf through the atmosphere of Earth you can see the different continents, new contexts, full of potential as you easily glide through the air, eventually finding this office here in New York. There you go (Shawn's previously cataleptic arms come to rest on the chair). It's time to sit and rest in this chair. Now your consciousness can drift out of the Silver Surfer so that you can see the body resting comfortably. The silver begins to flow out of that hand, receding to reveal your body resting comfortably there. That's it. And as that recedes to the space in front of you, taking the form of the Silver Surfer again, he can take whatever elements are less useful to you and while you keep the most important aspects of this experience.

Now when you're ready, as an awareness you can sink back down in to that you who is resting in the chair integrating fully and completely all learnings from this experience. And you could consider what is like for you moving fluidly from this context of trance to a waking state.

Or perhaps you would like to be curious about just how easily you will transition between roles and contexts tomorrow. After all I wonder what it will be like for you a year from now when you have practiced the art of changing contexts so well that is a part of who you are. That's right..

In a moment it will be time to come out of this trance but not yet. Next time you go into trance and DTI you can have a deeper and even more enjoyable experience where powerful changes can take place. That's right... Now in a moment I will count from one to three and when I reach three you can come all the way out of trance feeling refreshed, relaxed, and wonderful knowing that switching contexts can be as fluid as one... Two, coming all the way back now... And three, opening your eyes feeling simply fantastic!

In the example above we used a modified approach to the perceptual position DTI. Instead of the awareness associating into the model from third position, we had the modeler's body take on the characteristics of the model, then from third position associating back into first.

Comparing the Two Examples

In the first DTI with Wolverine, the modeler was given an open range of possibilities. She could play out the metaphor in any scenario her unconscious mind wished. In the second DTI the modeler was invited to have the same life experiences as the model in one particular comic book adventure, agreed on beforehand. Throughout this narrative the hypnotist kept going back to the modeler's specific words associated with his goal. This allows for the creation of a blended space in the modeler's experience. In this context we are guiding the modeler's unconscious mind to draw certain parallels and use the Silver Surfer's life experiences as reference points for developing the particular skill set and states that the modeler desired.

Either approach is good. This can be up to either the hypnotist or the modeler depending on context, familiarity with the character, and the client's particular preferences.

Summary

To review, the steps of this process are very simple. Once you have done the preliminary work, created the Event Matrix (for a more complete DTI), set the context, established unconscious permission for the DTI to take place, and induced trance. It's time to begin the trance process, as well as the unconscious activation. Invite the modeler to see the model standing in front of him. You can take some time to build up the visual characteristics of this experience. Next the modeler asks for permission from the model and dissociates from self. From third position the modeler can fully associate into the model and have experiences as him.

Take your time and allow the modeler to fully experience the powers and abilities of his model. This will stretch the client's perceptions of what is possible. Next, the model returns to the current time and place and the modeler's awareness can dissociate from the model. If you are doing an instant DTI at this point, you'll invite the unconscious mind to take what is useful and leave everything else with a model.

Finally the modeler can leave the Superhero and associate back into his own physical body. The modeler can then thank the model for the experience. The hypnotist can lead the modeler to future pace (i.e. practice) the changes in the context where the modeler wants the changes to take place.

Conclusion

The superhero DTI can challenge deeply held limiting beliefs about abilities. In this DTI the modeler experiences a world where the current laws of reality do not play a significant role, so the possibilities become unlimited. In the therapeutic context this type of DTI makes it difficult for a client to hold onto the problem in the same way. It causes a shift in perceptions. As we mentioned previously this also induces a spontaneous regression. As the superhero, the modeler is indirectly re-imprinting emotional states and skills, thanks to the regression. When he associates completely into himself as an adult, unconsciously it is as if he had had these capabilities and beliefs throughout his life.

One final thought about the superhero DTI, it's a fun lighthearted approach to change and can create an inability to be serious about a problem. After all, the less serious you are about a problem the less serious that problem becomes.

Chapter 28: Come to the Darkside - Super Villain DTI

Super Villain DTI as a Six Step Reframe

In this chapter we will explore a form of DTI that may seem counter intuitive at first glance. We will explore the therapeutic power of deep trance identification with super villains.

You may be wondering, why villains? Why supervillains!?! It seems like an unusual proposition to invite a modeler to step into the shoes of the bad guys. This particular approach while at first unusual, is a highly powerful way to help the client change in a short period of time.

When clients come in with a problem, it is multifaceted. By this we mean that it is never just what the client is naming. In NLP we have a presupposition that says behind every behavior is a positive intention. Every state and every behavior is motivated by the unconscious mind wanting something good for the individual. People make the best choices available to them. We can take, for example, a client who wants to stop smoking. At the conscious level the client believes that smoking is her problem. However, during the session we find their issue is the fact that they experience stress and the unconscious mind. Having the positive intention of producing more relaxation motivates the client to reach for a cigarette.

As you can see there is both the presenting issue as well as the unconscious motivation behind it. If you are familiar with the 6 Step Reframe from NLP, you will recognize this. So on a deeper level there is an unconscious intention that drives the state and behavior.

Clients may also create meta-problems in response to the issue for which they're coming to see you. In other words, they feel bad (or some other negative emotion) and then feel bad for feeling bad. These meta-problems cause the original problem to become locked into place because the client now avoids accepting and addressing the original problem.

In our example of a smoker, she feels stress, her unconscious wants relaxation, so her unconscious leads her to smoke. The smoker then begins to generate a commentary about the smoking behavior. She may think she shouldn't be smoking. "What's wrong with me, why can't I control my actions?" This type of thought-loop compounds her problem. By blaming herself, she creates a separate 'part' of herself that is responsible for the problem, and separates that part, blaming and rejecting it. The meta-problem puts a boundary line between the problem network within his mind, and the rest of his brain.

Think of it this way, if the client didn't have a meta- problem, she wouldn't have the problem because she would be happy as she is. An easy example to understand this is the smoker who comes in only because her spouse or doctor (or society) wants her to quit. For the client, she is happy with smoking. She has no meta-problem; no view of herself as having a problem, therefore no separate part is created. And if it's not a problem for the client, it isn't a problem for me as the client's advocate.

Because of this meta-problem, the client separates herself from the behavior, and as a result remains unaware of the positive intention behind it. If you were to ask a client's conscious mind about the positive intention, or what the part wants for her, she will typically respond with, "Nothing, it's just bad." She may think that part of her is either doing nothing for her, or is doing something that is purposefully detrimental to her.

The super villain DTI allows us to not only satisfy the positive intention behind the behavior, but also for the integration of that part, therefore dissolving the meta-problem.

In addition, the super villain often has access to resources that superheroes do not, and may be the exact resource that the client needs. For example, it is very common for supervillains to have a team that supports them. Superheroes, on the other hand, are often loners. Supervillains are skillful at lying out and following through on plans, while superheroes tend to spend more time in a reactionary position, responding to the plans of the super villains.

Super villain DTI allows for greater access to resources in the client's life that he may not have considered up until this moment. It allows him to use his neurology in highly resourceful ways, and very often ways that may have previously been rejected. If we look at this from the point of view of parts integration, this pattern takes the "problem" loop in the client's neurology, and attaches to make it part of a larger neural network that is more flexible and resourceful (this is an application of John Overdurf's Hidden Ability pattern).

The Traditional 6 Step Reframe

Before we go into the pattern itself we would like to take a few moments to discuss the traditional 6 Step Reframe. You will notice as we go forward with the super villain DTI itself that the elements of a traditional 6 Step are present, even though they may take on a less procedural appearance.

The first step is simple: get the problem. This is the same as starting any piece of change work. You want to establish the context in which the problem takes place, and the trigger that lets the unconscious know it is 'time' to begin the problem behavior, the state the client goes into when in the problem, and the behavior undertaken in the context. For the context, it is important to establish a particular time and place in which the problem is experienced. As hypnotist you should guide the client to be very specific about this, "I was in the office at 3 o'clock on Monday…" We want to activate the neural network associated with the problem. We do this because we know through

303

neuroscience that in order for neuroplasticity, i.e. change, to occur in a particular neural network, that network has to be active.

Next, you want to establish unconscious communication with the part of the neurology responsible for the problem feelings and behaviors. The traditional 6 Step Reframe does this by asking the client's unconscious mind to provide a yes signal. This could be a feeling, image, sound, or unconscious (ideomotor) movement. Some coaches may also use the increasing or decreasing of an emotion as the signal.

Having found the yes signal, we can then establish a no signal. The real secret to this is that we are calibrating to the client's unconscious communication, not necessarily what he is saying. He may consciously think he has a yes signal, such as hearing the word yes. At the same time he also has a finger twitching he is unaware of. We will use the finger twitch as the actual unconscious signal, although we may not make the client aware of that.

For the third step we ask the unconscious mind to identify and perhaps reveal the positive intention behind the problem state and behavior. The unconscious mind may choose to bring this to conscious attention, however that intention may stay in the unconscious throughout the process. The unconscious mind provides the signal when this is accomplished, with or without the conscious minds awareness.

Now that the positive intention is active in the unconscious, the client is able to generate more resourceful ways of meeting that intention. For this step we invite the unconscious to generate a large number of possibilities to satisfy the positive intention in different ways, ways that do not involve the negative feelings or behaviors. We may suggest that the unconscious mind generates, for example, 37 alternative ways of meeting that intention. We suggest a larger number because the conscious mind can only track 5 to 9 pieces of information at any given time, and we do not want the conscious mind involved in this part of the process. The conscious mind has tried to change the problem in the past, but unsuccessfully, therefore it has no business being involved now. Once again the unconscious mind will give you a signal when this is accomplished.

From all of these possibilities, the unconscious mind can now choose one to try on for a period of time. You, as the hypnotist can help the client's unconscious mind to doing this through a process of narrowing down the options; for example, from 37 to the 10 best options. Next he can narrow it down to the three top choices and choose the one that suits him the best. We also designate that it will be for a limited time, to test whether the new feelings and behaviors are really appropriate. This also allows him to test it to see if this new way of meeting the positive intention is ecological for him as a complete person.

Finally it is time for the ecology check, testing, and future pace. We may ask the client's unconscious mind if this new behavior fits in with the client's life and personality. Or we may ask if there is any objection to trying this behavior for the set period of time. If the coach gets a no signal, indicating this new behavior does not fit for the person as a whole (or a 'yes' that there is an objection, depending on how the question is phrased), then the hypnotist can have the client choose another new behavior. If the unconscious mind says yes this behavior is good, then we may suggest that the new behavior can be tried on for a week or two, and if this new behavior fits with the client at all levels, he may choose to keep it.

We can then test by having the client reimagine the context and trigger so that he may experience doing the new behavior. We follow this up with future pacing to give the client the opportunity to try this new behavior in a number of different instances, using his imagination, while still in office with the coach

This is a description of the typical approach to a 6 Step Reframe. In the next section we will explore the Super Villain DTI as a Six Step Reframe. Although at the surface it may not look to be the same, but when you look deeper you will see the same working parts.

The Mechanics of the Super Villain DTI

The first step of the Super Villain DTI, just as in the traditional 6 Step Reframe, is to associate the client into the problem state. We do this both to understand his strategy for the behavior, as well as to activate that part of his neurology, so that change can happen.

For example, we could consider a client who wants to quit smoking. In this step we associate him into specific times and places where in the past he would have felt compelled to smoke. This would give us important information about the state of his experience immediately before the smoking behavior.

It is typically during this part of a session that our client will express the meta-problem. In this case it could be the client feeling a deep sense of disappointment with his inability to consciously control the smoking behavior. He may also feel that part of him is weak or somehow flawed. It is important to begin to reframe this meta-problem, suggesting that the part indeed has a positive intention.

If the modeler has consciously expressed a connection with the metaphor of the superhero world, then you could simply ask him before the trance what villain represents the problem. Otherwise you can keep this at the unconscious level as in the example below.

The second step is to begin a formal trance process. With this type of DTI you may choose to do a formal induction, prior to using perceptual positions to associate the subject into the model. Once the modeler is in trance you may choose to provide some metaphors to pre-frame the experience he us having, or about to have. The following is an example of one way in which we can pre-frame the experience for the client to prepare his unconscious mind to create profound positive change.

> "So I know you are here today to make an important change and it's good to know that all you are is changing. It's true everything changes. Even right now your body is creating new healthy cells and your brain is rewiring itself. You are not only changing on the physical level, your thoughts and emotions are changing as well as a result of the experiences you are having right now, and will have in the future, including in the rest of this session.

When I was little I used to love superheroes. In fact we would spend many hours pretending to be this or that superhero with my friends. As a small child I always wanted to be the good guy. That means that someone had to play the super villain for the game to work.

I never wanted to be the villain until something changed; one day I was pretending to be the Joker and it occurred to me that this is a way more fun role. This is because I have a team and we got to make the rules. We make the plan, set the stage, and get to create the whole universe in which everyone plays. If you could play any super villain, I wonder who you would be. Which super villain can help you change easily?"

In the story above we suggest the idea that stepping into the shoes of the villain can open up new possibilities, and once you do, you have the power to create new realities. This also provides a nice bridge to the client regarding his problem because we have activated neural network associated with the problem, and now we trust the modeler's unconscious mind to make the connection between the problem and the villain.

It's now time to associate the subject into the super villain. We will use the perceptual positioning DTI process for this. Begin by helping the modeler build up a detailed visual representation of the super villain. Next, the modeler will dissociate from himself, so he can see himself as well as the super villain.

Then, when ready, he can associate into the super villain. Take a moment to help him orient into this new role. You can call his r attention to the different aspects of this sensory experience, including seeing himself over there, as we have demonstrated in other DTI examples.

The modeler as the super villain can then leave this space and have an adventure. We can do this very open ended, inviting the unconscious mind to transport the modeler to a space where he can act as the super villain, or in a more guided way.

As he has this experience of being the super villain this we call his attention to the beliefs, values, and resources of the character. It may sound at first counterintuitive to ask about values associated with a super villain, however, unconsciously it is very easy to find importance in the experience. The super villain's adventure is a reflection of the problem part of the client. This is an indirect parts integration. We may also place an emphasis at this point in creating plans and finding the one that will be the most efficient. This is still done completely at the metaphoric level.

Below is a brief example of this step. The modeler is a singer with stage fright who wants to feel calm on stage. He is associated into Magneto from Marvel's X-Men.

> Hypnotist: And as Magneto you can find yourself transported from this place to a space where you can change the future. You could find yourself on an adventure, perhaps fighting the X-Men or recruiting new mutants to your cause. That's right, take some time and enjoy this.
>
> (Hypnotist pauses for a few moments)
>
> Underneath the feelings of the moment, there is something powerful motivating you. And of course as Magneto you know the importance of protecting the mutants, keeping them safe. In fact there have been times when others have looked at you and you may have felt there was a judgment there.
>
> And yet now when you are calmly attracting things to you through your magnetic power I wonder who you are being, when you are someone who firmly in yourself and knowing you are safe?
>
> And of course as Magneto you don't just rush into situations, you plan. You calmly build a game plan

where you can act calmly knowing that the feelings that are truly important to you are being met. I wonder what plan you could put into place now so that you are calmly using your magnetic personality to draw people in.

In the example above we are mixing realities for the singer. Throughout the process we are taking motivations we know are a part of Magneto's character, such as the desire to secure a safe future for mutants. We know with this villain that the motivations at his core are good, although the behavior is not as resourceful, just as the modeler experiences. We also integrate some of the moving parts of the modeler's issue. For example, people with stage fright typically are unconsciously shifting perceptual positions with the audience and then mind reading their thoughts. We've switched positions to Magneto, being in his own shoes and drawing things in. This is ambiguous. Are we talking about Magneto attracting metallic objects, or the modeler attracting an adoring audience??

Once the adventure has concluded and the modeler has learned something of value unconsciously, represented by a physiological shift, he returns to this space where the modeler's body is. Now he can dissociate from the super villain and see both the character and himself. This is a middle point where he can leave behind anything that doesn't fit in with who he us as a person, and can take with him any new learnings that are useful.

Finally, the modeler associates fully and completely back into her or himself. Now we invite him to return to the context and trigger the old problem; this time with the new set of resources to experience how it is different. After testing, we can then future pace the client for success.

Here is the closing part of the Magneto DTI.

Hypnotist: There will be times and places in the future where you can enjoy calmly captivating an audience. And the cool thing is when you start with a base of calmness you can have high energy, low energy, and anywhere in between. It all depends on just how you want that audience to experience you. It could be like Magneto drawing in metal quickly, or taking his time, because you can be on that stage, and feeling the music as it pulls the audience in. I wonder just how magnetic you can be as a performer. Because it could be that you are in the audience watching you and completely captivated by your performance. And from this position you can feel being drawn in quickly and slowly. Either way you cannot help but be completely entranced by your performance. And who knows just how calm you can be as that song flows from you.

In this part the modeler is associated into the self and we return them to the context of the original problem, and trigger. This time we are using the Magneto experience to condition the change. We also do another perceptual position shift where the modeler floats into the audience, as he did before, this time though he us on the other end of the now magnetic performance. Keep in mind that we do not return to the context until we are sure there has been a shift. We are specifically looking for changes in breathing, symmetrical physiology, and to see if we form unconscious communication, such as finger twitches.

Unlike the traditional 6 Step Reframe, which is more procedural, this approach relies on the power of the unconscious mind to create connections between the metaphoric experience of the super villain, the problem state, and resources. The secret behind success with this approach is the hypnotist's artistry when it comes to weaving indirect suggestions throughout the experience. The use of embedded suggestions and ambiguities helps the modeler's unconscious make the connections.

If we were to look at this process through the lens of the traditional 6 Step Reframe, the first step for both approaches is the same, getting in touch with the problem.

The second step, establishing unconscious communication, in this context is different. The unconscious communication is established through the trance induction and the creation of the metaphoric landscape and character. The establishment of trance and the unconscious engagement with the process will lead to unconscious physiological shifts throughout the process. This is the unconscious mind communicating. Remember, we can't *not* communicate.

In this version we do not invite the unconscious mind to make the conscious mind aware of the positive intention. Instead this is more of an inductive learning experience. The modeler experiences the positive intention from the inside out when she or he begins to tap into the super villains values.

Similarly the generation and selection of resourceful alternative behaviors is done implicitly. As a super villain the client will have to choose one plan of action and try it in the metaphoric environment. This is a way of keeping the conscious mind out of the process of selecting the new resourceful behavior. After all, the conscious mind is tied up with the storyline of the adventure. It is the unconscious mind that uses the metaphors to communicate the application of new resources.

The final step occurs during the testing and future pacing. The modeler will go back to the time and place of the original problem and experience how it's different. We are letting the unconscious mind generate the new behaviors; in this part of the session *you can be pleasantly surprised to discover that the unconscious is automatically generating new ways of feeling and acting.*

While in this chapter we focused on the Super Villain DTI as being primarily a piece of change work, and in particular a DTI 6 Step Reframe. This type of DTI can also be tremendously generative. A super villain's work ethic and ambition can be used as a way of motivating a modeler to take action. You could think of a business person who already uses metaphors such as, "We're going to take over the world." He is already at some level making a connection with these types of super villain archetypes. He has the experience of stepping into them and using those mental states, the driving force behind the behavior

With that said, this is always tempered with the individual's personal ethics, values, and beliefs. The frame we use is that this is a learning experience, and a way to complement the client's values and skills. In a generative approach we will typically go through the matrix in order to establish that the unconscious mind is ready and comfortable with this type of generative experiments.

Chapter 29: Ancient Modeling: Animal DTI

What would it be like to be an animal? I don't just mean any animal. I mean another living creature who calls out to you on a deep level. How would it feel to be a swift cheetah, an unstoppable elephant, or a graceful crane? You could become curious about what type of lessons you would learn. After all, animals have tremendous skills and resources that we do not have reference to or even the necessary words.

If you could be a bird flying peacefully high in the sky, how would the problem you might be experiencing here on earth look to you? If you could dive as deeply down into the ocean as a killer whale, what hidden treasure might you find in that deepest of places?

Of course you or I wouldn't be the first people to ask these questions! Ancient peoples across the globe have wondered the same things. In ancient stories we hear of humans who become animals, shape shifters, as well as animals that become human. All of these stories teach important messages about resourcefulness, transformation, and hidden abilities. Animal DTI is a common cultural trance experience throughout the world. From the ancient Shaman of Siberia, to the legends of King Arthur, all the way to the practices of modern medicine men, and the modern western children's stories, this deep fascination has created a transcendent cultural narrative that leaves behind a trail of techniques in which this DTI experience is embedded.

As with any DTI we are working at the level of archetypes. It's certainly true that one benefit of DTI is leaving your own stuff behind so you have a clean slate. What you put on a slate is the model. The beauty of this is that animals do not have the same type of baggage and cultural hang-ups that humans do. Animals do not have the same facility with language, which means they are unable to construct, or hold on to, problems the ways that we do.

So associating into an animal is a completely novel experience and the modeler has no choice but to interact with the world in a completely new way. As unusual as this may sound, if you think about the common metaphors that we use in day to day life we often do you call on the archetype of the animal. For example some people view themselves as a shark in business, but a puppy dog at home with their kids. You can call to mind any number of animal nicknames given to children out of affection.

Associating with animals is something that happens unconsciously in our culture, just as other cultures have been doing for thousands of years as a means of healing, learning, survival, and spirituality. We will be exploring Animal DTI as a generative experience.

Consider a time and place where you'd like to have specific resource, it could be confidence, relaxation, playfulness, or anything else that is positive for you. Now consider what type of animal represents these qualities? We do not know exactly what it would be like to be that animal in that context, but we do know we could enjoy trying it.

Imagine becoming this animal. When you are this animal, what is your body feeling? What is it like to have no legs or arms, but just wings or even fins? I wonder what emotions you could be experiencing right now, and where in this body those emotions are felt. Does a tiger feel courage in his heart? Does a bird feel carefree in his wings? Is a monkey playful in her arms? Is a fish peaceful in his eyes?

These are impossible questions for the conscious mind to answer, and yet to the unconscious mind it would be fun to step or swing or crawl or fly or swim inside and really find out. You could think of a time and place where you want to have more of this animal experience, as a birthright. So experience the animal in a new way, and of course on your return you could simply be a human with a new understanding of how to be more like your animal.

This is a brief example of how you may use the animal DTI. At this point you have a number of different tools you can use to help the modeler associate into the experience. You could use a perceptual position DTI, Symbolic modeling, Tree of Life, BEAT DTI, or any other means of associating. In the example above we simply shifted positions by asking you to imagine 'as-if'.

We will give an example using the Perceptual Position DTI. You may also recognize some aspects of the BEAT pattern. This summary was taken from a client session:

- Select a context in which you would like more of a particular resource. The subject chooses confidence.

- Choose an animal that embodies confidence, and a context in which the animal demonstrates this confidence. The subject chooses a jaguar stalking a crocodile, a scene he had seen on a YouTube video.

- See that scene in your mind's eye, as if you are there watching it. What do you notice as a human spectator?

- Now float out of your body and, as pure consciousness, look down and see yourself watching the jaguar stalk the crocodile. Rewind the scene to the beginning and watch the whole thing again from this perspective. What do you notice now that's different to being the human observer?

- Rewind the scene once more. Now float down into the jaguar and experience the scene from the inside, feel how your body moves, how your legs are attached and coordinate with your spine. Notice the feelings inside. What are you paying attention to, and how? What thoughts are you thinking?

- Now float out of the jaguar and look down at the jaguar from above, you can see the jaguar and yourself as the human observer. From this perspective, what learnings do you wish to take back with you?

- Taking those learnings, float back into your own body, observing the jaguar.

- Now re-emerge into the here and now.

This approach is ideal for people who express a deep connection with animals or who hold a belief in spirit animals or animal guides. If the modeler should give you a metaphor, saying he would like to be like this animal in this situation, this is also another door into the DTI experience. Just as with any DTI we tie this experience to a specific context and trigger. You may find it enjoyable to explore how you can use animal DTI to enhance your outline, as well as helping your clients step outside of their normal model of the world to try on a new way of being. Just as with the superhero DTI, this encourages clients to have a flexible reality.

Chapter 30: Conclusion

Just north of Australia, deep in the Indian Ocean, there is a chain of thousands of islands separated by thousands of miles of water, called Micronesia. Micronesia is a fascinating place because since ancient times, without the use of maps, the locals have been able to navigate their way between the islands. This is no small feat considering they only have the use of their canoes as they move across large expanses of open water. The do not use maps, compasses, or GPS and yet they are able to literally feel their way to whichever island they wish to visit.

The way they do this is ingenious. They are able to triangulate their position in relationship to any one of the islands based on the positioning of constellations. They can look at two or more constellations and know where they should be in relationship to one or more islands. The sailors are able to safely and quickly navigate hundreds of miles of open water. This triangulation creates a mental grid-map on the ocean that they integrate with currents and other ocean markers so they know intuitively in which direction to sail.

From the moment children are able to learn the constellations they learn this ability. It becomes so ingrained in the unconscious that by the time they are adults they can feel the grid-line's in the ocean that connect islands. They know when they are on course and when they are not, based on how it feels. There are no landmarks to chart a course, yet the knowledge of the positioning constellations is embedded so deeply in the unconscious that Micronesians are able to feel the path to their destinations in daylight or darkness, fair weather or cloud.

At the heart of DTI is the understanding that modeling is much more than mimicking behavior. It is far more elegant than simply charting a course on a map. It is about fully integrating a new way of being in the world; integrating this into which you are on a deep unconscious level. When you have achieved this then everything becomes effortless. When you *trust your unconscious mind to take the lead using the stars, using your values to guide you, modeling is the easiest and most natural way to learn.*

In this book we have presented an easy to use protocol along with a number of different strategies, which make deep trance identification versatile, effective, and fun. Whether you are using this for your own personal development or to guide others on their modeling journey, you will find with each new DTI experience that modeling becomes a part of who you are.

When I (Jess) left that hypnosis training years ago I walked away with a treasure. This is something that only pure experience can teach. After that moment I knew I could step into any role and succeed. In fact, when I face challenges I automatically think, "You can pretend anything and master it."

As you go forward remember that living is learning. And no matter who you think you are, you are in all ways even more than that. When you know how to truly learn, there is nothing on earth that is out of your reach.

Beyond DTI: An Epilogue Trance About What's Really In It For You

If you've read this far, we're pretty sure your brain is buzzing with all kinds of possibilities you can experience using DTI, and all the other transformative processes in this book. And you know what? If you liked what you've been learning, know there is always more! Perhaps way more! Here are a few interesting examples as to what is possible.

Interested?

OK, hang with me for a bit.

Back in the 90's I (John) used to ask two questions at the beginning of the Hypnotic Modeling course I used to do.: "What is the greatest barrier to learning?" and "What is the greatest bridge to learning?" After going through a series of exercises, a number of which you've read about in this book, the answers would emerge pretty organically with the group. I did not have to say "and the moral of the story is..." The greatest barrier to learning? It's thinking we are separate from what we are learning. The greatest bridge to learning? It's temporarily dissolving boundaries to be able to *feel connected to what you are studying.* In other words, by having the experience, you are not separate from what you are learning. It is a part of you, just not in the way you thought!

Think about it...

Sometimes it takes processes like what *you are learning* in this book, where you identify with someone or something you consider outside of you, to *discover more* of who you really are. Each moment is an opportunity for you to discover *aspects of you* that you hadn't noticed that may, in fact, be beyond what you could have ever conceived to be you. Like a shifting beam of light shining on different facets of a diamond; you get to experience aspects of yourself you never knew were you, and do it from different points of view.

All through college in the mid to late 70's I was a student of Kripalu Yoga which was form founded by a Yogi named, Amrit Desai. I'd read many of his books and loved the simplicity and depth of his words, the product of many years of yoga practice, and of course, diligent study and reading of scripture—or so I thought.

Later in my twenties, I stayed at the ashram to hear the Yogi speak during Easter. During an interchange with a student he oft-handedly said, "I really ought to spend some time reading. I don't read very much." I was shocked; having thought he'd undoubtedly read numerous books, scriptures, etc. Apparently, not the case! He learned what he learned primarily through his ability to observe, his ability to both identify deeply and to de-identify, dissolving boundaries, to experience the essence of someone or something; whatever was the subject of study.

So, ultimately, learning the processes included in this book are ways to *exercise your brain* to be able to *Identify and de-identify, at will*, as well as being able to *shift your attention*, dissolve perceptual boundaries and also re-construct them, at will. No mean task, but then again, how would it feel if you knew *you are up to something BIG?*

It is through the mastery of these processes that we can experience our true selves and our interconnectedness to all things—and *be free—*

in the biggest sense of the word. In that way we can benefit from the resources we normally think are "outside" of us, because we can have the experience of them already being a part of us (as well as being a part of what is "out there."). We have the direct experience of something I have mentioned in my work. *"No matter what you think you are, you're always more* than that!"

In 2004, as a part of an exchange between the Dalai Lama and a group of western neuroscientists, an outstanding study took place. Essentially the Dalai Lama gave the researchers some of his best meditators that would be wired up to EEG's, as well as various brain imaging procedures to see what happens within their brains during meditation.

While being wired-up, each of the monks engaged in a specific type of meditation known as *compassion meditation.* The process involves going into an altered brain wave state (more about that in a bit!) while often choosing to focus on some group of people in order to actually "become" them. They would merge with them in a way for them to take on the "suffering" or "challenges" the groups may be experiencing. (I know, not a currently popular concept!) They would then use their own skills (similar to some of the NLP and Hypnosis skills you may know) to *transform* the suffering and challenges they had just taken-on from the group. In that way, they would be healing that group, by healing themselves. How cool and courageous is that?! But, there's more!

For most of us there is an area in the pre-frontal lobe of the dominant hemisphere of our brain, which is brightly lit when viewed through a PET scan. In fact, when we are in our waking state it is lit practically all the time. It is the area which makes the distinction between what is "us" and what it is "not us," what is "you" and "not you."

When the monks would go into the compassion meditation, this area in their brain went completely dim. They were able to turn-off that part of their brain and dissolve the perceptual boundaries of what is "I and "not I." In that way they could experience "no boundaries" and experience all that is "out-there,"; all the information and energy as being a part of themselves, using it to *better humanity*. DTI on another level, for sure, but there's still more!

Also evident in their EEG recordings was a high amplitude and high frequency band of coherence waves streaming across their brains, called gamma waves, which are frequencies of 24 Hz and up. Many of the monks exhibited gamma waves around 42 Hz.

So you might be wondering "What's the big deal about this?" Well, gamma waves are correlated with "Aha" experiences. You know when you get a flash of insight and really *"get it."* These waves are consistent with the brain being in amazing coherence and harmony - like a symphony, each player playing different parts, but all blending together to weave a tapestry of sound that is so much more than the sum of the parts.

It's like a web which connects far-flung areas of the brain so everything is firing as one, but each part is doing it's own thing (No metaphor there, right?) The result is a sense of *incredible clarity*: and "getting it" from many points of view, but all at the same time. It's the "aha" when everything comes together in a flash.

The difference between the monks and most of us is that they are creating this flash, this state, at will, and can maintain it for long periods of time. Even after they come out of the meditation, their brains continue to *sustain these changes* for a while. What do you think it would be like to *experience clarity* with on-going "aha" moments, one after the other for long periods of time?

Yes...take a moment... and enjoy what that might be like.

Remember, as neuroscience suggests, your brain is more like a muscle in your body, more than anyone had considered a generation ago. If you've bothered to read this far, you are "in," so you might as well *start your work-outs* now; if you haven't already....and *make a difference*, don't you think? Pick any one process in this book and practice it until it becomes natural and automatic. Then pick another and repeat. It will be worth it, if you put in the effort. There is no substitute for repetition.

So, it is our hope that reading this book will stimulate you to continue practicing these processes you've read... for a long time! The net result is much more than DTIing for fun, which has its merits, too. It's about going just *you can go* so much further...so why not? Right?

Remember...

You are part of the world and the world is a part of you.

So, because...
you are changing,
beyond the boundaries you once had about who you are, the world is changing...

...and in the process...
you can BE
discovering....
who you really are
which is all-ways changing.... in ways that are beyond what you can know, now and fully appreciate
but can look forward to... looking back on... with a smile (Oh, come on you can do it!) all off what you'll be discovering...
for the rest of your life...
remembering...
all the good
you can do
for everyone
includes
ALL
of
YOU, too!

Appendix I: Summary of the DTI Techniques

Below you will find a summary of each of the specific DTI techniques described in the book. When you are doing a DTI, either for yourself or with a client, you can use this chapter to decide which DTI technique is going to be most appropriate. Of course, you can also combine two DTI techniques, or mix and match as you see fit.

Each of the DTI techniques has pros and cons that we will also briefly outline in this chapter.

DTI using Perceptual positions

Perceptual positions are a tool of NLP. There are several perceptual positions available, and in the context of a DTI, these will include:

First position: being yourself, watching the model, or engaging in dialogue with the model.

Second position: seeing the world out of the eyes of the model. This is what you probably think of as DTI.

(Alternate) Second position: seeing the model from the eyes of someone the model interacts with.

Third position: observing the model from an impartial position, the 'fly on the wall' view.

Fourth position: observing the model within the organizational, cultural, social or societal system of which he is part.

'Quantum fourth' position: broadly meaning to observe the model within the context of all quantum possibilities, including the space in between everything that is, and everything the model might have been but isn't.

DTI, by its nature, involves experiencing the world from the point of view and perspective of the model. The very definition of DTI is that you 'become' the model while in deep trance. But Quantum Perceptual Position DTI offers a wider range of perspectives, and therefore the opportunity to learn more. You get to observe, and interact with the model, not just from the model's perspective, but also from your perspective, your perspective interacting with them (the DTI conversation with the model), the objective 'fly-on-the-wall' perspective, the perspective of the system, including other people they interact with (for example of serving Milton Erickson from the perspective of one of Erickson's patients), and the wider 'quantum perspective'. We would certainly encourage you to use a number of these different perspectives during any DTI!

Pros and Cons: Perceptual position is a 'go-to' technique within DTI and should be incorporated in some form in any DTI.

Event Matrix DTI

Using specific events from a model's life has been used as a modeling technique before recorded history. Even before Homer wrote down events from the lives of the ancient Greek heroes such as Odysseus and the great Achilles, orators would travel from town to town, and city to city, telling these stories as part of an oral tradition. Other cultures did likewise. Each of these stories was made up of specific episodes that illustrated the characters of the heroes.

Later biographical episodes began to be used as part of a more formal process, similar to DTI, for example by the Jesuits practicing the spiritual exercises of Ignatius, described in the chapter on the history of DTI. We believe that reincorporating this focus on specific biographical episodes into modern DTI adds a very important piece back into the puzzle.

The approach we have taken, which we call the Event Matrix, is to take specific biographical events from the life of the model, and consider each of these events using Logical Levels. Logical Levels is an NLP tool that enables you to think about events not only in terms of what took place and where it happened, but also in terms of emotional states of the people involved, their beliefs and values, and other attributes of their identity. So the Event Matrix involves gathering key events from the model's life and considering these events from the perspective of Logical Levels (or from the Tree of Life - see below).

Pros: Again, in our opinion, this should be a 'go-to' technique for most DTI's that you will do.

Cons: One disadvantage of the Event Matrix is that it takes a certain amount of research about the model's life to create a compelling Matrix. If you simply want to acquire one small part of the model's skills and abilities, rather than learning how they learned this skill, then the Event Matrix may be unnecessarily complex.

Counter Model DTI

Finding an alternative model can serve any one of a number of purposes. It can provide a way of measuring progress toward the goal of acquiring the model's skill, to 'fill in' gaps in the model's overall skills, or to provide flexibility in achieving those goals. It can even be used as a form of Six Step Reframe.

Pros: The Counter Model DTI provides a great deal of flexibility in the benefits of the DTI.

Cons: The Counter Model DTI adds some complexity to the DTI process because another model has to be chosen, and DTI'd.

Raikov DTI

Alexander Raikov is in many ways the father of modern DTI. He carried out extensive research on the effectiveness of DTI, and followed a strict and fascinating protocol. This protocol is mainly aimed at wiring a specific skill (such as the ability to play a musical instrument) into the subject's unconscious mind.

Because Raikov focused on one specific skill, he did not necessarily install the beliefs, values and other higher level attributes of the model that can be obtained from the Event Matrix, which in our view offers a more rounded view of the model.

Nevertheless, various elements of Raikov's protocol are enormously powerful, incorporating deep trance, regression, unconscious activation through physical movement, and specific techniques for conscious activation. His protocol can be used for a complete DTI, or elements of his protocol can be combined with the perceptual positions and the Event Matrix as we will discuss.

Pros: Raikov's DTI protocol contains some wonderful techniques and ideas not found elsewhere. These can be incorporated into any DTI to improve its power.

Cons: Because Reich's protocol involves deep trance and regression, it is mainly suitable for those with significant experience in hypnosis.

The BEAT DTI

The BEAT is an NLP pattern that I (Shawn) developed utilizing kinesthetic, auditory and spatial anchors to access a resource state.

The BEAT pattern can be used to experience a very rapid DTI, or to activate a more in-depth DTI installed through some other technique. The BEAT can even trigger a DTI in real-time, allowing the modeler to experience being the model, in real time, in the actual situation in which she needs the behavior.

Pros: The BEAT DTI is a simple and powerful technique, one that can easily be integrated with other DTI techniques. It can also provide a rapid DTI experience in less than a minute.

Cons: If used by itself, the BEAT does not provide the same deep trance experience of becoming the model as other, more deeply hypnotic, techniques do. Therefore it is best combined with other techniques.

Clean DTI

Clean Language and Symbolic modeling are powerful techniques developed by James Lawley and Penny Tompkins based on the work of David Grove. Clean Language can lead to a profound and deeply transformative experience that activates the unconscious mind on a deep level.

Combined with DTI, Clean Language will let you as the hypnotist create a powerful trance experience for the DTI modeler. Clean DTI installs the model on a deep unconscious metaphorical level.

Pros: Clean Language provides a very profound experience that can install the DTI on a very deep level.

Cons: Clean Language requires a certain amount of experience and expertise to apply effectively.

Tree of Life DTI

The Tree of Life DTI is an extension of the Event Matrix DTI. It provides a very sophisticated deductive modeling technique embedded within the DTI itself.

Pros: Provides a richer experience than just using Logical Levels.

Cons: Is a little more complex than Logical Levels.

Future-Self DTI

This is a powerful iterative process that allows the modeler to DTI with his ideal future self. You can use the Future Self DTI as a standalone technique to model your ideal self. For example, we have included it in this book as a technique whereby modeling the future-you who has successfully learned DTI.

You can also use the Future Self DTI as part of the future pacing for any other DTI.

Pros: The Future Self DTI can be very generative because it allows your unconscious mind to choose the attributes to be modeled.

Cons: The one disadvantage of the Future Self DTI is that it provides limited guidance to either the conscious or unconscious mind in regards to what is to be modeled. After all, there is no specific external model to consider.

Double Reverse-DTI

The Double Reverse-DTI is ideal when the model has physical or mental attributes that are simply not available to the modeler. For example, you could model Michael Jordan to improve your basketball skills, but it is very unlikely you would ever have the physical attributes Michael Jordan has, such as his height and athleticism. The Double Reverse-DTI allows you to use the skills of the model, but within your own physical limitations.

Pros and Cons: The Double Reverse-DTI is highly beneficial where the model has physical powers which are simply not available to the modeler.

Best Coach DTI

The Best Coach DTI provides the ultimate in personal resiliency. It allows the modeler to have the model available as a coach when needed. This allows the modeler to 'observe' his own behavior, and to make this observation from a very resourceful place.

Pros: The Best Coach DTI is a powerful resiliency pattern.

Cons: None.

Superhero and Super Villain DTI

The Superhero and Super Villain DTI are exactly what they sound like; the modeler chooses a superhero (or super villain) as their model. We (Jess and Shawn) have used the Superhero DTI extensively because of our interest in superheroes.

Pros: The superhero DTI can be an amazing experience where the modeler has an interest in comic book heroes.

Cons: If the model does not have an interest in comic books, then the Superhero DTI is unlikely to be of interest!

Animal DTI

We have not explored the animal DTI in depth. It offers a new take on DTI that can provide an experience very different from any anthropomorphic DTI.

Pros: The Animal DTI can provide a different experience that can shake up assumptions about how to perform a certain skill.

Cons: None.

Appendix II: Questions for DTI

Below you will find a list of questions that should be answered prior to beginning any full DTI.

By carefully considering and answering these questions, you will begin stimulating the unconscious mind toward change. So much so that there will be so much re-organization in your brain that the actual DTI could be redundant! We are not saying that you shouldn't do the DTI, of course, however these questions act as an exhaustive 'check-list' that will facilitate unconscious congruence and alignment with the changes. It's all in the set-up!

So take your time. Fully consider each question, do not just write down the first quick answer that comes to mind. Realize that whatever you may think the answer is, there is always more to it than that. Use your imagination to fully experience each answer. For example if you wish to DTI for creativity, ask yourself what kind of creativity? What will you be experiencing when you have that creativity? What will you be seeing? What will you be hearing? What will you be feeling? What will you be imagining? Answering these questions fully, begin to format your unconscious to accept the DTI itself.

Question 1: What is the skill you wish to obtain or improve from the DTI?

Question 2: What is the context or contexts in which this skill is to be used?

Question 3: What is your outcome in doing the DTI? How will you know you have been successful?

Question 4: Do you currently have 'blocks' or other negative associations with the skill to be learned, or the context in which it is to be applied? If so, what are these blocks?

Question 5: What do you believe about your own abilities now within the context in which you want the change to take place?

Question 6: Do you believe it is possible to achieve this outcome in this context?

Question 7: Do you believe it is possible to significantly improve skills or performance using the DTI process? Do you believe you are capable of doing so? Do you believe you are capable of absorbing the skills and abilities of the model using DTI?

Question 8: What is important to you about doing this DTI? What is important to you about having this skill in this context? And what is important about that? What will having this skill in this context do for you as a person?

Question 9: Are you committed to following through with the DTI process? Remember you're going to have to not only absorb these skills, but apply them in a real-world context. In short, you will have to take action in the real-world; are you prepared to 'just do it' when the time comes? [Note for the hypnotist: Is the subject congruent in his response?]

Question 10: What are your meta-programs in the context of the DTI? What are your meta-programs in the context in which you want to apply the skills gained in the DTI?

Question 11: Check to make sure you are unconsciously aligned with the DTI process and with your own goals. What was the result?

Question 12: What model is most appropriate for the DTI? Do you have sufficient information about the model, and if not where can you obtain more information?

Question 13: What counter model is most appropriate for the DTI? Do you have sufficient information about the counter model, and if not where can you obtain more information about him?

Appendix III: DTI Protocol

<u>Phase 1: Preparing for the DTI</u>

Step 1: Defining the Context For The DTI
Step 2: Therapeutic versus Generative DTI
Step 3: Choosing the model
Step 4: Choosing a counter model
Step 5: Are you unconsciously aligned with the DTI process?

<u>Phase 2: The DTI Experience</u>

Step 1: Building Rapport with the model
Step 2: Dream Incubation
Step 2: Selecting the DTI Technique
Step 3: Building and Absorbing the model
Step 4: Unconscious Activation of the model
Step 5: Conscious Activation of the model

<u>Phase 3: Integration</u>

Step 1: Connecting the model with the Real-World Context
Step 2: Integrating the model

Phase 4: Application, Testing, and Refinement

Step 1: Utilizing the skills in a real world context
Step 2: Identifying refinements to be made
Step 3: Rerun the DTI to install refinements

Appendix IV: Tree of Life

Below is a diagram of the Tree of Life for coaching. If you are familiar with traditional Kabbalah you would be correct in noticing that the Tree is reversed This is because it is your client's tree. Please consult the Tree of Life chapter to trace the "Lightening Path," as well as developing a deeper understanding of the Tree of Life

About the Authors

Shawn Carson

I was born in Lacashire, England, I moved to New York City in 1996. Since then, as an 'Englishman in New York', I have lived, loved, worked and taught in Manhattan.

Since childhood, I have been fascinated with the Mind. I began to study the application of NLP to sales and management in 1994. Since that time, my interest has grown and I have become a Master Practitioner and Trainer in NLP and Hypnosis Trainer, as well as seeing private clients. In addition I am a Clean Language Facilitator, Reiki Master and practitioner of EFT.

I began to teach NLP and Hypnosis in 2006 and opened the doors of our training and coaching business, IPH, in 2007.

Teaching and helping others in NLP and Hypnosis helps me to understand myself better. After all, at heart we all share the same fears, hopes, dreams.

Jess Marion

Hypnosis has been a life long passion for me. Ever since I was young I had a deep curiosity for how the mind works. I can still remember the first time I saw a hypnotist on T.V. who helped someone change their life, I was both amazed and hooked! Since then I have been on an incredible journey.

In 2010 I opened Philadelphia Hypnosis where I still see clients during the week. In 2012 I partnered with Sarah and Shawn Carson and am now a trainer at the International Center for Positive Change and Hypnosis. In addition to the NLP trainings and advanced workshops we offer, we are 3 of only 25 people world wide certified to teach Igor Ledochowski's Conversational Hypnosis Professional Hypnotherapy Certification Program.

I am also the co-author of "Quit: The Hypnotist's Handbook To Running Effective Stop Smoking Sessions", "The Power of Hypnotic Influence", "The Swish", and "The Visual Squash".

To discover more about Shawn and Jess and training opportunities please vist www.bestnlpnewyork.com

John Overdurf

John Overdurf is an internationally recognized therapist, coach, and Master Trainer of NLP and Hypnosis and also the Co-Developer of Humanistic Neuro-Linguistic Psychology. He is the co-author of the popular book *Training Trances: Multilevel Communication in Therapy and Training* which is used internationally in hypnosis schools, as well as university graduate and medical programs. He's also co-authored *Dreaming Realities,* considered to be a definitive text in working with dreams. He is known as a prolific developer of a long list of models and therapeutic patterns that are taught worldwide.

Since 1979, John has been doing therapy, coaching, teaching and training working with individuals and groups in virtually every imaginable setting.
There are very few coaches and trainers that have the depth and richness of experience that John possesses. Many he has trained over the last 30 years have gone on to become well-known, internationally respected coaches, hypnotherapists and trainers, themselves…*and you …never know how far a change will go.*

John and his fiance, Kirsten Farris, divide their time between Atlanta, Georgia and Phoenix, Arizona. When he is not teaching or coaching, you may find him mountain biking, making music, watching Kirsten compete in equestrian events with their horse, Lyle, or just hanging out, "taking it all in" and loving every minute of it.

http://www.johnoverdurf.com
john@johnoverdurf.com

Other Titles By Changing Mind Publishing

Quit: The Hypnotist's Handbook to Running Effective Stop Smoking Sessions
By Jess Marion, Sarah Carson, and Shawn Carson

The Swish: An In Depth Look At This Powerful NLP Pattern (NLP Mastery Series)
By Shawn Carson and Jess Marion

The Visual Squash: An NLP Tool For Radical Change (NLP Mastery Series)
By Jess Marion and Shawn Carson

Keeping the Brain In Mind: Practical Neuroscience for Coaches, Therapists, and Hypnosis Practitioners
By Shawn Carson and Melissa Tiers

The Meta Pattern (NLP Mastery Series)
By Sarah Carson and Shawn Carson

Other Titles by John Overdurf

Training Trances: Multi-Level Communication in Therapy and Training
By John Overdurf and Julie Silverthorne
Metamorphous Press

Index

CPSIA information can be obtained
at www.ICGtesting.com
Printed in the USA
BVHW01s1942211217
503398BV00020B/868/P